Drunks, Pests and Harlots

Drunks, Pests and Harlots

Criminal Women in Perth and Fremantle, 1900-1939

Leigh S. L. Straw

humming earth

humming earth
an imprint of
Zeticula Ltd
The Roan
Kilkerran
KA19 8LS
Scotland

http://www.hummingearth.com
admin@hummingearth.com

First published in 2013
Reprinted 2013, 2014
Copyright © Leigh S. L. Straw 2013

Photographs:
Esther Warden, Police Gazette Western Australia, 1911.
    Courtesy of the State Library of Western Australia.
Esther Warden, Police Gazette Western Australia, 1930.
    Courtesy of the State Library of Western Australia.
Mary Sweetman, Police Gazette Western Australia, 1911.
    Courtesy of the State Library of Western Australia.
Sarah Mattson, Police Gazette Western Australia, 1916.
    Courtesy of the State Library of Western Australia.
Sarah Mattson, Police Gazette Western Australia, 1930.
    Courtesy of the State Library of Western Australia.
May Ahern, Police Gazette Western Australia, 1916.
    Courtesy of the State Library of Western Australia.

ISBN 978-1-84622-042-5 Paperback

For Dad

I'll always love you as much as when I was the little girl dancing on your feet

Contents

Illustrations

Acknowledgements

This book started with a murder in Collie in 1929. The murderer is my husband's great-great uncle. That's a story for another time. In looking through the *Police Gazette* issues for 1929, trying to find a reference to Andrew Straw, I found myself drawn to the mug shots of female offenders. I didn't know a great deal about these women in Western Australian history and wanted to know more. This book is the result of that first curious look through the *Police Gazettes.*

Firstly, I would like to extend my sincere thanks to staff at the State Records Office of Western Australia for their ongoing assistance with court and prison records that have been a vital part of this research. Thanks also to staff at the State Library of Western Australia, particularly within the J. S. Battye Library of West Australian History. I would also like to thank the many regular researchers at the archives for guiding me through collections and making my task of locating obscure records so much easier. Your generosity is greatly appreciated.

From the start, colleagues at a number of universities have offered support and shared ideas around my research. A big thanks to: Quentin Beresford, Raelene Frances, Julie Kimber, Deborah Gare, Michael Sturma and Sean Brawley.

For humanising the stories even more, my thanks to Lynette McLaughlin for bringing her great-grandmother, Mary Ann Sweetman, to life in a deeply personal way.

Family and friends have supported me in a variety of ways through the research and writing of this book. Thanks are due to friends and family in Scotland and across Australia. Special thanks to my parents, Sandra and James, and my brother, Steven. Their love of history inspired me from a young age. I would also like to thank my mother-in-law, Debbie Straw, and Aunt, Janet Yetton, for their continued encouragement.

As always, the biggest thanks go to my husband, Tony, for being a wonderful husband, father and friend. Thanks for the many hours of play dates with Jack and Lawson while mummy worked on her 'criminal women'.

Introduction

'I think a little rest inside will do you good'[1]

Renovated warehouse apartments and terraced houses in the inner city streets of Perth and Fremantle will set you back at least half a million dollars these days. Real estate brochures speak of character housing lining picturesque alleyways close to pubs and shops with links to a bygone era. Back in the first decades of the twentieth century, these same areas were known as 'Dens of Dirt and Debauchery'.[2] They were home to a cast of poor, rough and criminal characters like Esther Muriel Warden. Esther, 'the worst female character in Perth',[3] was notorious for her many convictions for drunkenness, assault, theft, vagrancy, soliciting and property damage. By the late 1930s she had notched up over 200 convictions.[4] In Esther Warden's day, the now trendy city neighbourhoods were notorious haunts for criminals at war with the local police, authorities, press and public.

It is in these inner city streets that men and women were criminalised for offending the good order. They were a mix of violent, cunning, desperate and neglected people living a street-to-gaol existence. Some reformed their ways, but most remained in a cycle of offending that sometimes only ended with their deaths. As women, however, female offenders were further outcast from society for gender transgressions. Regarded as some of the hardest criminals in the state, they were neither murderers nor crafty fraudsters. At a time when Perth was establishing itself as burgeoning Australian city, to rival the other major centres across the country, women committing offences against good order were singled out as giving the city a bad name. Imprisoned for drunkenness, idle and disorderly, vagrancy, and other offences against good order, female offenders were marginalised from society by their inability or unwillingness to conform to ideals of the good woman.

Women photographed and scandalised in Police Gazettes, Prison Registers and leading newspapers of the day occupied a world where close police surveillance of their activities, criminal legislation, negative media coverage, incarceration and institutionalisation confined them to a life where they were stereotyped as the worst types of females. Their lives coincided with years of rapid change in Western Australia. The years from 1900-1939 followed the mining boom and the implementation of the *Police Act* in the 1890s and encompass years of growth, expansion, fears of social breakdown, a rising youth culture, war, depression and the onset of another war. For this alone they are interesting years to look at in terms of crime and regulation of particular behaviour in society.

In the words of the day, Esther Warden was a drunk, pest and a harlot. She lived a rough life on the streets at a time when society was unable to deal with women who did not conform. This book tells the stories of non-Indigenous women criminalised for public offences and seeks to humanise their experiences. Their lives also reveal criminal underworlds in Perth and Fremantle inhabited by push gangs, thieves, dealers and larrikin types claiming to rule the inner city streets.

Criminal Streets

The years from 1900 to 1939 marked a period of 'significant social change in Western Australia'[5] during which the metropolitan area rapidly expanded around Perth and Fremantle. While it still harboured a country feel, Perth was fast moving towards being a modern city with its growing Central Business District (CBD). Richer residents started to prefer the western areas to the previously favourable Esplanade and Adelaide Terrace. They moved further out to West Perth, Dalkeith and Claremont, most with riverside views. Subiaco, East Perth and Maylands housed more white-collar and skilled workers while working class people favoured eastern suburbs like Bassendean and Midland or the greater Fremantle area in the south.[6]

With more and more people moving to the suburbs to live in small workers cottages or family bungalows, living standards fell in the inner streets of Perth and Fremantle. King Street, for example, known today as an exclusive designer part of the CBD, was notorious in the early twentieth century for 'drunken orgies' and described as a 'disgrace to the town'.[7] Western Australia's urban poor congregated in and around King Street, across the railway tracks in Roe Street, North Perth, parts of Leederville and East Perth. In Fremantle, the very poor lived in overcrowded housing around Market, High and Pakenham Streets, now cosmopolitan café precincts. While crime was not restricted to poor members of society, these areas featured in apprehensions of drunk, idle and disorderly women. They were labelled streets of vice and well known to the general public.

As the metropolitan area increased in size, so too did criminal activities. Some streets were off bounds from the late afternoon. Local residents wrote into the papers about their evening mishaps and run-ins with local thugs. According to one resident of West Perth:

> Drunken men and women, with dress shamefully disheveled and using language that even devils would hesitate to use are the sights and scenes to which decent residents are compelled to see daily.[8]

The inner city slums around Murray and Hay Streets in Perth and Norfolk Street in Fremantle were said to harbour all manner of criminal types including thieving gangs and drunken standover men. Fremantle streets, it was said at the time, were lined by 'social outcasts'. They were the only ones game enough to live inner city.[9]

Most men and women facing criminal charges in the Perth and Fremantle courts were charged with drunkenness or stealing. Only a minority faced charges for the more serious crimes of murder, manslaughter or assault.[10] Historically, homicide accounts for only a fraction of all crimes whereas petty offences feature in general crime statistics.[11] Offences in the Western Australian Magistrates' Courts were categorised into five main classes: offences against the person, person and property, property, currency and good order. Over the period from 1900-1939 cases and charges for offences against good order vastly outnumbered other crimes, a little over seventy-four per cent of all crimes. Offences against good order were directly linked to social and political debates about drunkenness, containment of prostitution and social citizenship.

Criminal statistics, however, can only reveal so much about crime in society. Crimes that go unreported to the authorities or remain undiscovered cannot be known. This is what historians have called the 'dark figure' of criminal statistics.[12] In Western Australia, statistics show the number of charges and convictions placed against women arrested for offences against good order but their real number of crimes may be much larger if some offences were not reported. Esther Warden, appearing over 200 times in court, may well have been drunk in public and idle and disorderly many more times that went undetected. Recorded crime is still useful, however, in providing general crime trends.

National trends for crime over the twentieth century indicate the changing nature of crime discussions. Authorities in the early years of the century focussed on drunkenness, soliciting, gambling and Chinese opium dens. Statistical Registers in Western Australia included an additional column listing the 'cases attributable to drink', thus showing the emphasis on drunkenness as a serious social problem. Young women found in opium dens faced harsh punishment at the time. Maud Williams and Evelyn Hawkes were charged in June 1921 with being idle and disorderly in a Chinese den. They were lucky as first-time offenders to only get a week in gaol.[13] By the end of the century drug trafficking, burglary and violence featured more in examinations of crime trends. However, alcohol-related crime continues to be a problem today within the criminal justice system.[14] A major difference now is that public drunkenness has been decriminalised. Esther Warden had no such luck back in the years before 1939.

Rob Sindall, writing about street violence in the nineteenth-century England, argues it is best to see statistics not necessarily as indicative of what was actually taking place but rather 'what people believed was happening'.[15] In early-twentieth-century Perth and Fremantle, people believed drunkenness, soliciting and vagrancy were serious social problems increasing crime in the state. Policing practices also influence perceptions of crime and crime trends. Surveillance of drinking and vagrancy, for example, naturally leads to an increase in arrests for public order offences.[16] Increased policing of working class populations can affect perceptions of criminals, though statistically in the nineteenth and early twentieth centuries poorer people were more likely to commit petty crimes.

In terms of sex comparisons, men were more likely to commit crimes in Western Australia, as they were across Australia. Again, this is not surprising given historically three in four criminals are men.[17] Male crime, in dominating criminological data, helped to define female offending as unusual and deviant. In Western Australia, in the first decades of the twentieth century, men accounted for over ninety per cent of cases in the Supreme Court while women made up between six and nine per cent of persons charged in the Courts of Petty Sessions.[18] Yet, despite their reduced involvement in crime, female offenders are an important part of crime history as they provide a fuller picture of all crimes committed and the different people committing them.

Women Behaving Badly

In the first decades of the twentieth century, under new Police legislation and stricter social mores, women who were loud, drunk, loitering or generally leading idle lives could find themselves put away in Fremantle Prison for up to six months at a time. Just how criminal were these women? These days we might not see these women as criminals but this history shows they lived at a time when their bad behaviour was a criminal offence.

The majority of women charged and convicted in the West Australian courts from 1900-1939 were arrested for offences against good order. These accounted on average for around two-thirds of all cases before the courts, both Supreme and Petty. As much as any drunken, idle and disorderly, obscene or loud person was not tolerated in public in the first decades of the twentieth century, female transgressions in public were seen as unnatural and abhorrent. The female offender, though a minority of cases, failed to conform and was singled out as something 'other' to her sex. The overwhelming trend that most women conform to social expectations and are not involved in crime is important here.

The police and courts had little tolerance for offences against good order. Around ninety-five per cent of public order cases ended in convictions compared with eighty-per cent for property offences and fifty per cent for offences against the person. Women charged with offences against public order were almost guaranteed a conviction. In general they were sentenced to between three and six months' gaol with hard labour.[19] The average age for females tried in the Police Courts was around twenty-seven. The main entry point into crime seems to have been in the late teens and early twenties and from there at least half went on to lead lives of crime.

Habitual female drunks featured in court, police and press records but the authorities were unsure whether alcohol was a factor in their being idle and disorderly or a consequence of it. Either way, these two offences are linked to efforts to crack down on female drunks and vagrant women who were also engaging in prostitution. They were fallen women[20] and featured in the West Australian press for their drink problems and 'allied offences', namely prostitution[21] The idle and disorderly charge is naturally linked to prostitution through its use under the *Police Act* of 1892 (amended in 1902). This Act allowed police to prosecute prostitutes as vagrants under the idle and disorderly charge. Men were not liable to prosecution for soliciting but they were charged if living off the proceeds of prostitution.[22]

Female sexuality was defined at the time in the heterosexual, monogamous marriage. Soliciting on the streets undermined their respectable feminine identities. The state, churches and medicine all supported confinement of sexuality to marriage as the 'cornerstone of femininity'.[23] Prostitution was the 'extremity of failure in the monogamy test'.[24] The woman who broke the sanctity of the family was seen as a direct threat to society.[25] May Ahern, a well-known Fremantle prostitute, was arrested over the Christmas period in 1919 and sensationalised in the press as tempting men 'from the paths of virtue'.[26]

Females imprisoned as habitual drunks or as idle and disorderly vagrants were bad women and those who were married were bad wives and mothers. Motherhood was seen as the natural outcome of womanhood, as women were told from a young age. Family, friends, police, social workers and doctors monitored maternal behaviour. Importantly, it was the mother's responsibility to create a good child.[27] In August 1900 Helena Adams appeared before the Perth Police Court on a charge of habitual drunkenness. She was arrested after turning up drunk to a female home wanting her baby back. Helena's husband had given up on her and taken charge of their child. She was sentenced to three months in gaol.[28] Helena Adams failed in both her roles as wife and mother. However,

Helena's need to see her child remained. In June 1902 she was arrested and fined for property damage and obscene language after trying to see her child at the Industrial School.[29]

This study of female offenders uses criminal prosecutions of 'white' women in Perth and Fremantle traced through archival collections including: Magistrates Evidence Books, Police Complaints Books, Police Gazettes, Statistical Registers and general police files. Newspaper reports for over 2,000 men and women appearing in the Perth and Fremantle Police Courts have also been utilised and compared. From this a close socio-biographical study has been undertaken using births, death and marriage details for sixty female recidivists featured in press court reports. Evidence Books and newspaper reports offer the most extensive insight into how women were stereotyped, through inclusion of police evidence, eyewitness statements and at times testimony from the accused.

The Fremantle Prison Female Registers, held in the State Records Office of Western Australia, provide important snapshots into the lives of women criminalised for offences against good order. The Registers include personal identifiers for prisoners such as birth and marriage, employment, literacy and aliases used. I have been able to put together details of criminal convictions using a variety of public records but the Prison Registers are remarkable in their cataloguing of transgressions from respectable life. Women I had researched in the police records and in various newspaper reports came to life in prison mug shots and lists of offences, sometimes over several decades. Esther Warden's many convictions are detailed in four foolscap pages. Many times over she is identified as a vagrant, idle and disorderly and drunken woman deserving of weeks and months in prison. The futile nature of this cycle is evident decades after her last conviction in 1939.

Controlling Women

Women committing offences against good order in the inner city streets presented authorities with a particular challenge in how best to control women acting outside the bounds of society. In the first instance, it was the work of police officers to look out for women committing offences against good order. In their daily work of patrolling the inner streets of Perth and Fremantle, local constables were responsible for making sure idle, loud and drunken women were removed from the streets. The establishment of the Women's Police in 1917 created a system whereby women in positions of authority closely monitored women on the streets. Their role was clearly set out as controlling female public deviancy. Their main duties involved patrolling slum neighbourhoods, looking after drunken women and offering protection for them.[30]

When the police could not prevent public transgressions and prison had failed to reform, women were sent to Reformatories and Homes. Only a month after trying to gain access to her child, Helena Adams was taken into care at the Salvation Army Home in July 1902, after being caught soliciting. Magistrate Roe hoped handing her over to the care of the Home would prevent her from being brought up on another charge of idle and disorderly.[31] Helena was one of many female offenders sent to a Reformatory as a way to prevent imprisonment. It was a preventative measure aimed at reform rather than incarceration. It was also part of an overall effort to rescue womanhood and save the good mother.

The Reformatory and Industrial movement in Western Australia reflected a general move towards reform over punishment in the criminal justice system. Reformatory and Industrial Schools and Homes emerged in Britain in the nineteenth century with greater emphasis placed on self-discipline within social welfare programmes. From the 1880s Britain went through a process of decarceration, limiting the number of people sent to prison. Prisons were increasingly seen as a last resort for perpetrators of serious crimes and habitual criminals.[32] However, as research in New Zealand shows, women's homes and institutions created another female dichotomy: 'Magdalens and moral imbeciles'.[33] The former Fremantle Lunatic Asylum on Finnerty Street, changed in the early twentieth century to the Old Women's Home, was also used as another place to control female offenders. Women committing offences against good order were further controlled as lunatics and 'mad women' within the walls of the Asylum and Home.[34]

The Home of the Good Shepherd in Leederville featured in efforts to reform and ultimately control the lives of female offenders.[35] Established in 1902, it was based on the work of the order of the Good Shepherd with nuns working in the 'regeneration of fallen women of the State'.[36] When the convent on Adelaide Terrace grew too small for housing young girls and women charged with public order offences, operations moved to Leederville, looking over Mongers Lake (now Lake Monger). At its opening, the Reverend L. J. Smyth said: 'The inmates of the home may be wretched and sinful in the eyes of the world yet they were the children of Jesus Christ, with the same destiny as those who had not fallen, and redeemed by God'.[37] According to the ethos of the Home, women who had fallen could be redeemed but they were nevertheless punished harshly for their transgressions.

One stark reality at the time, however, was some women simply could not be reformed. Three days after Helena Adams was sent to the Home in July 1902, she was sentenced to three months in gaol. She had spent one night at the Home before again taking to the streets to solicit.[38] Some women made particular choices about returning to the streets and engaging in criminal subcultures.[39] Women portrayed only as vulnerable and requiring protection denies female criminal agency.[40] There were women in Western Australia in the first decades of the twentieth century who chose to drink and engage in illicit activities, regardless of any efforts to reform them.

'roaming the streets in the company of women of very low repute'[41]

Women offending the good order were regularly arrested in streets and outside pubs well known for vice and criminal activities. They inhabited a world where crime, poverty and social breakdown were inextricably linked. These were the crime streets of Perth and Fremantle avoided by the wealthy. They favoured the higher socio-economic neighbourhoods along the Swan River foreshore, out to Mount Street and further up to West Perth. The working classes and very poor congregated around the inner city streets of Murray, Hay, King, Wellington, William and Pier Streets. These parts were known for their poor sanitation, factories and drinking establishments. In these and other similar areas in Fremantle, women lived on the margins of society. Part of what can be termed an underclass in Perth and Fremantle, though some women fleeted between working class lives and the streets, the very poor on the streets suffered from persistent poverty and featured in public discourse about welfare, charity and the disreputable poor.[42]

Poor neighbourhoods were an accepted part of the expanding metropolitan area but criminality within these streets had to be watched and restricted. Living on the margins of society, poor women were subjected to greater surveillance of their everyday lives. As the police, charity workers and journalists patrolled the poorer parts of Perth and Fremantle their gaze fell on females. When poor women began living on the streets and were arrested for idle and disorderly, they became a part of a 'dangerous class'.[43] Their criminality and transgressions from bourgeois ideals led to stereotyping of criminal women as endangering the social order. The authorities, aware of the greater involvement of men in crime, did not expect women to engage in illicit activities so when they did, their actions were scrutinised more.

Police and authorities tried to contain female vice and crime within the inner city streets but by the first decades of the twentieth century, their drinking and disorderly behaviour was starting to encroach on residential areas. Immoral streets had to be contained and women taken off the streets. Women in the poorer neighbourhoods found their transgressions also led to further isolation from respectable society. Once labelled as troublemakers, the disreputable poor would find themselves further outcast from respectable society and this would lead them to gravitate towards other offenders for some sense of belonging and place.[44]

Mapping female criminal activities allows us to imagine the world poor, criminal women inhabited on the streets. What were their lives like and what led them to commit crimes? Were some women driven to crime through their poverty or did they actively seek out criminal activity? Esther Warden is one of a cast of characters making up the pages of this book. They include Cecilia Reilly who told a magistrate she hoped he would be dead when she got out of prison. There's Nellie Davenport, a public nuisance around Fremantle and described in court reports as a 'degenerate woman'.[45] Another, Annie Forbes, believed her only crime was her tongue. In 1918, Esther Miller was described in the papers as 'an awful character' and defied all attempts at punishment and reform.[46]

Women criminalised for offences against good order tell us much about social expectations of femininity at the time. Social codes 'defined the proper young woman as a frail but appealing, intellectually inferior but morally superior being, whose duty it was to be passive, decorative and sexually pure'.[47] As Perth entered into the twentieth century, Victorian feminine ideals continued to impact on female lives. Women were expected to live up to the ideal of the perfect lady, regardless of their socio-economic background. As much as this ideal was flawed in its application to working-class women who had to work outside the home to earn a living, there remained the expectation of 'the reputable working class and the deserving poor'.[48] The good Australian woman was constructed into the twentieth century as, 'domestic, home and family-bound, pure, clean and rationalised'.[49] Some Australian feminists also incorporated a maternalistic approach into their work creating a 'new social order' in the first years of the twentieth century.[50] In this way, mothers were a key focus for emphasising the moralistic female citizen.[51]

The last years of the nineteenth century witnessed a surge in nationalism in Australia based on masculine identities. It was the era of the heroic, egalitarian bushman adhering to a strong sense of mateship. Australian manliness was defined by physical strength, patriotism and a militarism defending the nation.[52] Female activists campaigned against this gendered, male-centred citizenship. From this, 'maternalistic and reforming' feminism sought to give women an identity within the nation, influencing the Woman's Christian Temperance Union (WCTU) and using women's moralistic identity in particular to deal with vice within society.[53] This continued on into the first decades of the twentieth century. In 1903 Rose Scott, Australian feminist, activist and suffragist, argued women needed to be the moral upholders of a righteous nation.[54]

Women could nevertheless negotiate their feminine identities and express themselves in varying ways in Australia into the twentieth century. In the years after the First World War, for example, dancing and entertainment shifted the line between good and bad women when some females used pleasure as a way to engage with the modern times.[55] Early twentieth-century Australian feminists also argued for greater recognition of women's 'sexual embodiment'.[56] In this way, the dichotomy of the good and bad woman was not utilised as much as was the campaign for equal moral standards and 'the right of women to control their bodies'.[57] Melissa Bellanta's work on female larrikins in Brisbane,

Sydney and Melbourne from the late nineteenth century shows how young women 'rejected demure femininity' through their involvement in gangs, prostitution, and popular entertainment.[58] Some young women told the authorities in reformatories they had 'no desire to be respectable'.[59]

The feminine ideal accorded little attention to working-class identities where femininity was re-fashioned to suit the needs of local communities. There persisted in Australia from the late eighteenth century acceptance in working-class communities of female sexual identities, prostitution, drinking, and general rowdiness.[60] Prostitutes in the first decades of the twentieth century generally lived and worked in their local communities and were recognised as a part of the community and not necessarily outcast as they were by middle and upper-class opinion.[61] Lilly Doyle was labelled a common prostitute by police in Fremantle and vilified in the press over the course of the first decades of the twentieth century. However, Bill Marks, who grew up in South Fremantle at the same time, remembered a drunken Doyle walking the tramlines late at night and singing. For Marks she was one of the local characters with a feminine identity that was not entirely at odds with expectations of the local community.[62]

Yet, while all women have a sense of their femininity - 'what it is to be a good woman, and what it is to fail'[63] - female criminal lives represent deviant femininities.[64] Female criminality is interpreted as 'a form of deviation from natural or normal womanhood'[65] and the women featured in crime stories from the streets of Perth and Fremantle were shown to have deviated from 'normal womanhood'. The extent to which impoverished, marginalised women living on the streets of Perth and Fremantle were able to negotiate constructions of femininity was limited, however. Poor, criminal women were directly impacted by sexism, defined as negative evaluations based on their gender.[66] With minimal or no familial or financial support and caught in a cycle of offending and incarceration, criminal women were confined to a life more or less decided by legislation, the courts, police and press. Institutionalised sexism stereotyped them as bad women. Court authority was upheld over the female accused through magistrates consulting with police and women rarely being represented by counsel. Forced to reveal private aspects of their lives in public, female offences were then interpreted by magistrates, based largely on police evidence, and then interpreted again for the public in newspaper reports.

Criminal women captivated the West Australian public. Some became court identities and household names through their lives of crime. Reporting proceedings at the Police Courts (the courts sat six days a week), papers singled out repeat offenders, several appearing for the hundredth time in court. In March 1920 Lilly Doyle faced a charge of creating a disturbance around High and Market streets in Fremantle. She had appeared in court more than 130 times. In the court story that followed her appearance she was labelled a 'Police Court Identity'.[67] Tales of criminal women helped to sell newspapers using sensationalist headlines to ' shock, frighten, titillate and entertain'.[68] It also involves society measuring itself against the outsider.[69]

Female criminality in Perth and Fremantle was not restricted to poor women. However, criminal convictions were clearly decided along class lines. The women in this book all share similar histories as poor, urban females caught in a cycle of offending. Gaol terms ranging from weeks to months failed to curb their offences against good order. On numerous occasions women were discharged from Fremantle Prison only to be sent back days later. That most arrests resulted in lengthy prison sentences is evidence of the cyclical relationship between poverty, drink and homelessness and the part that imprisonment played in perpetuating the cycle.

The cycle of offending also brought women together on the streets through shared experiences. Women arrested about the streets were regularly in the lock up together, made court appearances on the same day and spent months near each other in cells in Fremantle Prison. While it is difficult to establish their full associations, given the lack of extensive personal evidence, we can at least imagine a world they inhabited on the streets together. Weld Square and the Fremantle Esplanade, for example, become meeting places for outcast women looking to drink with other street women or share their stories of trying to survive amid the poverty of their circumstances. In the heat of summer or bitter cold of mid-winter, they met, talked and associated on the streets for years.

What can *Drunks, Pests and Harlots* offer to our understanding of history? Located within the broader scholarship of crime history, this book engages with a variety of approaches to the past and demonstrates the transdisciplinary benefits of crime studies to broader historical scholarship. Crime history allows the historian to work across different areas of study to gain a wider understanding of past lives and experiences. The criminal case studies in this book combine various approaches, including women's studies, sociology, philosophy, media and communications, law, criminology and justice studies. In particular, historical perspectives have much to offer to criminological research. Historical study contributes to understandings of how crime develops over time, the ways in which it is understood within society, and links historical contexts to ongoing debates about crime, justice and punishment. What crime history shows us is the value of applying a variety of approaches to understanding the past in an effort to better capture the essence of the people who populated it.

There is a particular story being told in the pages that follow. The lives of women with long criminal records reveal a great deal about the society in which they lived. Their experiences show a West Australian society trying to maintain the social order and consensus at a time of strikes, fights for equal rights, war, materialism, emerging youth identities and depression.[70] Crime added to anxiousness about modern society and from this concerns about female deviants on the streets of the growing metropolitan area. Offences against good order were seen as a serious social problem by authorities in Perth and Fremantle. Public behaviour in the inner city streets was closely monitored for any deviance that would signal a fall in social standards. Good order offences were deemed serious enough to warrant gaol terms in Fremantle Prison from days to months at a time. Men and women alike faced similar public scrutiny for their offences against good order. If they were repeat offenders, the police and courts were less likely to show any form of leniency. However, women were more closely scrutinised in a society that did not expect to see them involved in crime.

These stories are located within Western Australia but they represent a broader history of efforts to control women's public identities. Any deviance from what was thought to be respectable femininity in the first decades of the twentieth century was firmly dealt with. We could also ask the question of whether much has changed? Are women still judged differently in public when drunk, disorderly and/or using obscene language? Is society still more outraged when a woman is drunk and violent in public, compared with a male counterpart? We may judge the judicial system as harsh back in the early twentieth century but social expectations continue to be placed on women in public.

Drunks, Pests and Harlots is written with particular questions in mind. It is not an institutional history, though Fremantle Prison, Fremantle Asylum and Homes are a part of the story being told. This book is more concerned with street life and constructions of women based on their public actions. Public discourse in the first decades of the twentieth century clearly set out social constructions of female deviance. Women offending the good order are bad, immoral women; they are neglectful wives and drunken mothers. Therefore, what follows is a history of female criminality as told in the stories of women frequently arrested, charged and imprisoned for the main crimes of drunkenness, soliciting and vagrancy. It is also a history of the role of the media in sensationalising female court appearances and turning female offenders into 'court identities'.

Ultimately, this book is an examination of the person of the female criminalised as a drunk, vagrant or idle person. Who were the women criminalised for offences against good order? Did they conform to any criminal 'type'? How did society perceive them? How did they perceive themselves? Some women appearing in court provided tales of their lives, tried to gain understanding and also contested authority. Their voices help to further humanise female criminal experiences. There is more to this public story, too. Reconstructing the lives of women featured in criminal records provides an opportunity to study female outcasts in Perth and Fremantle and give some meaning to their lives on the fringes of society. *Drunks, Pests and Harlots* humanises female offenders with life stories beyond mug shots staring out from the prison and police records.

1. Crime Streets

'Haunts of the Undesirable'[71]

Edward Rudolph was 'looking for a woman' one evening in June 1900. By the end of the night, he wished he'd just stayed home. Walking along King Street in the centre of Perth, he met Mrs Alice Chute. From there they went to The Royal Hotel and various other pubs that night. Around one in the morning, he and Alice went back to her rented house at 66 King Street. Shortly after, another man came through the bedroom window, joined by Mrs Chute's husband. Edward lay in bed, quietly, expecting Alice's husband to throw him out. When nothing happened, he wandered into the kitchen where he found several men going through his cigar case. When he challenged them he was hit over the head with a frying pan. Stumbling out of the house, Edward looked for a passing police officer but when none appeared, he went home. A few hours later, members of the same group broke into his house and knocked him out again.

The case was dismissed a month later in court, due in large part to contradictory evidence. There were gaps in the stories and Rudolph was hesitant to make public the full details of his evening with Alice. Well known to the authorities, this King Street group bore the brunt of scathing comments from the Police Magistrate, Augustus Sanford Roe. Son of John Septimus Roe, first Surveyor General in Western Australia and among the first colonists, Roe had had enough of the Chutes and other dubious characters appearing before him from King Street. He described the Chute house as 'one of those pestilent spots that wanted wiping off the face of the earth'. The area was a disgrace with its constant disturbances and 'drunken orgies'.[72]

Two months after the Rudolph case, the Chutes and their associates were again mentioned in court when police produced a damning report on properties in King Street. Well-known prostitutes and gamblers were listed as living in houses along the street. The Chute house was singled out as a place 'harbouring convicted thieves' and 'a number of low characters'. According to Constable Love, it would be 'a blessing to the neighbourhood' if the occupants of these houses were turfed out.[73]

In the first decades of the twentieth century, King Street was one of the most notorious streets in Perth. It's a far cry from King Street today. Located in the trendy West End, the area is home to exclusive designer shops including Louis Vuitton, Prada and Chanel. Old warehouses have been converted into exclusive apartments, legal offices and stylish restaurants that mask a sordid, criminal history. This once 'pestilent spot' has become a trendy inner city street. Inner city development over the last couple of decades has led to a reinvention of Perth and Fremantle precincts. Town planning experts have worked hard to rejuvenate areas that were once notorious for drunkenness, soliciting and vagrancy. The stories now seem locked in behind the renovations but it was in these parts that women were regularly arrested. Tracing the lives of women committing offences against good order in the first decades of the twentieth century firstly involves a geographical history of the streets they inhabited. These are the crime streets of Perth and Fremantle.

*

Crime was not new to the streets of Perth and Fremantle in the twentieth century. Fears about increasing levels of crime dated back to the earliest days of colonisation. In this 'land of sin and sorrow',[74] new arrivals tried their best to manage sandy, poor quality soil and evade starvation in a distant, isolated part of the world. The first colonists stepped ashore in Fremantle in 1829 after weeks camping under makeshift tents on Garden Island.[75] Grand pianos and ornate furniture, elegant dresses and clothing of the finest silk were bundled onto the beach. It was not long before the more desperate started pilfering these goods. Punishment was swift. Petty thieves were placed in 'stocks', their hands locked in place through two planks of wood, and publicly humiliated on the corner of Barrack Street and St George's Terrace.[76]

Early criminals in colonial society, mainly drunks, thieves and fraudsters, were said to inhabit a close criminal world on the inner town streets. In April 1847 *The Perth Gazette* ran a column criticising proposed improvements for the town of Perth. Small cottages, it was argued, would be 'occupied by the very lowest grades of society' and would ultimately create 'nurseries for the worst kinds of vice, crime and disease'.[77]

Crime was also closely observed in Fremantle. George Fletcher Moore, an early colonist, wrote in his diary of 'dissatisfied' colonists 'who plod through the sand from hut to hut, to drink grog and grumble'.[78] Doctor Thomas Braidwood Wilson was scathing in his portrayal of Fremantle in October 1829. He characterised the town as a 'very bad place, owing to the idleness, roguery, and thieving' of the people there.[79] Offences against good order were such a problem that the *Marquis of Anglesea*, one of the first ships arriving in the colony with settlers, servants and military men, had to be converted into a prison.[80] The hulks of the old world had made their way back into the lives of the British colonists. Things were little better by the last decades of the nineteenth century. Governor William Robinson described Fremantle in 1873 as a 'seaport lockup for drunken sailors and prostitutes'.[81]

Streets known for crime developed from a growing divide between rich and poor. Land ownership in the colony favoured a minority of wealthy colonists able to claim land in the best parts of the foreshore and inner Perth area. The concentration of wealth in the town was apparent from as early as 1835 with seventy houses built along St Georges Terrace and Adelaide Terrace and valued at £200 each. This had the effect of excluding labourers who had originally lived in these parts.[82] The Terrace became an exclusive part of Perth where the likes of the Forrests and Shentons, prominent families, vied for the best land on which to build large homes. An example of this is the replica of Alexander Forrest's home at 221 St Georges Terrace, now Rigby's Bar in the Forrest Centre.

Rents in Perth were already high by the middle of the nineteenth century leading some owners to subdivide and profit but also maintain as much space as possible.[83] Money also ensured the rich could influence town planning. When the Colonial Hospital was originally planned for the centre of Perth, wealthy residents argued against this and were successful in having it built further east. They preferred the hospital, with its 'lunatic' cells, to be built closer to the less expensive parts of the town.[84] Real estate prices worried Perth residents as much in the nineteenth century as they do today.

With government and banking buildings, gardens and large colonial homes, St Georges Terrace and The Esplanade contrasted with the cottages, shops and hotels further back from the foreshore. The 'serving class' was forced to look for land in the less favoured parts of the town.[85] This land was located around Murray, William, Wellington and Roe Streets, areas that were regularly flooded through the nineteenth century. Only in the 1870s was drainage improved in these areas.[86] Cottages in Wellington, Milligan and Murray Streets were rented out to labourers and small artisans who also preferred cheap rentals in East Perth. Bronte Street, near the cemetery, was popular.[87] Shops, bakeries and factories – central to working-class communities - were mainly situated in Beaufort and William Streets.[88]

Class spatial differences had much to do with Perth's rapid expansion into the twentieth century. It was fast becoming a burgeoning Australian city. The gold rushes from the late nineteenth century contributed to a huge spike in immigration to Western Australia. In 1891 the colony numbered close to 50,000 non-Indigenous people. By 1911 it had risen to over 280,000.[89] Perth directly benefited from the movement of people into the city from the Goldfields. Not only a stopping point for people moving out in search for gold, the city was a favoured attraction for the growing number of visitors to the state in general. Perth's population increased from 27,553 in 1901 to over in 56,000 in 1911.[90] At the census of 1921, out of a state population of over 335,000, the city of Perth population was over 64,000 compared with a population of over 25,000 in Fremantle, inclusive of its east and north areas.[91] By 1939 Perth people numbered over 87,000 souls, with Fremantle increasing to over 28,000 out of a total population of over 460,000.[92] At all major censuses before 1940, over seventy per cent of non-Indigenous West Australians lived in the metropolitan area.[93]

Perth's expansion in the twentieth century shared much in common with urban expansion across other major western cities. A Central Business District emerged around central Hay Street, St Georges Terrace and Barrack Street. Transitional, industrial and declining neighbourhoods now surrounded the CBD. Housing in this area was a mix of rundown small cottages and boarding houses. The next sector belonged to the respectable working classes, followed by a middle-class residential sector and further out a commuters area.[94] In 1904, one-third of the city centre was residential but by 1911 it had fallen to around one-fifth. Commercial premises increased from twenty-three to over forty-per cent of all buildings in the city.[95]

Perth was fast becoming a city but it retained some of its market town identity into the twentieth century. The New Market on Wellington Street, site of the present bus station, was built in 1897 and served as an important market centre for local residents, businesses and visitors from the surrounding areas. Street sellers were also regularly trading about the inner streets. Stalls selling fruit and vegetables, meat, cloth and shoes lined Hay and Murray Streets. Mainly working from wheelbarrows, street sellers lived off the steady traffic in people flowing in and out of the city. Cattle were also a common sight in St Georges Terrace, taken through Perth on their way to the Subiaco Abattoir. The New Market didn't see out the 1920s, however, and was pulled down in the 1927.[96]

The town of Fremantle developed out from Arthur Head. Settlers first came ashore here in 1829 and from then on it became an important strategic location. With its jetty jutting out from Bathers Beach, this was the main colonial entrance into Fremantle.[97] From the late 1830s, High Street ran from the Round House in the west of Fremantle up to St John's Church in the east. As the main street of the town, it served as a central point for the street planning on either side of it.[98]

Fremantle town was planned out in symmetrical blocks. It was town planning of a type brought by surveyors from Britain. Like the New Town area of Edinburgh, for example, street blocks ran either side of a main street that intersects with one or two other main thoroughfares. This streetscape is the same today. High Street in the West End intersects with Cliff, Mouat, Henry and Pakenham Streets on its way to Market Street and through to King's Square. If you stand at the base of the Round House today and look east up High Street, you can imagine John Septimus Roe, Government Surveyor, standing on the same spot in 1829 and devising plans for the town.

Fremantle's character was different to Perth. Government officials and newspapermen worked in Fremantle from the 1830s while Perth remained the colony's government and business centre.[99] Fremantle became an important mercantile centre for the colony with an economy based on the shipping of goods. Dominated by wooden houses, the town was home to merchants, innkeepers and artisans. It was also home to cesspits in the backyards of High Street and, briefly, plague brought ashore by its international shipping business. Seven people died of plague in Fremantle in 1900.[100]

Similar to Perth, the wealthy showed a preference for certain parts of Fremantle. Rich residents and businessmen lived and set up large offices in limestone buildings along Cliff Street. The Samsons were among the first to do so and set a standard for the street from the 1830s. By the second half of the nineteenth century, wealthy businessmen dominated the streetscape. These 'Merchant Princes of Fremantle'[101] included shipping entrepreneurs like James Lilly who ran his shipping company from inner Fremantle.[102]

Fremantle's port identity was well established by the late nineteenth century. With the opening of the Inner Harbour in 1897, designed by C. Y. O'Connor of Pipeline fame, Fremantle was able to welcome large steam and sail ships into its harbour. Shipping and insurance offices lining Phillimore Street and its Square were testament to the identity of the town. Phillimore Chambers and the P & O Building were both part of the precinct by 1903, further adding to this as a shipping precinct.[103]

Though regarded as a large town by the turn of the twentieth century, Fremantle was developing into a city. Electric trams were introduced in 1905 and Market and Bannister Streets were developed as new areas where shops and hotels clustered around the growing population.[104] Fremantle was officially registered as a city in June 1935[105] but its earlier character as a 'predominantly working-class community' remained.[106] While elite merchant families like the Mannings and the Batemans dominated town business in the nineteenth century, working-class people remained a key part of the Fremantle life.

Poor Streets

Perth's nineteenth-century colonial elite liked to boast that Perth society was respectable and free from the vices of other colonies and the old country. Though at best a 'shabby-genteel society',[107] their respectability was important. As the city became more urbanised and commercial from the 1890s, Perth's elite looked beyond the city centre to continue on in their respectable ideal. They wanted larger houses with more land space and so left much of the inner city parts to working-class residents and the very poor who were unable to afford higher rents and larger mortgages in the outer city streets and suburbs.

One of the main goals of urban planning is to foster a healthy, respectable lifestyle for residents in good communities.[108] Perth was well on its way to achieving this in the early twentieth century but it was located in its surrounding parts. By the 1910s, West Perth was mainly residential and suburban in character. East Perth, by contrast, was a mix of residential areas, factories and workshops. It was effectively made up of poor people living in an industrial area.[109] The commercial precincts of Murray, Wellington and William Streets were still surrounded by residential areas but they were increasingly crammed into small blocks.

Residents of West Perth and further out in Claremont did not have to live next to industrial sites and commercial congestion. Here they could live on larger blocks, in larger houses, and away from the expanding business and commercial centre of Perth. One resident of Claremont referred to it as a model suburb in a letter to *The West Australian*.[110] Crammed into small properties and surrounded by factories and businesses, poorer people lacked the space and comfort of the suburbs.[111] One member of Parliament in 1937 reflected on this class difference in Perth when he asked: 'Why should not the poor man of East Perth have the same privilege as the wealthy resident of West Perth?'[112]

Urban expansion led to a class struggle over housing. Middle and high class residential areas around West Perth and Claremont, and to an extent parts of Subiaco, meant working-class people were restricted to housing in East Perth, Victoria Park, Leederville and North Perth.[113] 'Housing classes' were now more apparent in the expansion of the metropolitan area and with housing restrictions came increasing poverty. One reporter for *Truth* newspaper was sent out over a number of evenings in February 1904 to investigate the conditions of Perth's homeless. On the Esplanade, the 'roofless palace of Perth's poor', he found numerous men sleeping against the fences (one of whom he noted for loud snoring). One of those sleeping rough claimed it was better than what was on offer in the lodging houses.[114]

Growing poverty in the city streets also led to debates about the state of living conditions and slums. Members of a Child Welfare Conference in 1919 were shown slides of slum conditions. One half-acre housing block in East Perth contained eleven houses.[115] By the 1930s, the debate about slums had intensified. In September 1935 the Town Planning Commissioner, D. L. Davidson, gave a lecture to the Young Labour League in Perth. Something needed to be done in terms of housing in the capital. Perth was well on the way, he argued, to housing congestion with little consideration for the very poor. Slums were a direct result of flats created in inner city parts without proper building programs. Davidson cited people living in a stable in Adelaide Terrace as one of the worst examples of slum conditions.[116] The debate continued through the next year. C. H. Boas claimed in June 1936 that slum conditions were no better in Perth than they were in Melbourne. The Chairman of Health in Perth then went on to deny this, claiming there were some bad houses but slums did not exist in the metropolitan area.[117] For the very poor, slum conditions were a reality of life.

Newspapers and local councils publicly singled out Perth's impoverished areas. Slums and shelters dominated corners and laneways around George and Wellington Streets, while 'hovels' were an eyesore in King Street and Melbourne Road (later renamed Milligan Street). In these inner streets you could reportedly find 'houses of the worst slum type'.[118] Another article in *The Sunday Times,* also in 1920, drew attention to slums in Pier Street and around William and Roe Streets containing '[r]agged, half-clad children and women…about these hideous dens and habitations'.[119] It was 'one of the worst portions of our fast growing city'.[120] From there the article descends into an almost Dickensian world of poor families 'glad to ave ad a pitch with yer'.[121]

Some of the worst slum conditions in Fremantle were said to exist in Norfolk Street and nearby streets where 'housing conditions are seen at their very worst'.[122] One two-storey building was likened to a barn but with three dwelling houses within, 'hardly fit for cattle'.[123] At the turn of the century, papers in fact referred to Fremantle as a port of 'Beastly Backyards and Stinking Slums'.[124]

The very poor, without a roof over their heads, tended to gather around the inner city streets closest to the Men's and Women's Homes, including the Mt Eliza and Pier Street establishments.[125] Sometimes they saw out the night in in a secluded part of the city and port, in a park or shed. Police frequently came upon men and women sleeping rough in sheds behind businesses and houses. Amelia Louise Scanlon, described in court in 1927 as an 'old, shrivelled woman', was charged as a vagrant after regularly sleeping in old sheds in the laneways of inner city Perth.[126]

In Fremantle, poor residents inhabited small cottages and boarding houses in the inner streets. The wealthier favoured the riverside streets of North Fremantle and parts of East Fremantle along the Inner Harbour. South Fremantle came to be known as home to 'the racehorse and the battler' with limestone and wooden cottages also having stables out the back.[127] Fremantle Smelting Works was also located nearby along South Beach. Opened in the early years of the twentieth century, it employed hundreds of people from Fremantle and around the surrounding region.[128] Yet in comparison to Perth, Fremantle took on a larger, more expansive working class identity in its urban geography.

The message in debates about slums and the living conditions of the poor was clear. Perth and Fremantle could not sink into the same depths of overcrowding as other parts of the world. People in the growing metropolitan area had to be rescued from the 'hopeless and deteriorated' conditions of slums.[129] The authorities feared the ongoing perpetuation of what we now call an underclass. It refers to the long-term unemployed and impoverished families.[130] Persistent poverty more than just unemployment is a key element in understanding people who are very poor.[131] It can also be socially constructed in terms of being linked to the poor, the welfare poor and disreputable poor.[132] While it can be fluid, the underclass almost always live in poorer conditions and neighbourhoods and differ from the regularly employed working class.[133] Importantly, the underclass had to be prevented from becoming criminals and members of a 'dangerous class'.

Dangerous people

Men and women who were frequently out of work and wandering the streets were regarded as the undeserving poor, not part of a respectable working class.[134] While the undeserving poor image has increased since welfare systems were introduced in the aftermath of World War Two, the 'social benefit scrounger' has been around since at least the sixteenth and seventeenth centuries.[135] By the second half of the nineteenth century, rapid urbanization increased concerns about poverty and its links with criminality.[136] When the very poor engaged in crime they were labelled the 'dangerous class'.[137] The very poor were thus excluded from social citizenship ideals and ostracized for not contributing to society.[138]

Perth and Fremantle harboured a dangerous class of men and women from the late nineteenth century. In 1880 the Chief Justice told various offenders that he would not stand for the 'depredations of persons of your class' in a community that was 'industrious, hardworking, and, I hope, thrifty'.[139] Criminals were outsiders who threatened the fabric of decent society. By the 1920s underclass criminals were increasingly seen as a social problem after an, 'age of classic social investigation' into them.[140]

The dangerous class concerned authorities in terms of their habitual criminal lives. Attorney General Thomas Walker, addressing parliament on the introduction of a criminal bill in 1911, made a clear distinction between criminals and recidivists. According to Walker criminals were 'creatures to be pitied and specially treated'. Repeat offenders, on the other hand, were 'diseased morally' and needed to be 'isolated from the rest of the community'.[141] In 1912, an editorial on the United Charity Organisation in Western Australia argued against

> charity that all too frequently, goes to the undeserving at the expense of the genuinely distressed or needy…Every large city has its quantum of wastrels who cadge their worth less way through life, and the blackest part of their offending is that their practices divert relief from deserving cases, and tend to foster cynicism in the often victimised'.[142]

Five years later another editorial warned: 'Big cities are growing, and with them slums. And with the slums is ignorance, and dirt, wretchedness material and moral'.[143] There is a fine line here between the deserving and undeserving poor.

Authorities had a very clear definition of who the deserving poor were in Perth and Fremantle society. From 1911 to 1913, there had been a thirty-three per cent increase in the number of adults and children assisted with money or kind through the state. The Superintendent of Public Charities declared in 1913 that it was the duty of charities to provide assistance to those who were destitute either from age, infirmity, or some other sufficient reason'. Lack of employment was cited as a sufficient reason. He also listed five types of deserving poor: ' (a) Widows, (b) mothers with sick husbands, (c) mothers with husbands in the asylum (d) mothers with husbands in prison, and e) mothers deserted by husbands'.[144] Those engaging in criminal activities were quite clearly the undeserving poor.

West Australian concerns mirrored international anxieties about the dangerous class within urban centres. In Columbus, Ohio in the late nineteenth century, there was a preoccupation with how to keep the dangerous class away from respectable people.[145] In struggling to understand poverty and crime, authorities and charitable institutions were faced with a reality that many criminals were reduced to poverty because of their crime as were 'paupers driven to crime by their poverty'.[146] This led to a twentieth century idea of paupers as driven to crime.[147] In March 1930, George Bootmaker told the Perth Police Court that he was 'desperately hungry' when he stole a bag in Barrack Street. He had nothing to eat all day and 'nowhere to go except the Esplanade'.[148]

The idea of the undeserving poor is useful to those who are not poor. Characterised as responsible for crime, the image of criminals as impoverished people provided the better off with a stereotype of those responsible for criminal activities.[149] The idea of the predatory criminal class within the non-respectable working classes also gained popularity from the nineteenth century.[150] In December 1928, the scandalsheet *Truth* referred to Detective Sergeant McGinty's fight against 'Perth's battalion of predatory women' stealing from shops in the city.[151] These women were sensationalised in the press as part of an undeserving poor, pilfering from respectable society and engaging in 'street criminal activity and other aberrant behaviour'.[152]

Underclass criminals were said to profit from fraudulent shops and businesses in the back streets of the city. In August 1903 *Truth* ran a story on second-hand clothes stores in the back alleys of Perth accused of selling stolen goods:

> Any visitor to Perth cannot but notice that many of the back streets are small Petticoat Lanes. In every street of Perth, sometimes running door to door, are secondhand or "old clo'" shops…something very sinister about the whole business.[153]

People selling stolen goods were labelled crafty Fagins and the back alleys likened to parts of East End London. Poorer parts of the city, as sensationalised at they were in the press at times, were well known as haunts of urban criminals. Police regularly raided a number of businesses on Barrack, Beaufort, Murray and Wellington Streets for illegal betting offences, mainly for keeping a betting house in the back of premises. Illegal betting in the streets also presented police with frequent disruptions to both pedestrian and motor traffic. Trafalgar Road and Short Street in East Perth were frequently brought to a standstill by Two-Up contests. James Duffy was brought before the authorities in September 1929 when his street betting interfered with pedestrian traffic in Charles Street.[154]

Street betting and betting houses kept the police busy and hindered traffic in the city centre but sly grog shops, assaults and thieving gangs were a greater source of concern for authorities. Sly grog shops operated out of regular businesses, coffee palaces and homes and contributed to public drunkenness. Eva Shearer, a widow, was charged in June 1911 with the illegal sale of alcohol in a shop on Wellington Street, adjoining the Kensington Hotel. She was caught when a police informer purchased stout from her and returned with a search warrant. Eva's lawyer pleaded guilty on her behalf but argued she was not in the habit of selling alcohol. Her shop was recognised as one of a growing number of Sunday hotels operating outside of liquor restrictions.[155]

Some shops were also a front for sly-grog selling. One fruit shop in Pier Street was referred to in the press as a notorious place for buying colonial beer far cheaper than in the hotels. Some of its frequent customers, it was alleged, included 'police delinquents' in plain clothes.[156] The sly grog trade flourished at a time when hotels could only sell liquor up to the early hours of the evening. People wanting to drink on into the night had to go looking for the sly grog sellers down alleys in at the back of shops.

Customers at the Central Café in Hay Street were often treated to a liquor raid on the premises. In March 1916 the proprietor fronted court on a charge of illicit dealing in liquor. A probationary constable had dined at the café with a female. When he asked for a beer he was told a young worker had just been sent out to get a dozen. Upon the lad's return the officer was given some beer and placed a sample in a jar. It wasn't the first time the constable had been served alcohol at the café. The proprietor had been convicted of illicit sale of liquor in January 1915 and so was heavily fined in this case.[157]

Inner city cafes were the cause of some concern to authorities. In June 1907 the proprietor of the Café Anglais fronted court for breaching the licensing law. A case was made against John Goldsworthy for having 'permitted reputed thieves and women on evil fame to remain on his premises'.[158] Police alleged the café was a well-known place for 'persons of bad character' and 'half-drunken' women.[159] Criminals were making themselves at home in the local cafes and the authorities would not tolerate it.

There was a growing belief by some in the press that Murray Street had in fact turned the criminal corner in 1912. *The Sunday Times* published an article in July outlining its 'metamorphosis'. Taken on a tour of the street only a few years earlier by a member of the CID, the reporter told of seeing one of the worst criminals being pointed out on the street. It was also apparently a site for 'draggled women'.[160] The street had apparently changed considerably by 1912. The Catholic Church now stood where it could look down the street, along with the new building for the Commissioner of Health and 'big warehouses and business premises of importance'. It was becoming one of the 'finest business thoroughfares in the city'. [161] Not everyone agreed with an improvement in Murray Street. One writer to *The Sunday Times* in 1920 asked those who doubted the existence of slums in the city to take a walk down Murray Street where the conditions people were living in made the writer 'sick'.[162] It was sensationalist in some respects but backed up by other reports and letters to the papers.

Crime continued to be a problem along Hay, King and Wellington Streets into the 1930s. It was generally off-bounds from the early evening. Hay Street, up towards Cathedral Avenue, was described in court in 1933 as 'a scene of frequent trouble' which 'provides more work for this court than it should do'.[163] The trouble continued. James Dalton was badly injured in Hay Street when he was assaulted by a group of men in October 1937.[164] Hay Street's narrow and congested layout, seen as aiding criminal activity, remained the same until the 1970s.[165]

Hardly a week passed when a crime was not reported in Wellington Street. The street was notorious from the late nineteenth century for garrotting attacks. Perth residents read numerous stories in the papers about individuals attacked with a weapon, held tight with an arm around their head and then robbed.[166] In May 1935, three men set upon William McGilvray, a resident of the Salvation Army Home, while he stood in Wellington Street one evening.[167]

Melbourne Road, intersecting Murray and Wellington Streets, was also notorious for crime. It was claimed 'scarcely a day or night passes but a case of assault and battery takes place, and the locality is converted into a veritable pandemonium for the time being'.[168] It was not the type of place you wanted to be in the late hours of the day. Two 'reputable citizens' found this out firsthand in September 1912 when two bullies who were 'lying in wait in the shadows' attacked them. According to press reports, they were 'lucky to escape with a few bruises and their silver intact'.[169]

Narrow laneways and parks were also off-bounds. James Keoughran was robbed one night in a case of mistaken identity. As he walked along Pier Street two men took hold of him outside the Goldfields Club Hotel and took off with money and cheques from his pockets. In January 1938 Clarence Paine was attacked with a knife in a lane off Pier Street.[170] Weld Square between Beaufort and Stirling Streets was almost a no-go area most nights. James Kennedy fell asleep in Weld Square one evening in November 1905 and was robbed of his watch, chain and pocket-knife.[171] Almost a fortnight later a man was stabbed in the Square after a disagreement with another man. He had escaped his assailant in

Weld Square and was found bleeding from the face in Wellington Street but refused to give police the name of his attacker.[172]

Thieving gangs were notorious in Murray, Pier and the inner areas of Fremantle. Some used females as decoys. Minnie Forrester played a central role in a thieving gang that targeted men in the alleyways of Perth. She would lure men into the alleyway with promises of a good time where they would be confronted with male members of the gang who would assault and rob the unsuspecting male. *Truth* claimed in 1904 that one victim of the Murray Street gang committed suicide – or was murdered perhaps – after his attack. He was lured into an alleyway off the street by a woman of 'evil-repute' and then set upon by the group's ringleaders.[173]

On the northern side of the city, over the railway tracks, in what would later be named Northbridge, certain streets became synonymous with criminal or immoral activity. Roe, James and Fitzgerald Streets were notorious for brothels, soliciting, Chinese Dens, gambling houses and public drunkenness. This was the stomping ground of shady characters such as William O'Shea and James Dunn. The pair frequented hotels like the Great Western Hotel (now the Brass Monkey), thieving from customers, 'lay about' in Russell Square and 'kept company with bad characters of both sexes'.[174] Like the park areas near the city centre, Russell Square regularly featured in police records. In March 1900, police arrested Mary Lloyd for abusing passers-by from a seat in the Square.[175]

By the first years of the twentieth century, some members of the public became quite vocal in their responses to crime streets. One letter to *The West Australian* in 1909 provides a vivid image of what the author calls 'Lawlessness in the Streets'. Responding to a previous letter in the paper arguing for low levels of crime, 'Justice' asks the writer of that letter is they had heard of:

> the shooting affair in East Perth. Did he hear of the man who was knocked down and killed near the Bohemia Hotel? And what about the police-constable who was set upon by some young roughs near the Great Western Hotel and received such a severe handling some months ago? The garrotting on William-street bridge, one of the chief thoroughfares of the city? And again, the arrest of two ruffians in Wellington-street for house-breaking etc? He

probably never heard of the person who was waylaid near Weld-square…Another person set upon in Stirling-street…I saw a powerful man stop his buggy in Murray-street and rush up to an old man standing on the footpath and knock him down, leaving him bleeding in open daylight, and drive off as if nothing happened.[176]

'Justice' hoped the letter would do 'quite enough to convince any lover of justice that there's more lawlessness in Perth than some people would imagine'.[177]

Crime streets also impacted on Fremantle life. By the twentieth century it was the kind of place where you could find a brothel between two churches, as *Truth* reported in 1903. Scathing in its description of the port town, the paper stated: 'Fremantle was never of good repute as a sanitary town, and it is even of worse repute as a moral one'.[178] In July 1926 *The West Australian* reported magistrates taking issue with a 'crime that is much too prevalent in Fremantle'.[179]

By its very nature as a port town, crime in Fremantle was different in some ways to Perth. Thieving gangs centred their attentions on the shipping sheds and yards rather than department stores favoured by some thieves in Perth. The wharves provided dishonest lumpers with opportunities to steal items from cargo arriving regularly in the port. Police and Customs raids on houses in North Fremantle late in December 1902 failed to turn up six cases of tobacco stolen from the 'B' Sheds at Victoria Quay.[180]

The port did, however, share much in common with crime in Perth too. Crime in laneways also concerned people in Fremantle. In April 1924 the Head of the Fremantle Criminal Investigation Branch expressed his concern in court that the absence of lights in the laneways behind businesses was 'an inducement to boys to embark upon careers of crime'.[181] Speaking at the trial of three boys charged with stealing from Fremantle shops, he declared unlit lanes provided a cover of darkness for raids of shops, during what the paper termed a recent 'epidemic of thieving' in the port town.[182] Fremantle was no different to other Australian cities that harboured crime in unlit streets and dark alleyways.[183]

Pakenham, Leake, Bannister and Market Streets all featured regularly in criminal cases and reports in the papers. One police raid in Fremantle in May 1903 provides an insight into some of these streets. In an effort to deal with the problem of prostitution and houses of 'disreputable character', police raided a number of houses over the course of a weekend. Houses in Norfolk, Arundel, Pakenham and Bannister Streets were the main targets. In court the actions of the police were commended in aiming to 'rid the town of its undesirable characters'.[184]

South Beach, further out from the centre of Fremantle, also took on a criminal identity into the 1920s. Fremantle's attraction as a resort town meant visitors gravitated towards South Beach for swimming, outdoor films and general entertainment.[185] John Curtin, Federal Member for Fremantle and future Prime Minister, opened the Summer Season at South Beach in 1928.[186] He didn't expect the entertainment to be so criminal. *Truth* used a court appearance that same summer to alert its readers to a pickpocket problem in the area:

> To be a pickpocket, lifting a wallet from a coat, whose owner is inside, needs a certain amount of courage, cleverness and deftness, which brings the action close to art…crooked art. But to dive a clumsy hand into the pocket of a coat whose owner is diving in the sea at a good distance away is a cowardly action which has no grace at all.[187]

The thief in question was condemned as both criminal and not artistic enough for the trade.

Criminals were also more mobile then they had ever been. Like other urbanised parts of the world, Perth experienced two major eras of change influencing its urban geography from the late nineteenth century. From the 1870s, during the Age of Steam and Steel, Perth's railways network increased, particularly with the opening of the Central Railway Station in 1881. The overhead electric tramway extended Perth's urban planning from 1899 and by 1911 was taking passengers to suburbs outside the city. Automobiles expanded the metropolitan area even further from the 1920s.[188] Such technological advances meant criminals could travel further more easily and had more options when trying to escape from police.

Prohibited Streets

Despite their poverty and criminal activities, very poor non-Indigenous people were treated better than Indigenous residents. The centre of Perth also included a large Noongar prohibited area from 1927-1954. Aboriginal people were only allowed to enter and walk through the main streets of the city centre with a pass. The exclusion zone extended from along the waterfront down at the jetty, along up Spring Street, Milligan Street, past Russell Square north of the city centre, along Newcastle Street, Lord and Royal Street in East Perth and down Bennett Street, intersecting with Adelaide Terrace. It excluded Noongar from all main parts of the city, including businesses, parks and access to the waterfront. Wellington Square, an important centre for a number of Aboriginal groups, was in the prohibited zone. It explains why today this is such an important meeting place.[189]

Men and women socialising with Aboriginal men and women, even before the creation of the prohibited zone, could be charged with consorting. Under the 1905 Aborigines Act, and subsequent amendment act of 1909, supply of liquor to Aboriginal people was prohibited. Lilly Morris was sent to prison for three months for supplying alcohol to an Aboriginal man and woman on a vacant block in Wellington Street.[190] Lilly Morris was frequently drunk and idle in the inner city streets and had dozens of convictions again her name[191], but she was never excluded from Perth and Fremantle based on race, something quite different to Aboriginal experiences. Non-Indigenous people could be hauled off the streets if their activities were viewed as criminal. However, a major difference is, they were not excluded entry into the city. No matter how drunk or violent Esther Warden acted in her life, she was never prohibited entry into the city based on race.

Criminal Invasion

There's an interesting argument behind some of the debates about a dangerous class in Perth and Fremantle in the early twentieth century. Newspapers used court proceedings to argue criminals from other places outside the state had invaded Western Australia. One article in *The West Australian* in May 1903 detailed a 'Western invasion of criminals' from the eastern states. These 'undesirable characters' were exciting feelings of terror amongst suburban householders worried about the future of the metropolitan area.[192] In May 1904, *Truth* argued the gold rushes from the late nineteenth century turned the state into a 'dumping ground of notorious criminals from every portion of the globe – especially the Eastern States'.[193] Some of the 'most expert and daring ruffians in Australia' were said to inhabit the streets of Perth and Fremantle, hanging around public houses and forming gangs menacing respectable business owners and residents.[194]

There is some truth to anxieties about crime from other places taking root in Western Australia. By 1901, due in large part to gold rush immigration from the late 1880s, the state's population had increased from fewer than 30,000 in 1881 to over 184,000.[195] Perth's metropolitan population alone had increased from 6,000 in 1884 to over 87,000 in 1911.[196] The population in both the capital and the state was a largely immigrant one with those born in WA a minority of the population. Most Australian migrants came from Victoria and New South Wales.[197] A quarter of all non-Indigenous people in 1921 were born overseas, nearly eighty per cent from the British Isles.[198]

Western Australia's crime statistics, as indicated by the press, reflected the largely immigrant population. Analysis of individual cases relating to warrant notices in the various *Police Gazettes* from 1900-1939 show as many as two-thirds of warrants were for people from overseas. However, they were mainly for crimes committed outside Western Australia. The majority of warrants, particularly in the years before World War One, were for men from Scotland, England, Ireland, Germany, Finland, Sweden, Russia and the Malay Peninsula. Many tried to use a career as seamen to avoid facing criminal charges.[199] Their crimes show the ongoing problem of transitory crime, as was evidenced also by those on the run from charges in the eastern states.

A better indication of crime *within* Western Australia from 1900-1939 is the details for prisoners gaoled for crimes committed in the state, particularly cases before the Courts of Petty Sessions where the conviction rate was higher.[200] On average over forty per cent of prisoners were born in the eastern states, mostly from Victoria and New South Wales. At least half were men migrating from the Victorian goldfields hoping to make a quick fortune from WA's gold boom. Instead they found themselves down on their luck and turning to crime. A further forty-five per cent of gaoled criminals came from overseas, notably Britain, Finland, Sweden and Germany. Around ten per cent of criminals were born in Western Australia.[201] What needs to be taken into account, however, is possible bias within the taking of details. Police and prison staff may have made greater note of non-West Australians to emphasise crime as a problem brought into Western Australia. In at least ten per cent of cases where origins were not listed, the criminals were from Western Australia.[202] Regardless of their origins, however, by the first years of the twentieth century, the inner metropolitan streets were home to many criminals and criminal groups.

Criminal women on the streets

The inner city and port streets were home to a number of female criminals. While male crime dominated, close to ten per cent of criminals in Western Australia were women. They were also predominantly local girls. Around three-quarters of women arrested for offences against good order were from Western Australia or had lived in the state for some years. Those born elsewhere, around half of all women convicted, were mainly from Victoria, New South Wales, New Zealand, England and Ireland.[203] As a whole, they were a recognisable part of the community and known to police.[204]

Women came to the attention of police in inner city streets well known for crime: Murray, Wellington, upper Hay, Pier, Newcastle, Fitzgerald, Roe and Lake streets in Perth and Leake, Bannister, Market, High and Pakenham Streets in Fremantle. Drunkenness, petty theft, soliciting and assault tended to be local offences. There were obvious benefits to committing local offences. Soliciting near home, for example, allowed women to engage in sex away from the chances of being caught by the police. Caroline Salvetti was known to pick up men in pubs or on the streets then take them back to her house in James Street. By the 1930s her impatience with exacting quick payments led to her attacking men in her home, something that brought her business to the attention of police.[205]

Drinking was usually the entry point into crime for female. Over seventy per cent of women facing court for offences against public order were charged with drunkenness.[206] Drinking introduced women to criminal haunts and bad company. However, their histories also show women who were a part of pub culture in working class areas but when they pushed it too far and got out of hand, they were excluded.

A tour of these drinking streets is important to imagining the places criminal women frequented in the early twentieth century. Women favoured the pubs closest to the main nightlife streets of Perth and Fremantle, not unlike their male counterparts. With the boom from the mining sector, hotels became more 'opulent' from 1890-1911.[207] Wellington Street, closest to the Railway Station, was a favourite drinking haunt for women. Hotel numbers in fact increased in Perth and Fremantle around the railway stations to accommodate people travelling on trains and commuting to work.[208] Grand Central Hotel, now a Backpackers at 379 Wellington Street, attracted many of the women featured in this book. Esther Warden, for example, drank too much here one night in February 1903. When the licensee tried to move her on, she struck him in the nose. She was still half drunk at her court appearance.[209]

Moving along the street to the west, the Imperial and Globe Hotels, opposite the Railway Station, were frequented by numerous women, including Mary Tite. By 1939 she was prohibited from entering the Imperial Hotel but was found there one evening by a plain-clothes policeman. Her need for a glass of beer and a chat with friends got her three days in gaol.[210] The Royal Hotel, at 531 Wellington Street, was convenient up until the late 1920s for its location across from the Wellington Markets. You could come out of this pub and wander around to William Street where on the corner the Bohemia Hotel stood.

City Hotel, further along Murray Street and on the corner of King Street, was another favourite pub for women. It was frequented by the likes of Mary Richardson, a well-known identity about Murray Street. Known as 'Roughie', she was held responsible in the press for starting the 'War in Murray-Street' in February 1900 between her partner, a neighbour and an arresting officer[211] and was frequently thrown out of the City Hotel.

For those living near Melbourne Road, the Melbourne Hotel (still standing) was a favourite. Women who did not want to drink up Murray and Hay Street often kept going along William

Street towards the Terrace to have a drink at the Palace Hotel, now Bankwest.

Women coming into the city centre from the direction of East Perth frequently used the pubs lining the eastern end of Hay Street. The Grosvenor Hotel, built at the turn of the century, was favoured along with the Criterion Hotel at 560 Hay Street and the Metropole Hotel (now in the mall).

Across the railway tracks, on the northern side of the city, The Great Western Hotel at 209 William Street (now the Brass Monkey) featured in crime reports in the press. Drunken women were regularly confronted with police outside the pub. Only a walk away from the Police Station and Lock Up on Roe Street, it was one of the main areas of the police patrol each evening, something that naturally impacted on criminal statistics. Further up James Street, on the corner of Milligan Street, was the Victoria Hotel, now Rosie O'Grady's. This was one of Esther Warden's favourite drinking places.

Fremantle is known for its collection of various pubs lining the main streets. All of the main pubs were there in the early twentieth century and frequented by a collection of female habitual drunks. Oddfellows Hotel on South Terrace (now the Norfolk Hotel) and Freemason's Hotel (now the Sail & Anchor) were favoured by female drinkers. Esther Warden was notorious in pubs lining the streets off the Terrace. At the Duke of York Hotel on Bannister Street, the licensee moved on Warden in October 1913 after she had had too much to drink. She retaliated by throwing a stone at his head and spent the next month in prison.[212] High Street, a main thoroughfare one block across from Bannister Street, was Esther's favourite drinking street. It was close to where she had set up a house of 'ill-repute' (a brothel) in 1900. She was a regular at the Commercial and Cleopatra hotels but saved some of her most drunken, violent sprees for the Orient Hotel, cornering Henry Street.[213]

You were much more likely, however, to bump into a drunken woman on the *streets* in Perth and Fremantle in the early decades of the twentieth century. Public drunkenness was the main target of police and authorities. In at least half of the drunkenness cases, women were arrested in public, outside of the pubs. Jane Sleeman was found drunk in the Esplanade in Perth in 1913 in possession of a child's go-cart. Unsure as to how exactly she came by the stolen item, Sleeman, in a drunken haze, thought she might have taken it from outside a shop in William Street.[214] Sarah Gundry was arrested in Fitzgerald Street in March 1918 brandishing a beer bottle and telling anyone who would listen that she had been released from gaol that morning. She was sent back inside for another fortnight.[215]For Sleeman and Gundry, as women, their drinking immediately signalled a lack of respectability'.[216]

Street prostitutes worked similar streets, lurking in the shadows of popular thoroughfares or more upfront and confident in streets known for the sale of sex. Women soliciting for sex on the streets, outside of the brothels, could be found anywhere along the main streets of Perth and Fremantle but there were identifiable preferences.

Around the CBD area, women sought out businessmen. *Truth* ran a story in July 1903 on the prostitutes parading 'Barrack and Hay-Streets about 5pm every afternoon'. Anywhere from ten to twenty women paraded along these streets and were often led into work offices by men who, the paper stated, should have been at home with their wives and children.[217] The paper even claimed that 'respectable' St Georges Terrace was 'turned into a regular prostitutes' parade'.[218]

On the other side of the railway tracks, working-class men favoured Roe Street brothels. The first brothel, Nera, was on the corner of Roe Street and Melbourne Road.[219]. As more and more women were pushed off the streets into brothels, Roe Street became an important centre for prostitution in Perth. Street prostitution here was mixed in with brothels near boarding houses and single workmen's cottages, distanced from the respectable areas.[220] Debates raged during the war years about the increase in prostitution in Perth. In the first two years of the war there were twice as many convictions for soliciting than any year before that.[221]

The authorities looked to further regulate the sex trade. It was easier for police to tolerate illegal sexual activity if it could be contained within designates areas.[222] Brothels, for their part, were easier to control. Their close proximity to the Central Police Station in Perth, for example, meant the sex trade could be closely monitored and prostitution contained. By the 1920s only a few scattered brothels remained in outlying suburbs.[223] The regulation of the sex industry greatly benefited the madams who were able to profit from the localisation of prostitution within a few brothels in Roe Street.[224]

Fremantle had its own houses of ill-repute in Bannister and Pakenham Streets but they never took off as much as the brothels in Roe Street, Perth. However, these Fremantle streets had their fair share of well-known prostitutes. Rachael O'Brien was also well known to police for soliciting in Bannister Street. An old offender, she was rarely out of trouble in 1902. Suffolk Street also featured as a street for immoral purposes. One house adjoining another house of ill-repute, off Marine Terrace, was mentioned in a shooting incident in 1902.[225] The same house featured in another shooting case a few months later in 1903. The link between violence and soliciting was meant to serve as an example to readers of the low-life people living in the area.[226]

Streets associated with criminal activities were also known to harbour homeless women who were criminalised for vagrancy. These women mainly slept rough in the back streets of Perth and Fremantle, in parks and sheds at the back of properties. Notorious spots included Wellington Street, near the Markets, and Hay, King and Pier Streets. More women favoured park areas such as Wellington, Weld and Russell Squares. In an age when women were expected to be at the centre of family life and uphold the morals values of the household, the vagrant female was seen as a failure in society. The press ran regular stories about these women, as in the case of Alice Sullivan, found in an unoccupied house in John Street, West Perth in 1919.[227] Interestingly, when Mary Govan appeared in court on charges of vagrancy in a Perth park, she claimed there were women who were more of a nuisance in the park and couldn't understand why she had been singled out.[228]

Women committing offences against good order were also known to sleep rough on Heirisson Island at the Causeway in Perth. There they slept in shacks with other homeless people, forming a community of vagrants. Mary Ann Reardon was rescued from the river in 1902 drunkenly trying to get to her lover on the island.[229] Mary Ann Sweetman was also known to sleep there regularly.[230] Further south, as South Beach in Fremantle, women slept near other homeless people in the scrub nearby or in huts on the beach. It was a favourite sleep-out spot for Esther Warden.[231] Lilly Doyle, too, was a regular at the vagrant humpies on the sandhills between South Beach and Robbs Jetty.[232]

Despite the persistence of crime in inner city streets, if crime could be contained within particular territories of the inner city streets of Perth and Fremantle, the more respectable citizens of the growing metropolitan area could take comfort in knowing crime had been contained, dealt with and its expansion prevented. However, when it encroached on respectable communities outside of the main streets, the public outcry was quick and fierce. Criminals, particularly criminal women, could not be allowed to encroach on the better suburbs of around Perth and Fremantle. Believing they were under threat from vice and crime, suburban residents used the press as a means to gain public attention for their plight. It was a question of decency, not a call for assistance for the impoverished of Perth and Fremantle. Good communities, residents argued, should not be threatened by vice and crime, particularly from women. One resident of George Street in West Perth argued:

In the interests of decency I would like to call the attention of the authorities to the disgraceful sights and sounds in George-street, West Perth. Drunken men and women, with dress shamefully disheveled and using language that even devils would hesitate to use are the sights and scenes to which decent residents are compelled daily to see daily.[233]

Residents close to Charles Street, just out of the inner city area, didn't appreciate their evenings and weekends disrupted by females who 'endeavoured to paint Charles-street red with their language'.[234] As a regular meeting place for the less appealing members of society it was the job of the police, one letter to *The West Australian* argued, to clear the streets of these unsavoury types. Sisters, Millicent and Lucy Webb, enraged residents of Kimberley Street, Leederville in January 1918 by using bad language in the presence of locals. They were characterised by police as bad characters who, together with some young men in their company, regularly caused a disturbance and used 'filthy language'.[235] Residents of Mount Hawthorn also complained to authorities about Dorothy Iolanthe Smith 'sleeping in the open air' around residences. Her vagrancy was in direct opposition to respectable suburban life.[236]

* * * * * * *

In the first decades of the twentieth century, Perth and Fremantle had clearly identifiable streets known for criminal activities. There was a general social understanding that some streets were off-bounds by the late afternoon when they would start to attract a regular crowd of drunks, thieves, prostitutes and gamblers. Esther Warden, Minnie Forrester, Mary Ann Sweetman and other women who make up this book frequented the inner city streets at all hours of the day. However, as we will see, these streets also brought together small communities of people who had nowhere else to go or did not want to go back to their homes. For people like Mary Ann Sweetman and Sarah Mattson, the inner city streets became a home of sorts and a place to meet other women in similar circumstances. Perth and Fremantle streets have many stories to tell, among them women criminalised for offences against good order. Our story starts with Esther Warden, one of the most feared drunken women about the streets of Perth and Fremantle.

2.

'A Perfect Fiend'[237]

Some of the most notorious female criminals in early twentieth-century Perth and Fremantle were drunks. Characteristically seen outside pubs, on street corners and wandering around the inner city parks, they could also be found in shop fronts, back alleyways, stables and beach shanties. Their beer, wine or port came from the local pubs and sly grog sellers who were willing to make some extra money out of the desperation of a hard drinker. Drunken women didn't usually talk to people passing by. They danced and shimmied about the streets trying to entertain invisible audiences but more times than not abused pedestrians and hurled beer bottles at them. Empty or full, it didn't matter. Each evening police roamed the streets looking for stray women who either had no place to go or were too incapacitated to run a mile when they caught sight of the local constables. Until the start of the twentieth century, the drunk on the streets was a nuisance and signalled a break from respectable society, but they were not regarded as criminals. It was only with the new legislation under the *Police Act* that they became a criminal menace, just by being drunk in public. It was into this world that Esther Warden entered the Perth and Fremantle criminal scene from 1900.

Esther Warden usually fought all the way from the streets to the lockup, to court and prison. In one case, she was arrested for assaulting another woman in Murray Street on the Saturday morning of 17 January 1914. A local constable arrived on the scene and found a man trying to pry two women apart, one of whom was Warden. When Constable James got hold of her, she thrashed about and kicked him in the shin; a wound he later showed in court. Only hours earlier she was run out of the Great Western

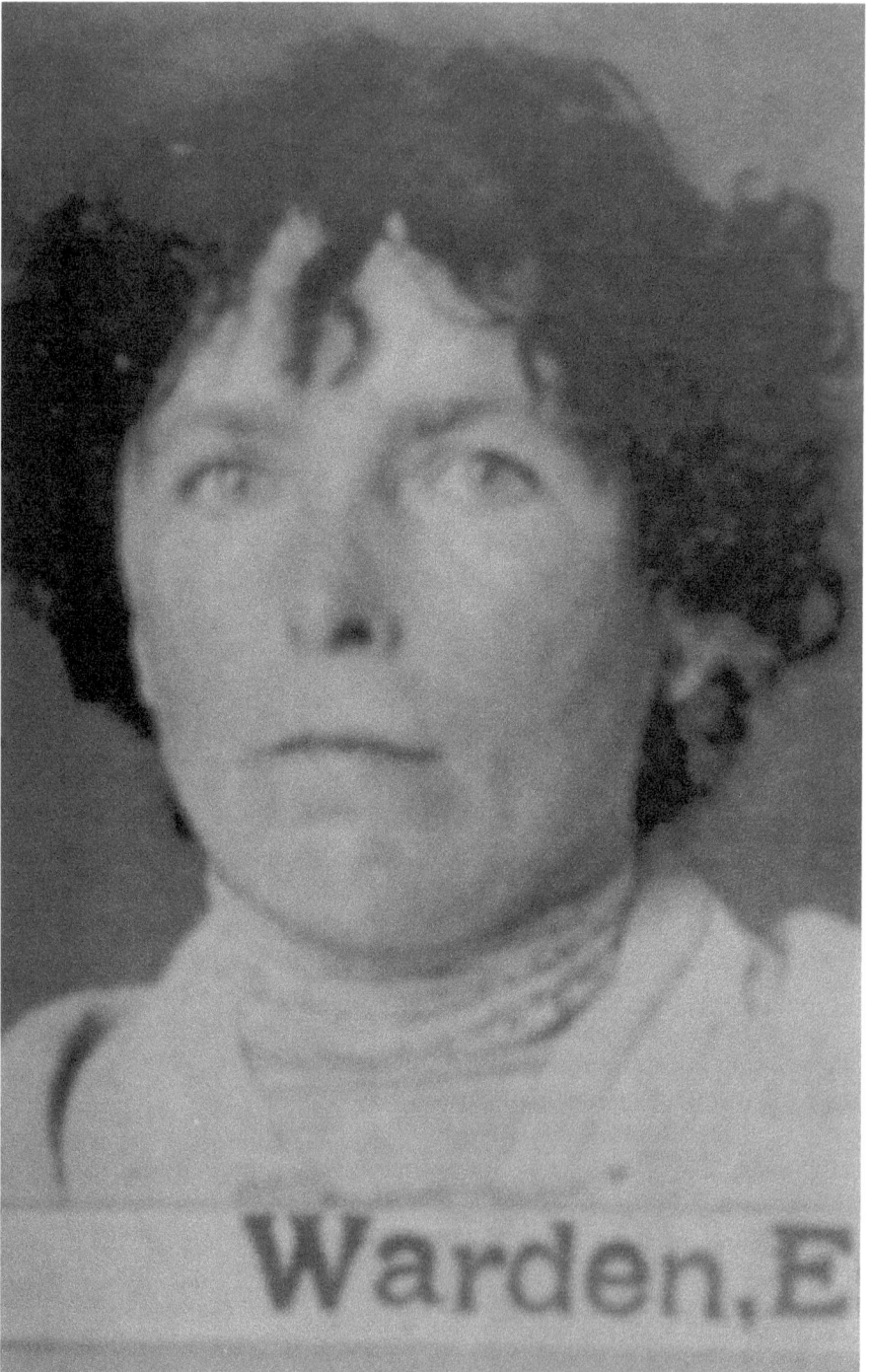

Esther Warden, 1911

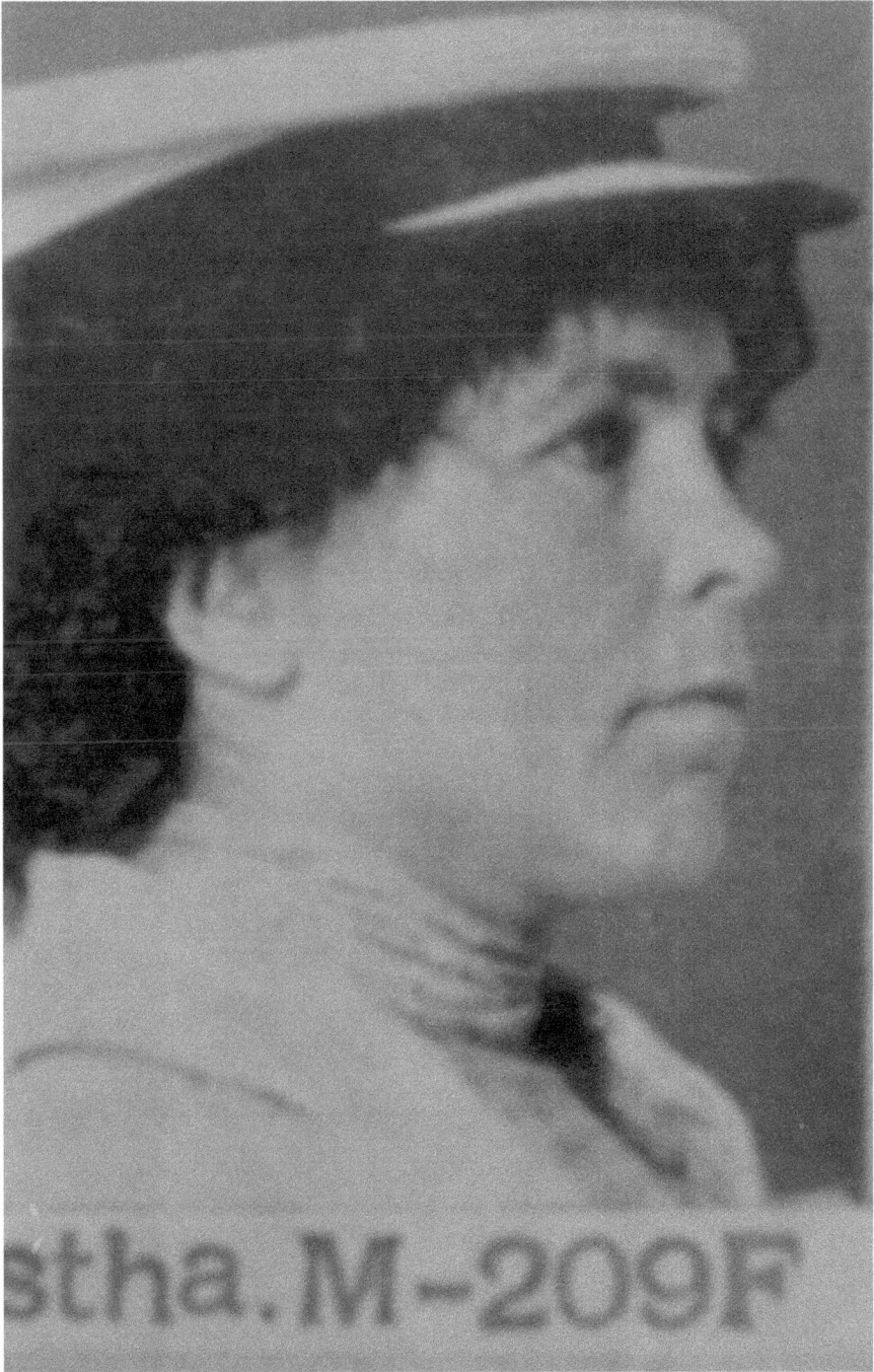

Hotel on William Street for assaulting a man with a hatpin. At the lockup police confined Esther in a solitary cell. For the two disorderly charges, Warden was sentenced to twenty-eight days in prison and a further two months for the assault.[238] Esther Warden regularly started a new year like this.

Esther knew the drill well at Fremantle Prison. She probably knew the rules by heart, having listened to female prison officers recite them to her for many years: 'A prisoner who shall use improper language or be guilty of swearing, quarrelling, fighting or making a false statement or giving a false reply to any question either verbally or in writing…'[239] Even with numerous convictions to her name by 1914, Esther Warden knew it was going to be another tough prison stint. The rules were always a problem, whether she spent weeks or months inside. She could handle the prison cell and even go without a drink for weeks at a time, knowing always that on release she could quench her thirst pretty much straight away, but banning her from using improper language, swearing or fighting with the other women was a hard rule to follow.

Prison officers had long ago given up hope of not seeing Esther Warden again. Now in her early forties, Esther listened to no one and tolerated the judicial system insofar as she served her sentence only to return to the streets and commit a crime. Esther was also a product of her circumstances. Her husband and former partners were long gone and she had few friends willing to help her out. Esther rarely played the victim card though. She was one of the toughest women about the streets of Perth and Fremantle. Warden was the local drunk you crossed over the street to get away from and police feared having to run her in. Notorious was an understatement.

Esther Warden's real battle was with alcoholism, made worse by recent legislation against public drunkenness. People caught intoxicated in public could find themselves sentenced to gaol terms of anywhere from weeks to six months at a time. Worse still for Esther, she was a female drunk in a society where people wrote letters to the press about drunken women 'lounging about the streets…to the deep degradation of their sex'.[240] As we walk the streets with Esther and try to make sense of the life she led in the first decades of the twentieth century, her long criminal career reveals much about a society in which women found drunk in public faced harsher sentences than if they had assaulted a person or stolen property. The drunk was a direct threat to the social order; as a female drunk, Esther Warden also transgressed strict moral codes. Esther's unwillingness to conform to social mores led to her being cast out from society.

*

Esther Warden was born Esther Muriel Wingfield in Carlisle, England in 1873.[241] With prison staff, however, she seems to have had a bit more to say on that. Over the course of her prison sentences, she identified herself as from Carlisle in England, Galway in Ireland and Victoria, Australia. At one point her religious affiliation is Roman Catholic but even this is changed to Church of England. [242] It seems likely, based on the repetitiveness of England as a birthplace across the records, Esther was from England but probably of Irish heritage. The Victorian connection is an interesting one. Warden regularly claimed in court that she had rich family members in Victoria and brothers who were willing to take her to Melbourne. She claimed in 1918 that rich relatives from Melbourne sent her money when she was out of gaol but this was in defence of a vagrancy charge and used as evidence she had legal means of support.[243] The Victorian family members are never named, do not appear in court in her defence and she never attempts to use any money to go to Victoria.

Esther's life before 1900, when she first appears in police and court records, is something of a guessing game. Sometime between her birth in 1873 and first known conviction in 1900, she arrived in Western Australia. The closest record for Esther's arrival in the state is a female migrant listed at Fremantle in January 1884, having docked on board ship from the eastern colonies.[244] Even if this was not Esther, it is possible she was lured from Victoria to Western Australia by the gold rushes of the late nineteenth century. She was not alone. The gold finds around the Kalgoorlie, Goldfields and Murchison regions from the 1890s brought many keen prospectors to Western Australia. The state's population had increased drastically from 29,708 in April 1881 to over 184,000 by March 1901.[245] This rapid movement of people west also left a trail of abandonment. Desertion records in the *Police Gazettes* detail the many wives and children left behind.[246] Western Australia also experienced a boom in prostitution as rapid urbanisation and heightened immigration increased the demand for sexual services. It wasn't just men who contributed to an increase in prostitution. Women looked for better business in the West, some wanting to escape police attention for their soliciting elsewhere in Australia.[247] Esther Warden may have been chasing gold and sex like many others before her. Esther's first conviction in Western Australia was in fact for keeping a house of ill fame (a house used for prostitution) in Pakenham Street, Fremantle in December 1900.[248]

Around this time Esther also gave birth to a stillborn son.[249] The child's birth record is significant as it lists one Alexander Carl Warden as the father. However, little is known of Esther's husband. By 1901 she was linked to another man, Plunkett O'Sullivan (aka Richard Plunkett) and no mention is made of a husband. By 1923 she is listed in the Prison Register as a widow, yet no certificate exists in Western Australian records for the death of Alexander Warden. Perhaps he moved interstate or overseas after 1900? Another possibility is Esther married before she came to Western Australia, fell pregnant but was then estranged from the father before she arrived in the state. Whether it is Wingfield or Warden family members in Victoria she is referring to later in court is not known.

What is clear is by 1901 Esther was involved in a violent relationship with Plunkett O'Sullivan. Plunkett was a clerk from St. Kilda in Victoria but listed 'traveller' as his trade.[250] Warden and O'Sullivan were notorious about the Perth and Fremantle streets, pubs and houses for their open battles with each other and anyone who got between them. Court, press and prison records reveal a long list of appearances on assault charges. In February 1901, they both appeared in court after Plunkett had beaten Esther up and tried to suffocate her with a pillow. According to Esther, assaults were regular and her black eye, on show for all to see in court, was just one of many. O'Sullivan was fined and in default faced seven days in prison.[251]

Two months later, Esther Warden's house in Melbourne Road (now Milligan Street), was the site of another violent confrontation. Two young girls, Ella (Eva) Claffey and Bella Dalrymple, were living with Warden in the house at the time. Judging by Claffey's criminal record[252], it seems likely Warden was using the house for prostitution. Local thief, Fred Dawson, entered the property and after some words with Warden started smashing lamps. Plunkett O'Sullivan arrived home at this point and intervened, leaving Warden to run out onto the streets and call down police. Warden was no shrinking violet though. She took to Dawson and O'Sullivan with a bottle in an attempt to clear them out of the house. It was Esther who actually brought the case to court, claiming O'Sullivan had assaulted her. For his part, Dawson claimed he had been living with Warden at the time and was trying to 'reclaim' her. The case was dismissed and the two girls were sent to the Salvation Army Home.[253]

The incident at Esther Warden's house in April 1901 was only the start for Eva Claffey. Over the course of the next sixteen years she was convicted numerous times for vagrancy and loitering for prostitution. *Truth* used one of her appearances in court in 1904 as an example of degradation of the inner city. Eva appeared with two other young women in court that January on idle and disorderly charges and were said to be in company of 'thieves and suspicious characters'. Yet their worst digression from respectability was frequenting a 'Chinaman's place in Stirling Street' in the city. There is an interesting twist to the story, however. The court preferred one of the women's associations with a Chinese man, against popular racial thinking at the time, to her mother who was said to have been largely responsible for her downfall.[254] Eva Claffey's mother had been sentenced to gaol as an idle and disorderly person on a number of occasions. In 1902 a magistrate, in sentencing mother and daughter, said Mary Claffey was responsible for her 'daughter's degradation'.[255] Eva had also supposedly suffered at the hands of her brother who ran a low-class brothel in Highgate and forced her to 'sell her body to Chinese men'.[256] It seems Esther Warden was but one of many people close to Eva who used her in the sex business.

Despite their own violent relationship, Plunkett and Esther were fiercely loyal to one another, as many hotel workers found out:

A Woman's Wiles - Esther Warden and Richard Plunkett, alias O'Sullivan, were jointly charged with having assaulted George West, licensee of the Grand Hotel. Mr. N. K.

Ewing appeared for the prosecution. The evidence of the complainant tended to show that the female accused was a general nuisance about the hotel. On the night of the assault she was very drunk, and he was putting her out, when she struck him on the nose. She could not stand properly, and tripped once. O'Sullivan then joined in the assault. A man named O'Sullivan gave evidence for the defence, after which O'Sullivan entered the box, and stated that West had thrown the female accused on to the path. She had bruises all over her body. Mr Roe reminded O'Sullivan of former advice which he had given him, and said that Warden had brought him to his present condition. O'Sullivan was fined with £1 15s. 6d. costs. Warden, who was half-drunk, was remanded till Friday.[257]

While no conviction is recorded in the Prison Register for this court appearance, O'Sullivan had to vouch for Warden only weeks later when she appeared on a vagrancy charge.[258]

It wasn't long before Esther was again before the Police Court. Three months later, in July, she was sentenced to one month in prison as an idle and disorderly person.[259] Police gave evidence in court that she associated with prostitutes and convicted thieves.[260] Warden's association with O'Sullivan did little to aid any reform. His financial support for Esther was unreliable based on his own cycle of offending and incarceration. Esther pleaded with a judge in June 1904 that she could not be held responsible for her vagrancy: 'My husband is in gaol, and the police say I have no visible means of support. Well how can I have any means of support if my husband is not out?'[261] While they were not legally married, it appears Esther thought of Plunkett as her husband. He had been convicted for a number of stealing offences in Kalgoorlie in February 1904 and sentenced to over two years in Fremantle Prison.[262] Released early from this sentence, he was in prison again in April 1905 for another stealing offence.[263] Plunkett was a crafty thief about the streets of Perth and Fremantle and could dodge arrest better than he could in Kalgoorlie, though usually not with Esther in tow.

By 1906, Esther and Plunkett were back in court together, this time appearing on 5 April 1906 to answer another charge of assault.

Police arrested the pair in Fremantle the previous month after they assaulted a man who was near-blinded in the attack. O'Sullivan was released but Warden was found guilty and sentenced to seventeen months in prison. Evidence presented to the court argued Esther was the main instigator and had inflicted the horrific injuries. Magistrate Roe, who had seen O'Sullivan and Warden in court many times over the last few years, told Plunkett he had warned him six years ago that his association with Warden would lead to trouble. This is interesting given O'Sullivan's stealing offences in Kalgoorlie in 1904 were committed while Warden was back in Perth. Roe was right, however, in his comments about Esther's character, claiming she 'was a woman who when she had a "little drink in her" was of an ungovernable temper'.[264]

While her abusive relationship with Plunkett O'Sullivan did her little good, alcohol was the root of Esther's problems. In February 1909 she was arrested for using bad language around two men in the city while drunk. She was taken to the lock up where by midday on the Sunday of 21 February she was fighting with other inmates and had to be detained in the refractory cell. She was sent back to prison for one month and fourteen days.[265] Within two weeks of her release she was back inside on another drunkenness charge.[266]

Four months later Warden asked a magistrate in court if she could leave Perth instead of facing another gaol term for idle and disorderly. The magistrate refused and sentenced her to over two months in prison.[267] A year later she was something of a local drunken identity in court:

> Muriel Warden Again - Esther Muriel Warden made her 90th odd appearance in a police court dock on a charge of drunkenness. She has appeared in the Port Police Court on 25 prior occasions. According to the police. Warden when arrested was in the street minus her boots and one stocking. During the Court proceedings she expressed the hope that she "wouldn't be hung for the offence." She was fined 5s or 21 days' imprisonment.[268]

Esther Warden arrived in Western Australia at a time when drunkenness was cast in the press as a 'Upas which poisons our whole social system'. Drink was the 'demon that was devouring the heart's blood of the colony'.[269] Debates raged throughout the second half of the nineteenth century about the 'multiplication of public houses [as] one of the most certain means of multiplying drunkenness and crime'. [270] As with discussions about narrow lanes and town improvements, public houses were likened to 'nurseries of crime'.[271] By 1889 West Australians consumed twice as much proof alcohol as the other Australian colonies. The colony ranked ten per cent higher in alcohol consumption than the United Kingdom and consumed more alcohol than most European countries. Consumption increased a further fifty per cent by the final years of the nineteenth century.[272] In Western Australia, alcoholism was the most common metabolic disease.[273] The increase in population with the gold rushes and the disparity between male and female numbers contributed to Western Australia's increased consumption of alcohol.

By the first years of the twentieth century, there were a growing number of arguments for the link between drunkenness and addiction. Questions were asked as to whether it was 'a moral vice, a bad habit, or a mental disease?'[274] In Britain, the United States and Australia excessive drinking featured in medical debates about habits and disease:

> The craving for alcohol, which is a symptom of disease, is intensified by a short period of compulsory abstention; and in some cases the sudden cutting off of the drink supply amounts to positive cruelty. The world, including the medical profession, has been slow to arrive at anything like a general agreement that inebriety is a disease not a misdemeanour.[275]

> Such debates inspired legislative changes in Western Australia. By the first years of the twentieth century, inebriates came under the Habitual Drunkards Bill, introduced into parliament late in 1898, and finally passed as the Western Australian Inebriates Act in 1912. The thinking behind the Act was to allow for better treatment of habitual drunks and break the cycle of unemployment and alcohol abuse:

It is better, however, that inebriates of the vagrant, unemployable type should be kept under merciful detention for an extended period than that they should oscillate between the streets and the gaol.[276]

The Act allowed for the placement of habitual drunks in Inebriate Homes, the first one opening at Whitby Falls in 1914 for men. There were no female inebriate retreats so women found themselves in gaol or one of the Homes for women. Some convicted drunken women were sent to the Claremont Asylum for the Criminally Insane.[277] Well into the twentieth century, however, the preferred treatment of inebriates remained gaol terms and periods of time in reformatories.[278]

Esther Warden's excessive drinking was thus defined as different to drunkenness. Defined as an inebriate, she had lost control over her alcohol consumption and, in turn, her life.[279] As much as habitual drunks might be pitied at the time, as in the case of the twenty-five year-old woman appearing in court and described as bedraggled and looking more like fifty[280], they presented a social problem through not contributing to society.

Yet, Warden was not only an inebriate; she was also labelled a dipsomaniac. A report in *The Sunday Times* in July 1927 referred to her as a 'female dipsomaniac'.[281] Based on late nineteenth-century medical thinking, alcohol consumption, for the dipsomaniac, was part of a disease that required control and treatment against the 'irresistible, uncontrollable, morbid impulse to drink stimulants'.[282] Drunkenness was now directly associated with insanity and could also be explained as a 'degenerative nervous disease often rooted in family history'.[283] Dipsomania was different from usual habitual drunkenness due to the imbalance within the person's mental state.

Dipsomaniacs were differentiated from habitual drunks from the late nineteenth century at a time when there was increasing focus on eugenics and defective biology, particularly within criminology.[284] Criminologist, Cesare Lombroso, published *The Criminal Man* in 1876 and argued a large number of offenders were born criminals.[285] Legislation in Western Australia in 1903, relating to the Lunacy Bill, decreed that habitual drunkards could be placed in a 'hospital for the insane' if a judge consulted with two medical practitioners who agreed to this. They could be placed there for a period not exceeding twelve months.[286] In this way, habitual drunkenness was linked to defective biology and dipsomaniacs were treated in similar ways to cases of insanity.

At times, the press used dipsomania stories to invoke sympathy for habitual drunks. In February 1905 the *Sunday Times* ran a story about a man sent down to Fremantle Gaol from Kalgoorlie. He was 'an unfortunate dipsomaniac, deserving of infinite pity and humane care and treatment'. Addicted to alcohol, he had been sentenced to over three months in gaol. Described in the Police Court as a 'disreputable drunk', the man pleaded he had 'committed no crime except against myself'.[287]

Defined as an inebriate, dipsomaniac and general alcoholic, the authorities were clearly looking for some sort of explanation as to why Esther Warden could not control her drinking, nor reform her ways. This negative public profile in the courts and press also brought her to the attention of members of the Temperance Movement in Western Australia. A letter was presented for Esther Warden in court in January 1914 confirming the Woman's Christian Temperance Union was willing to offer support towards her recovery from alcoholism. It was dismissed on the grounds that Warden was beyond reform.[288] She was, however, an ideal candidate for assistance from the Temperance Union.

The temperance movement was active in Australia from the 1830s. Advocates looked to education and reformation of the individual as key aims in dealing with the social ills of excessive drinking. Their efforts were closely linked to ideas about the regeneration of society through dealing with the vice of drunkenness.[289] This was a key topic of discussion at the Inter-colonial Temperance Convention in 1881.[290]

Temperance societies were part of a larger 'conservative force', aiming 'to keep Western Australian society as clean and wholesome as possible in the face of an increasing number and range of evils'.[291] Church groups, the Woman's Christian Temperance Movement and the Women's Service Guild, headed the social reform movement in the metropolitan area. Members were mainly from the middle-class but were led by Perth's elite, targeting 'the rough and unrespectable working-class'.[292] The WCTU, starting in the United States in 1873, was widely established across Britain and Australia only a few years later.

Temperance campaigns also inspired women to campaign for social reform and have a voice in society at a time when women there were 'among the few avenues of activity open to them'.[293] Miss Jessie Ackerman, a prominent member of the WCTU in America, went on a tour of Fremantle Prison in November 1910. Afterwards she used the local press to detail her thoughts on drinking to the West Australian public. Prison staff took her on a guided tour through cells and the main blocks of the female part of the prison. Jessie claimed she had 'rarely seen a set of harder faces'.[294] She came across women who had been in gaol more than twenty times each and had entered the prison worse the wear for drink. Ackerman, though praising the move towards reforming women inside and outside prison in Homes, worried that women were 'turned out again, victims of themselves' and with little help in trying to overcome alcohol abuse.[295] Jessie Ackerman's hope for female drunks was that they could be 'fully restored to womanhood and become useful citizens'.[296]

Ackerman had already toured Western Australia back in 1892 and was instrumental in setting up the WCTU in the state. By May 1910, when she arrived in the state ahead of her tour of Fremantle Prison, Ackerman was pushing for women's suffrage and the extension of women's voices into Australian public life. Jessie Ackerman encompassed the twin concerns of the WCTU: total abstinence from alcohol and women's suffrage as a means to bring in legislation to meet the needs of the temperance movement.[297] The WCTU believed in the nuclear family as the ideal in society. Female respectability was central to its moralistic drives. A Mothers' Day banquet in 1933 celebrated the 'importance of "mother" within the home and nation'.[298]

West Australian women joined Jessie Ackerman *en masse* to address the problem of drunkenness. Women began protesting in public against alcohol and in Australia visited houses, hotels and factories in an effort to raise public awareness of the 'evils' of drink.[299] Like the temperance movements in general, the WCTU was an evangelical movement aimed at educating people and enacting reforms through legislation. Mainly made up of middle class female members, the Union saw children as an important target of education; they were impressionable and had not started drinking so could perhaps be convinced not to start.[300] Grace

Ferguson, President of WCTU (WA), gave an address in 1903 stating: 'We are not fighting the publicans or the brewers, or the distillers especially, but we are fighting the drink traffic. We must do our best to teach people, especially children, of the bad effects on their health and lives'.[301]

With Perth headquarters in Barrack Street from 1898 and Willard House in Aberdeen Street after 1923, the WCTU women were in close proximity to public drinking places in the city. At the Barrack Street premises, in the first years of the twentieth century, meals and short-terms stays were arranged for people discharged from hospital or gaol.[302] WCTU members visited the lockup on Sundays.[303] In Fremantle, WCTU work, run out of Somerset Lodge, centred on prison visits and work around the main inner streets and close to the harbour.[304]

The WCTU was successful in 1923 in having drinking age increased from eighteen to twenty-one and a ban on sale of liquor within twenty miles of Perth on a Sunday.[305] Yet, despite temperance efforts in general and the work of the WCTU, the first years of the twentieth century showed little reform of Western Australia's drinking problem. Offences 'attributable to alcohol' still accounted for over forty per cent of cases brought before the Petty Sessions.[306] Histories of drinking in Australia also show that Western Australia was 'the exception to Australia's growing sobriety'.[307]

In response to temperance and community pressure, the West Australian government implemented an overall program of regulation and reduction from 1912-1927.[308] The Labor Government, under John Scaddan, headed a program for state hotels, as a way to regulate drinking establishments. A system of controlling and inspecting hotels also coincided with greater emphasis on the 'duties and obligations of licensed persons'.[309] A Licensing Amendment Act of 1922 set out that hotels in Perth and Fremantle would only be granted a license if they had twelve bedrooms, two sitting rooms, bedding and furniture and one bath and closet for every ten lodgers. There was also a tax on all goods in hotels.[310] Hotel licensees were now directly responsible for making sure hotels were used more for accommodation than drinking.

The Australian temperance movement was also responsible for achieving a six o'clock closing time for pubs across five states during and after the First World War. While Tasmania ended the early closing time in the 1930s, it continued on until the 1960s in Queensland, Victoria and South Australia. Western Australia never experienced a 'six o'clock swill', instead bringing in an early closing time of nine o'clock. Regulation of hotels and new closing times stemmed some of the flow of alcohol but wine shops remained popular in Perth and Fremantle. Fruit shop owners were also given wine licenses in the early twentieth century. Sly grog selling was also linked in with drunkenness debates. Men and women supplying alcohol outside of the regulated hours were portrayed as only adding to the ongoing social problems of alcohol abuse.[311] Sly-grog sellers inhabited a world on the streets of Perth and Fremantle directly aiding drunkenness and profiting from it.

While there were greater efforts across Australia to favour inebriate institutions over gaol terms for drunks,[312] in Western Australia, gaol was still the preferred punishment. Esther Warden became a notorious criminal largely based on the new legislation of the day. Criminalisation of drunkenness came under the *Police Act* of 1892, not under the Criminal Code.[313] Drunkenness was listed as an offence against good order and allowed police to monitor public behaviour.[314] Sections 53 and 54 of the *Police Act* set out persons found drunk or disorderly could be gaoled for anywhere between twenty-one days to six months. This was specifically drunkenness in public: 'in any street or public place'.[315] Criminalisation of public drunkenness was thus seen as a way to deal with the state's alcohol problem.

The first four decades of the twentieth century witnessed particular patterns in charge rates for drunkenness. The rate for drunkenness charges declined during World War One but had an even more noticeable decline during the Depression years from start of 1930s to 1936.[316] All offences, aside from property offences, also declined during Depression, brought on by a lack of employment and government regulatory activities.[317] Australian drunkenness statistics then witnessed an increase after World War Two, more to do with the return of servicemen and increasing prosperity.[318] Public drunkenness was the most common non-traffic offence in Australia over the century, accounting for two-thirds of all offences.[319]

Western Australia, having started the century with the highest rate in all the states for drunkenness charges, witnessed a drop by 1905, but then an increase up to 1910. A major trough was apparent during the years 1915-1920 matched by a consistent decline through the 1920s and into Depression years.[320] If anything, crime statistics show that 'the active policing of particular behaviour demonstrates more clearly the concerns of the day...'[321] Part of the decline of certain years can be attributed to the passing of the Inebriates Act in 1912 and the keeping of statistics up to 1937 attributing crime to drunkenness.[322] The war years of 1915-1916 played host to a major campaign against illicit sale of alcohol from 1915-1916, spurred on by state and national debates about controlling the supply of alcohol as a means to deal with public drunkenness.[323] Pressure, too, from the WCTU and other Temperance organisations meant drunkenness was regularly on the public radar.

The 'Terror' of the West End

Esther Warden and Plunkett O'Sullivan appeared in court together in March 1908. On the day of their arrest they had an altercation with a man named Ryan and O'Sullivan came off worse for wear with a black eye. Later that day they went to Ryan's house in Murray Street and started breaking the windows. Their disturbance created a scene, drawing a crowd of onlookers and also two plain-clothes policemen. In court, Esther and Plunkett admitted to long criminal records but said they intended to leave the state.[326]

Esther Warden was alone by the end of the year. She spent six months in prison on an idle and disorderly charge, along with damaging property.[324] When he got out, O'Sullivan skipped the state, probably returning to Victoria.[325] Despite their abusive relationship, Plunkett at least offered Esther some security in terms of regular companionship. When he left, she had no one. Any family that she did have at this time were either thousand of miles away in England or over east in Melbourne. Brothers she claimed looked after her were said to work out of town on the railways and mines so could offer little direct support. Esther Warden was left to her own devices. In an habitual drunk prone to violence, this was disastrous for Esther and people on the city streets she frequented.

Throughout 1909 Esther Warden regularly appeared in the Perth and Fremantle Police Courts, living between the street and prison. In September of that year she faced another charge of being an idle and disorderly person. According to police she was never with any respectable person and had been seen drunk and in the company of a man in his sixties or seventies. Esther said he was her brother and along with four other brothers, was planning to take her to Melbourne. Roe was having none of it and sentenced her to one month in gaol.[327]

Augustus Roe knew Esther Warden too well to trust she would leave the state. Since her first conviction at the start of the century, they had met one another across the courtroom on dozens of occasions. During one appearance in September 1910, and still drunk, she tripped up the steps to the dock. Magistrate Roe ruled that she be detained another few days to recover before a sentence was decided for the charge of idle and disorderly against her. Before she left the court, Esther gave a little performance for the magistrate. According to the papers she 'executed a daring fandango in the ante-room, and remarked that she didn't care a _____ something or other'.[328]

In June 1912, Roe told Esther, again disgraced in court, that she was 'an incorrigible nuisance'.[329] Charged with being disorderly and using obscene language, Esther had to be tackled to the ground by police while trying to use a hatpin as a weapon. She hoped for a fine this time but the magistrate sent her down for another two weeks inside. She had only just got out of prison for a lengthy sentence imposed in February for taking charge of a Saloon Bar when the owner refused her a drink. Esther then took to him with a penknife, inflicting an inch-long wound on his hand. Constable Smythe, a man who had detained Esther on numerous occasions, described her in court as 'a filthy, vile, dangerous woman'.[330]

The police had little time for Esther Warden by this stage. Police Constables Houston and Foley worked regular shifts together around the streets of Perth. By the second decade of the twentieth century, they expected to bump into Esther on the streets in a drunken condition, yelling obscenities or tussling with someone over money she had stolen. If it was a relatively quiet night and Esther was nowhere to be seen or heard, she was most likely in prison, In October 1911 the two policemen appeared in court and gave evidence they had known Esther for some years and was a 'menace to society'.[331] Esther, for her part, claimed the 'police are all against me'.[332]

With close to 100 convictions by the start of 1912, the police had reason to be suspicious of Esther Warden's every move. She was now a notorious woman around inner city Perth and the years of fleeting between the streets and prison were starting to take their toll on Esther's appearance. Described in the press in 1907 as a young woman in early thirties,[333] only three years later *The Daily News* reported her 'charms are visibly vanishing'.[334] The years following Plunkett's desertion in 1908 show a rapid descent for Esther Warden into a drunken, loitering, violent lifestyle. It brought her directly into contact with local police and repeatedly landed her lengthy gaol terms as a repeat offender. It also made her something of a criminal celebrity in the newspapers at the time. Readers looking for sensational tales of crime in the inner city streets were regaled by the latest tale of Esther Warden's brush with the law. In 1913, Esther became known as the 'terror' of West End pubs in Fremantle.

Fremantle was a hive of activity from the turn of the twentieth century. Someone like Esther Warden, loud and drunk in public, would not have escaped the attention of the many people going about their lives and work around the town centre and port. From the end of the nineteenth century, Fremantle developed into an industrial centre, spurred on by gold rushes. Fremantle Port served as a gateway for new arrivals, from which they travelled overland to the goldfields. East Fremantle's population soared as prospectors, unable to find accommodation in town, set up canvas tents along Marmion and High Streets.[335]

Fremantle's boundaries were further expanded by the settlement of British migrants from 1903 (part of a government scheme) and those looking for work along the Great Southern railway[336], which would link Albany in the state's south with the main settlements up to, and around Perth and Fremantle. Supplies brought in by ship to Albany's deep Port could then be transported to the industrial and agricultural districts around the south and south-west of the state.

The industrial and working-class life of Fremantle appealed to Esther Warden's Carlisle origins. The Eight Hours movement dominated labour life in the port town by the first years of the twentieth century. The Fremantle Trades Hall to this day contains the figures '888' above its entrance, signifying the campaign for an eight-hour working day. Unionist processions were well known in Fremantle and viewed with a sense of pride by local people who supported community crafts and trades.[337] This was a town where working men built houses for their families from scrap timber.[338]

Fremantle's cosmopolitan identity also flourished from the 1890s with the gold rushes and an influx of seamen from around the world. Men from China, Japan, Sweden, Germany, Britain and America regularly disembarked at Fremantle to enjoy town life. Italians took to fishing in Fremantle and set up market gardens while other European food producers, many of them from Greece, established businesses along Market Street and South Terrace.[339] Local workers and new arrivals with a thirst for beer also brought about the building of new pubs as a means to keep up with a rising clientele. It was also during this time that some of Esther Warden's favourite drinking haunts were built, including the P & O, National and Fremantle hotels.[340] These pubs, and the many others lining the inner streets of Fremantle, drew in Esther Warden.

Esther Warden was known as the 'terror' of the West End in Fremantle. Policemen knew her on sight and publicans scrambled to clear their pubs of glasses before she descended on the premises. They could usually hear her singing along the street or if she was in her usual mood, hurling abuse at people walking past. Hotelkeepers, it was said by *The Sunday Times,* feared a visit from Warden. She 'had a nasty habit when she was on the loose, of throwing glasses, bottles or anything she could place her hands on, at the frontispieces of the bar-tenders who refused her liquor'.[341]

Fremantle publicans were keen to prevent any further attention placed on their establishments. At a time when hotels were increasingly regulated and encouraged to mainly serve alcohol to those with accommodation, drunken locals brought too much attention from police and residents with a tendency to report disturbances to the press. The West End pubs of Fremantle were also known to occasionally harbour criminal types from the last decades of the nineteenth century. Police frequently apprehended thieves as they tried to evade arrest in the local pubs. In one case, detectives in Fremantle followed two thieves in September 1909, after they stole two portmanteaux from a man in High Street. From there they watched them go from pub to pub looking for a place of refuge, or perhaps to sell their goods. When they came out of the Orient Hotel, they were nabbed.[342]

The Orient Hotel was one of Esther Warden's favourite pubs. Back in 1876 the pub was known by its Irish name, the Emerald Isle Hotel. It was here that an initial plan was hatched to free a group of Irish Fenians from Fremantle Prison. This plot was made possible by the support of an Irish patriot living in Boston. Born in Drogheda, Ireland, John Boyle O'Reilly was transported to Western Australia aboard the *Hougoumont* and arrived in the distant colony in January 1868. Transferred to a road gang in Bunbury, O'Reilly plotted his escape and was successful in hiding out on an American whaler in February 1869. From there he hopped from ship to ship until he boarded the *Bombay* in Liverpool and set sail for Philadelphia.[343]

It was through O'Reilly that the escape of Irish prisoners was arranged from 1875. He purchased an American whaler, *Catalpa*, and had it wait in Bunbury for the arrival of the six Irish escapees who were on route in a whaleboat they had commandeered after their break from prison. Nearly caught by government officials while trying to escape the West Australian shore, the group made it safely to New York where they were welcomed ashore.[344] J. B O'Reilly went on to fame as a journalist, editor, poet and lecturer. He became an icon in Irish-American cultural life and was one of President John Kennedy's favourite poets.

Despite her Irish heritage and fondness for the pub, Esther Warden was regularly evicted from the Orient Hotel. In January 1915, Esther became violent and abusive inside the pub when she was asked to leave. She had been released from gaol that morning and was enjoying a drink to celebrate her release after three months inside. The party ended too soon for Esther. The arresting sergeant described Warden as 'a dangerous person when under the influence of drink'.[345] Esther was sent back to prison for another three months.[346]

'the worst female character'

A Vagrancy Charge - Esther Warden (48) was charged with being an idle and disorderly person. Evidence was given that the accused, who was the worst female character in Perth. annoyed residents of West Perth by her riotous manner and unbearable conduct. The accused, who had never been known to do any legitimate work frequented Chinese dens. In denying the charge, Warden said that a Chinaman, who earned from 15s to £1 a day as a cook end herbalist, gave her every penny he received. When she was out of prison, where she was for long periods, rich relatives in Melbourne occasionally sent her money. Sergeant Leen, who prosecuted, stated that not one of -the charitable institutions which had had previous experience of the accused would take her back. The accused, who had several previous convictions against her, was sentenced to six months imprisonment.[347]

In the years that followed Plunkett's desertion, Esther Warden descended further into a drunken life outside of her repeated terms in prison. In October 1911, police described her in court as a 'menace to society'. Without means of support and idle about the streets, she was sentenced to three months in gaol and made the front page of *The Daily News*.[348]

Esther now inhabited a world where she rarely escaped the attention of police and crime reporters looking for a good story. Her only secure home was Fremantle Prison. Esther claimed in June 1912 that she had a home in Melbourne Road (Milligan Street). In fact she told Magistrate Roe she would hold him responsible for this house while she was away in prison.[349] How Warden was able to keep a house in Perth is unclear. In and out of prison and with little or no work, how could she afford the rent? Did she own the house? Esther claimed in one court appearance in 1918 she had wealthy family in Melbourne who sent her money.[350] Perhaps she did and they paid for her rent or had helped set her up in a house in Perth. The reality, however, is regardless of whether she had a home or not, Esther spent most of each year in gaol.

In the years that followed, Esther Warden was labelled a danger to the state. The reality, however, is Esther was the least of the state's troubles as the time. When Britain declared war on Germany on 4 August 1914, the Australian government offered its support, determined to defend Britain. Federation in 1901 created an Australian nation but it remained one with close ties to Great

Britain. Australia gained a measure of independence through Federation but it remained committed to political, economic and social ties with the Mother Country. While there was some uncertainty as to the full nature of the European conflict, Britain was successful in drawing on support from the outer reaches of its Empire. West Australians were enthusiastic enlisters in the war, outdoing other parts of the country in terms of initial numbers. It had devastating impacts. Over 6,000 men were killed and close to 16,000 injured. Some battalions experienced loss of life or severe injury to over seventy per cent of their men.[351]

As WA played its part in the First World War, Esther Warden was fighting her own battles about the streets of Perth and Fremantle. Despite initial hopes the war would be over by Christmas, there was a growing realisation as December approached that the war was only getting started. The conflict in Europe from 1914 was but a larger extension of deep divisions and competitive interests that had dogged European history since the sixteenth and seventeenth century with the rise of competing empires. By the nineteenth century, France, Germany, Britain and the Austro-Hungarian empires fought for control of the seas, particularly around the Black Sea. The Crimean War of the 1850s had failed to keep in check the mistrust between the France and Britain and their German and Russian rivals. As these competing forces increasingly targeted the Ottoman Empire, the scramble was on to take advantage of the Balkans. The Crimean War settled nothing and left deep divisions between the dominant powers in Europe. In many respects, the First World War came out of these rivalries and a deep desire to settle old scores.

Police about Perth and Fremantle had their own battle to fight. Bracing for the festive season, they took to the streets to lock up roughs and hooligans and anyone idle about the streets. Warden was arrested at the start of the festive month for idle and disorderly. Attacking people during the day with a hatpin and thrown out of shops, Esther was apprehended by police in a Chinese smoking den in Perth on 2 December. Police reckoned they had caught one of the most dangerous women in the state.[352] She was drunk, violent and abusive in public and police had reached their limit in terms of looking for ways to reform her outside of prison. She was beyond reform.

Esther spent most of 1917 in prison. Described by P. C Foley in January 1917 as 'one of the most dangerous women in Western Australia',[353] she was seen as a danger to the community. After months in gaol on different offences, usually committed within days of her release from Fremantle Prison, Esther was sentenced to three months behind bars on a charge of idle and disorderly. Esther was a regular fixture on the crime pages of the papers. As *The West Australian* reported in October 1917:

"A Dangerous Woman."- Esther Muriel Warden (47) was charged with using obscene language and also with being an idle and disorderly person. After hearing the evidence of Plain clothes constables Baumgarten and Maingay accused, who was described as a dangerous woman, was sentenced to 14 days' imprisonment on the first charge, and to six on the second, the sentences to be concurrent.[354]

Esther Warden knew she was caught in a cycle of offending. In April 1918 she told a magistrate she had no idea how she was meant to avoid being charged with vagrancy: 'The police say I don't work, but I can't, because I have to spend a lot of time in gaol'.[355] From the start of 1914 to the end of 1918, Esther Warden spent a total of four months out of prison.[356]

Facing the reality that not all female criminals were weak, some women were characterised as something 'other' to their sex. One woman appearing on a charge of drunk and disorderly in Hull, England in 1836 was described as 'of Amazonian build' and 'conducted herself more like a fury than anything else'.[357] The same characterisation was still being made in the twentieth century. When Alice Kelly appeared before the Perth Police Court in May 1922 on a disorderly charge, she was described as a 'muscular woman of generous proportions' who trashed about in court and had to be detained.[358] Violent women, especially when drunk, were seen as unnatural to the social and gender order of the time.[359]

Esther Warden publicly challenged notions of the respectable female. *The Daily Mail* ran a story on Esther Warden's latest antics in August 1918 under the title: 'HAILED LIBERTY BY SMASHING WINDOWS WARDEN GOES BACK TO GAOL'.[360]

Esther Warden celebrated getting out of prison on the Saturday by getting rollicking drunk and smashing windows of a shop in Lake Street in Perth. On the Monday she again faced the Police Court and went straight back to gaol for three weeks.

The female drunk on the streets

Esther Warden was violent, abusive and obscene but her greatest transgression was as a female drunk. It was a sign of the times. When two young women were charged in November 1926 with what papers described as a 'police mobbing incident in St. Georges Terrace', they were identified as female drunks. Both in their early twenties, Gertie and Beatrice were arrested for being too drunk at Gordon's Hotel, made worse when Gertie told a constable to 'go to hell'. In court the prosecuting Sergeant declared 'these girls are going to the dogs and we are seeing if we can do something to keep them off the streets'.[361]

Women drunk on the streets of Perth and Fremantle sparked numerous commentaries in the press. In March 1904, *Truth* published an article under a partial heading of 'Sickening and Degrading Sights' in which the writer tells of the 'very large number of women to be seen in our principal thoroughfares under the influence of liquor'.[362] The paper claimed drunken women could apparently be found in hotels drinking all day until closing time. One reporter told of four drunken women who 'lurched' out of a city hotel in front of him. One tried to dance but fell over, giving her friends a good laugh. According to the report, these scenes were a regular occurrence in the city.[363]

A major cause of social deviance is unachievable goals for those lower down the class structure.[364] In this way habitual drunks were directly linked with an underclass in Perth and Fremantle singling out the deviant as a 'non-productive liability'.[365] Lower class individuals are in fact more likely to be treated as criminals deserving punishment.[366] Drunkenness was increasingly linked to poverty and social vices.[367] The world of the working-class public house was thought to harbour all manner of vice not found in the more respectable parts of growing metropolitan areas by the end of the nineteenth century.[368]

Drunkenness cut across all sections of society in Perth and Fremantle but the wealthier members tended to drink at home or

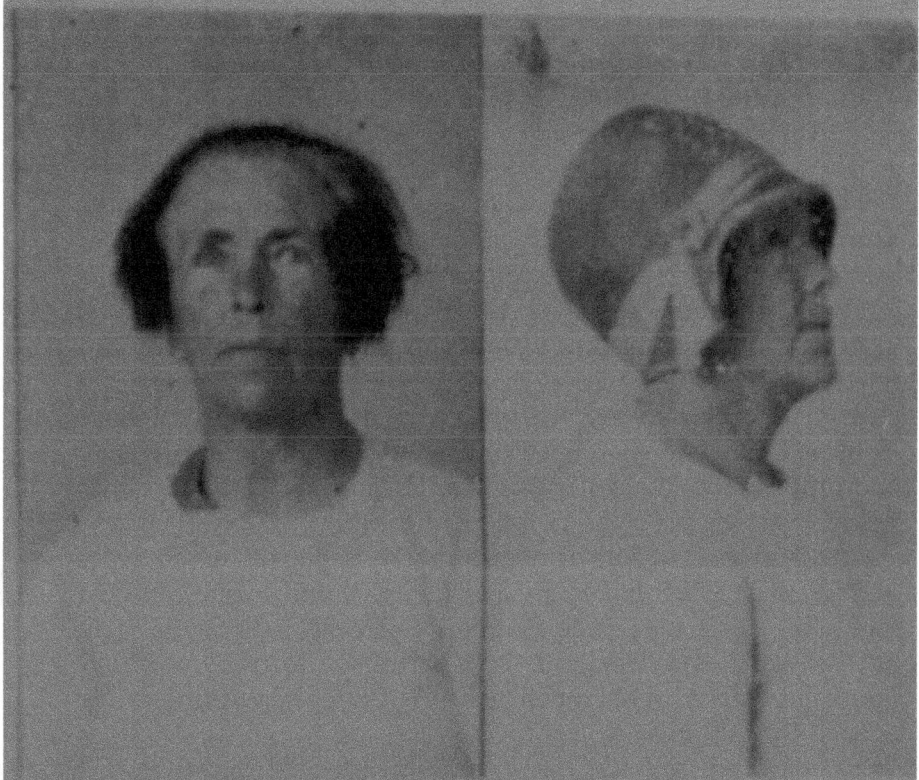

F-18.   F-209.—WARDEN, Estha Muriel.
(Disorderly conduct.)

Esther Warden, 1930

67

at social functions. Their drinking was kept behind closed doors. At times the press reflected on such class inequalities. A 1905 article in *The Sunday Times* argued: 'The rich can be screened, their lapses are condoned, and in the worst of cases they can secure nursing and protection. But the poor are just kicked into the dungeon the moment they fall'.[369] A police memo of 1924 reveals a class basis to arrests and evidence:

> Respectable members of the community, who may have become implicated in some trivial offence, strongly resent having their fingerprints taken, and it is not intended that the practice be enforced in such cases, as no good purpose would be served thereby.[370]

Wealthy transgressions were also dealt with differently. Women's homes for middle and upper class inebriates, for example, began to spring up across the urban centres of Australia into the twentieth century.[371] The 'Green Place' was opened in 1916 on the Mosman Park waterfront, outside of Perth city, for unconvicted women with a drink problem.[372] In this there is a clear distinction between the unconvicted and convicted female drinker. Drunkenness was an offence in public, not in private[373] and brought the likes of Esther Warden into direct contact with police.

The convicted female drinker publicly displayed her deviance and was seen as a threat to gender roles.[374] Women were expected 'not to be seen in the principal streets, especially in broad daylight but confine themselves and their patronage to the low public houses in their own neighbourhood'.[375] One local, writing to *The Sunday Times*, stated:

> It would give me very great pleasure to see a drunken woman bundled away into safety the moment she set foot into our public thoroughfares, instead of being allowed to spend the day lounging about the streets, to the deep degradation of her sex.[376]

Esther Warden provided ample evidence for those lobbying against female drinking. Unable to control her drinking and frequently violent in public, she assaulted men and women alike and was never shy in telling the authorities what she thought of them. She was not alone, however. Esther Warden's group photo in March 1911 features another woman with dozens of drunkenness convictions: Mary Ann Sweetman.[377]

3.

Drunken Mothers

You could be forgiven for thinking Mary Ann Sweetman didn't like cricket. On a Saturday afternoon in March 1917, while Claremont and North Perth battled it out at the WACA ground, Sweetman hurled abuse at people watching the game.[378] She was long gone by the time a local constable arrived. P. C. Turner decided to head towards Adelaide Terrace, knowing it was a favourite spot for Sweetman. It was there he found her entertaining a gathering crowd on foot and in passing cars, 'her skirts tucked up, dancing in the street'.[379] The dancing quickly turned to aggression when Sweetman caught sight of her employer at a nearby hotel and abused him for allegedly not paying her wages. Turner stepped in and made his arrest.[380] The show was over.

When Mary Sweetman turned up in court two days later, the magistrate could hardly believe it. She had only just come out of gaol having served three months for habitual drunkenness. 'Every time you are free', Police Magistrate Davies told Mary Ann, 'you seem to break out on one of these excursions of yours'. She was sent back to prison for another seven days.[381] Five months later she reached her century. Unlike the cricket game she had disrupted, this century was for criminal convictions, mainly for habitual drunkenness.[382]

Around the same time Mary Ann Sweetman was hoisting up her skirts and dancing in the street, visitors to the city were describing it as a 'city of drunken women'.[383] When J. J. Simons, leader of the Young Australia League Boys, returned from a trip to the United States in 1917, he addressed the Women's Service Guild in Perth and told them: 'Perth is the most beerlogged city we have seen. Anyone who cares to walk Cameron lane up at this moment will, I believe, see in five minutes more "drunks" than we saw in the whole of San Francisco'.[384] He continued:

> I have seen more intoxicated women in the city of Perth in one day…than I saw in eight months in the United States, and I have to confess this to my shame, since it is a reflection upon the community at large. If there is one work of outstanding importance which the woman of Perth are called to take up it is the removal of this blot upon our fair name and the impression which it is bound to create in the minds of a large percentage of the travellers who pass through the city every year.[385]

It was sensationalist but it went a long way in drawing more attention to women who were drunk in public; women like Mary Ann Sweetman. Another message is clear here: women needed to rid the streets of other women who were not conforming. It was their civic duty.

Perth suffered bad press in the early twentieth century for its drunken women. In 1922, one visitor described it as a sinful city where women patronised the many wine shops and then went 'reeling up the street' drunk.[386] Habitual female drunks regularly provided the papers with material on which to base stories of drunken outrages. The state might worry about its inebriety problem but it was far worse for it to also suffer from a female inebriety problem. In 1927 *The West Australian* included a letter from a Mount Lawley resident disgusted at the number of drunken people in the city. In particular, it was 'more pathetic to see the number of women staggering homeward along Barrack and Beaufort Street…'[387] Things were little better by the 1930s. One Salvation Army officer claimed in 1933 there were more drunken women in Perth than she had seen in twelve years of work in the eastern states.[388] Of all the drunks the Army tried to reform, the officer claimed, women were harder to convert.

The majority of women charged and convicted in the West Australian courts were arrested for offences against public order, over two-thirds for drunkenness.[389] These were the women most reported in the newspapers. The press used cases of female habitual drunkenness as a form of social control, targeting a public world where 'intoxication and drunkenness are firmly located in social spaces'.[390] Drunken women were reminded in regular newspaper reports that their antics were not tolerated in Perth and Fremantle.[391] The drunken mother, however, was especially outcast in public discourse. The police, courts and public were readily willing to cast aspersions on mothers who drank too much and ended up in prison. A fuller life history of the women involved is most lacking from this social commentary. Mary Sweetman and Sarah Mattson, two women featured in this chapter, suffered greater public scrutiny as drunken mothers. What is not detailed in the social commentary is the wider life story contributing to extensive criminal records.

*

When Mary Ann Haynes married Benjamin Tolfrey Sweetman in Fremantle on 24 April 1887[392] she thought her life had taken a turn for the best. The Sweetmans were a well-known Fremantle family involved in the local shipping and wool business. Benjamin built and repaired boats and also worked as a storeman for Elder Shenton & Co., a forerunner of Elders Limited as it is known today.[393] Before it was the Woolstores Shopping Centre, the old wool building on the corner of Cantonment Street in Fremantle was a hive of activity for the wool business back in the first decades of the twentieth century.

Benjamin's family had been in Western Australia since the first years of the Swan River colony. His father, Thomas Sweetman, arrived virtually from the first months of colonisation and his mother, Emma Mould, came from Hampshire, England as a servant to the Bussell family in the south-west region.[394] When Thomas deserted his family and moved to South Australia in 1857, the same year Benjamin was born, Emma was left alone to raise ten children. [395] His father's abandonment left in Benjamin a determination that he would not do the same thing when he had his own children. It also contributed later to his lack of support for his wife, Mary Ann, when she regularly left the family home to drink at pubs or on the streets.

Benjamin and Mary Ann Sweetman moved into a house at 8 McCleery Street, Beaconsfield, just south of Fremantle town centre.

In the first fourteen years of their marriage, Mary Ann gave birth to seven children, including two sons who fought in and returned from World War One.[396] Beaconsfield back in those days was similar to South Fremantle with its streets lined by cottages, some with stables out the back. When the Sweetmans moved into their house it was in an area fast expanding with the recent population growth in and around Fremantle. The local Beaconsfield Primary School on Hale Road was a new building back in 1890 and was only down the end of the street for Benjamin and Ann's children. It was a working class area, close to racecourse and the wharves.

Despite their efforts to set up a close-knit family home, Mary Ann descended into the life of a repeat offender, frequently before the courts and in and out of gaol. In January 1902 she appeared in court after being arrested for threatening her neighbour, Sophia Nelson. The two were known in the local area for abusing each other but things had come to a head when Sweetman threatened to get a gun during their dispute. The case was dismissed when it was shown Sweetman had no gun and the magistrate hoped this would be the last he would see of the neighbourhood quarrel.[397] It wasn't. One month later Mary Ann was back in court on a charge of assaulting her neighbour and was fined.[398]

Like Esther Warden, Mary Ann's main problem was drink. By February 1904 she was described as an habitual drunk in court and sentenced to seven days in prison.[399] A few months later Mary Ann was becoming disorderly with her drinking and sentenced to three weeks' hard labour in prison.[400] Despite her gaol time, Mary Sweetman was something of a local identity in Beaconsfield for her sociability at the local pub, the Beaconsfield Hotel, on the corner of Hampton Road. There were moments, however, when staff and clientele didn't quite know how to take her. One story told by family members is Mary Ann joked around one day with bar staff and offered up one of her children for a beer or some money.[401]

Interestingly, it was Mary Ann Sweetman who took her husband to court in January 1905. She accused Benjamin of persistent cruelty. On release from gaol in December the previous year, she had gone home, argued with her husband and he put her out on the streets. After sleepless nights on the beach, she repeatedly returned to their house but was sent away, hungry and alone. Mary claimed her time in gaol was due to her family's neglect. All she wanted was to be with her children and have her husband made responsible for her.[402]

Robert Sweetman, their teenage son, told another story. The seventeen year-old gave evidence that 'at times he had had to use force to keep his mother inside the house so that she would not annoy anybody'.[403] He also stated the family was at a loss in terms of what to do with his mother when she was drunk. She was uncontrollable and could not be restrained. Presenting evidence to the court on behalf of a case now against Mary Ann, two medical men declared her a dipsomaniac. Having gone to court to make her husband face his responsibilities, Mary Ann now faced a disorderly charge for being loud and obscene outside her home. She was sentenced to six weeks in Fremantle Prison and publicly declared a dipsomaniac.[404]

It must have been humiliating for Mary Ann. Acting out of desperation, she had taken Benjamin to court in an effort to make him open the family home to her once again and see her children. But he was having none of it. His own father deserted him as a child and Mary Ann's frequent excursions into the city to drink away from her family might have reminded him too much of the rejection he, his siblings and his mother experienced. Mary had spent almost half the previous year in prison for drunkenness and disorderly charges.[405] Benjamin Sweetman had clearly had enough of her drinking and the consequences it brought to their family with a mother absent for weeks at a time.

Mary Ann did not want to abandon her family. Even though she was not welcome for long periods in her house, she was known to sleep in the paddock at the back of the property. She also slept in the door of a butcher's shop near the house on the corner of South and Solomon Streets. Mary Ann wanted to be close to her family but could not control her drinking. She is said to have watched from afar some days as her children arrived home from school and one of her sons, Cecil, often brought blankets to her during the night.[406] The separation from her children was a greater hardship for some than hard manual labour in prison. One visitor to Fremantle Prison in 1937 reported, 'in some women, whatever their failing, there is the ache for the presence and prattle of children'.[407]

Mary Ann Sweetman, 1911

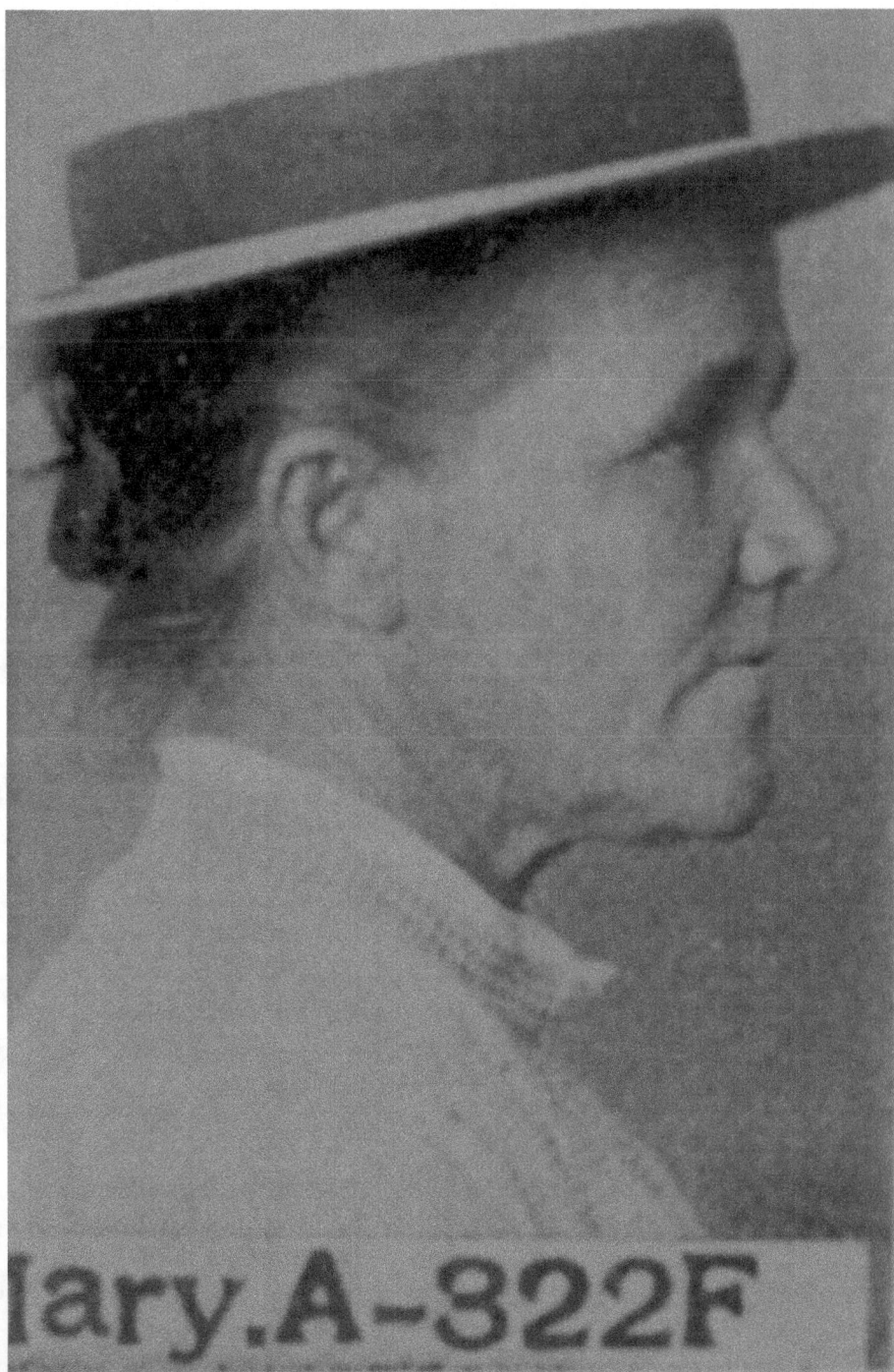

lary.A-322F

Later, in November 1909, Mary Ann again sued for maintenance and charged her husband with desertion. The case was dismissed and Mary Sweetman was again singled out for her drunkenness and inability to control her drinking.[408] She had been recommended for medical treatment back in March 1907 but it had done little to curb her drinking.[409] In July 1909, before the maintenance case against her husband, Mary had been arrested for drunkenness and obscenity in West Perth. She was said to have gathered with a group of women and was drunkenly holding her child in her arms. Despite Mary's plea she had just bought the child sweets and was on her way home, she was sent to prison for three weeks.[410] She also claimed in court in November 1909 that she would 'not hurt a hair of my children's heads'.[411]

Despite her protests in court, Mary Ann Sweetman could not control her drinking nor keep her family life together. As a female drunk she was labelled a weak woman. A common theme in press reports, social commentary and court records was the linking of female drinking with a weakness of the will. From the eighteenth century, drunkenness was seen as a moral problem attributable to those weak of will and susceptible to vice.[412] According to Victorian historian L. O. Pike, writing in 1876:

> women are less criminal than men not only because they are physically weaker now, but because they were physically weaker generations ago. The habit of mind has descended with the habit of body, and the cumulative effect of ages is seen in modern statistics.[413]

The prevailing Victorian social and judicial view that women were less culpable than men in relation to crime and more troubled than troublesome continued on in Western Australia in the twentieth century.[414]

Nineteenth-century thinking, continuing to influence into the first decades of the twentieth century, attributed drunkenness to 'the frailty of women's bodies'.[415] When it released details from the Superintendent's Fremantle Prison report of 1914, *The West Australian* titled its piece, 'THE DRINK HABIT. WEAK WOMEN'.[416] According to the Superintendent, habitual female criminals were 'of weak will'. He claimed they frequently tried to keep off alcohol 'but their wills are too weak to withstand their temptations and environments'.[417] Another prison report revealed one female prisoner at Fremantle had been in court and gaol for the last ten years with only one year when she had not fronted a magistrate. She was in the dock on average six times a year, mainly for drunkenness.[418]

Research into drunkenness and wives shows 'women who drank were deemed incapable of setting a good moral example for their family (drunken women were often placed prostitutes at the bottom of the social/moral scale)'.[419] Havelock Ellis argued in *Studies in Psychology of Sex* in 1911 that 'drunkenness invariably leads to a laxness of moral restrain in women'.[420] But the drunken mother, like Mary Ann Sweetman, was a far worse candidate for someone who has fallen into the depths of society's outcasts. In January 1915 *The West Australian* argued greater reform was needed for habitual female drunks. Eighty per cent of the women, it reported, were married on their 'first acquaintance with the gaol' but were now 'lost to themselves and dangerous to their families'.[421] The greatest tragedy was they were 'potential and probable mothers'.[422]

The female inebriate posed a particular dilemma for society: weakness of the will in women, it was argued, had a direct impact on the next generation. Degenerate theories of the late nineteenth century identified heavy drinking - 'part vice, part disease' – as directly affecting offspring and thus poisoning future generations.[423] Annie Owens, arrested for drunkenness and falling about in the street in Royal Street, Perth while holding a baby in her arms, was proof for the press of the degenerative effects of alcohol abuse. Annie had allegedly given the ten month-old baby some wine.[424] Owens' actions undermined her role in populating the nation with healthy children.[425] Unlike today, in the early twentieth century, 'heredity rather than the conditions of pregnancies' was emphasised.[426]

Characterised as a weak woman – a dipsomaniac – and a bad wife and mother, Mary Ann Sweetman was a well-known drunk on the streets of Perth. What the magistrates, press and public did not see, however, was a woman with a troubled past. Key events in Mary Sweetman's early life could explain why she went on drunken excursions around East Perth. Mary Ann was new to the Beaconsfield and greater Fremantle area from the late 1880s. East Perth, where she was born and grew up, held more meaning for her and kept the ghosts from her past. It was here that she regularly returned during her drunken excursions. It was this past that haunted her.

*

Mary Ann was born in Perth in 1866 to Henry and Ann Haynes and in time became older sister to Charles Henry and George Robert. Mary's mother, Ann Clough, arrived in Western Australia in 1864 as a domestic servant to Governor Hampton. While working for Hampton, she fell in love with Henry Benjamin Haynes and they were wed in Perth in August 1865.[427] Henry was a local tailor but had been transported to the colony in 1861 for a murder he committed in Winchester, England.[428] He received a conditional pardon in 1870 and the family moved from a house in Cemetery Road, East Perth (now Forrest Avenue near the East Perth Cemetery) to a cottage on Wellington Street close to the Colonial Hospital (Royal Perth Hospital). Henry kept up his tailoring work in the cottage while Ann turned the front room into a small shop that was popular with people walking past in Wellington Street.[429] The Haynes shop was situated in a bustling part of town where small shops were formed in other cottages nearby, alongside butchers' shops, small factories, clothing stores and blacksmith's shops. The Colonial Hospital, Victoria Square and various churches bordered the streets near the Haynes house and offered a steady traffic in people going to and from the city centre. There was also no shortage of local pubs, something Mary's father enjoyed after long working days. The Haynes family were not always struggling but neither were they comfortable. The tailoring business paid the rent but Ann's work in the front shop kept them from missing payments during tight periods.

Despite Benjamin's criminal past, the Haynes family appeared to be a loving one where husband and wife spoke well of one another and supported their three children as best they could. Mary and her two brothers were schooled while young but were put out to work before their teens. Mary often worked in the shop with her mother. John Cole, a shoemaker and neighbour to the Haynes, later said 'they seemed to live together very comfortably'.[430] Henry

Haynes' recent convict past left a large chip on his shoulder, however, and eventually caught up with him.

Convicts were a regular sight about the emerging city streets in the 1870s and 1880s. Transportation to Western Australia had only ceased in 1868 and the city continued to use convicts to build new roads, houses, government offices, as well as extend the railways. Convicts helped to build Perth Town Hall on Barrack Street and not far from the Sweetmans on Wellington Street.[431] Though he was now a former convict, the regular flow of convicts around the area was a constant reminder to Henry Haynes of his convict background. He had originally tried to hide it from Ann. When they first met through her work with Governor Hampton, Ann thought Henry was a tailor, not one of the convicts, until her employer informed her otherwise.

Tormented by the demons of his past and a strong drinker, Henry Haynes spent increasing amounts of his free time at the Horse and Groom pub along the road from their house.[432] When the family lived back at Cemetery Road, Henry spent a few weeks in the Colonial Hospital after an illness affected his movements and speech. Excessive drinking was starting to take a toll on his health. After this he had tried to commit suicide on four occasions and was then taken to the Fremantle Lunatic Asylum.[433] In contrast to her husband, Ann Haynes was a mild mannered woman who went peacefully about her work and looking after their family. Despite their differences, neighbours and friends described the Haynes marriage as a love match.[434]

All this changed in September 1883 when Henry was found guilty of embezzling cloth from a customer. Despite protesting his innocence, Haynes was sentenced to one month in prison. [435] Henry believed Ann had informed on him and spent much of his month in Fremantle Prison turning over in his head why his wife would have given him up to the authorities. There is no evidence to support Ann having informed on her husband. When Henry was released from gaol in October 1883, Henry stormed into their home and grabbed his wife, screaming that she was responsible for his time in prison. As she was used to doing when Henry flew into one of his rages, Ann tried to calm him with a bath and some food. It seemed, for the time being, that the pair had worked through their differences. However, in the days that followed,

Henry's drinking brought out the accusations all over again. He was drinking heavily and demanding more money from his wife for beer.

On the morning of 12 October 1883, Henry sat down to breakfast with his family. He went out later that morning and returned home with a coat that needed cleaning for a client. Ann said she would clean the garment and went to the back room to open a kerosene tin. Henry followed his wife into the room, sat on the couch and started demanding money for beer. Mary Ann had also joined her parents in the back room but a customer, a young girl, came into the shop at the front of the house. Mary went to serve her. Moments later Mary heard her mother scream and rushed to the back room. There she found her mother on the floor in a pool of blood. Her father stood near the body with a hammer in his hand. Henry Haynes had killed his wife.

When the case came to trial the following January, Henry Haynes, described as 'respectably-dressed peculiar looking man', pleaded not guilty to the murder of his wife. His defence tried to establish grounds for insanity. One of Haynes' clients, Frederick Spencer, said he had known Haynes for over ten years but 'had always looked upon the prisoner as having something peculiar about him – a strange look about the eyes, but he did his work well'. Dr Barnett, a colonial surgeon in Fremantle who had known Haynes at the Lunatic Asylum, testified that a 'wild look in the eyes' was one of the main symptoms homicidal mania. He also said those suffering from this condition were more likely to inflict injury on loved ones. The court had to decide if Haynes was sane, particularly at the time of the murder, and responsible for his own actions.

Mary Ann Haynes was seventeen at the time of her mother's murder. As a key witness, she gave evidence in the trial of her father in January 1884. Standing in the dock and recalling the horrors of that day back in October, Mary Ann showed clear signs of trauma. When she described the moments leading up to and after the attack on her mother, she had to stop for some time to compose herself. In the papers she was described as seeming 'to feel her position very acutely'. In the days leading up to the murder, Mary Ann had 'noticed a wild appearance' about her father's eyes but she had not suspected him of plotting to kill her mother. When she rushed into the back room on the day of the murder, she told the court, she screamed at her father, 'Father, oh father, what have you done to poor mother?' Other witnesses would also testify she had called her father a brute for killing 'my poor mother'. Ann's head wound was confronting for her teenage daughter, as much as it was for the doctors who tended to her afterwards. Doctors at the Colonial Hospital described horrific head wounds. Mrs Haynes' skull was fractured and her brain protruding in one part. Doctors found five wounds on left side of the head, two if which fractured the skull. Wounds were also located on the left temple and right cheek. This was what Mary Ann walked into and witnessed.

The Chief Justice was not convinced by the Defence case for insanity. He asked Dr Waylen if other causes could lead to a wild look. The doctor answered: 'Yes, toothache for instance'. The Attorney General then asked if drunkenness would contribute in large part to Haynes' depressed and nervous state and the doctor agreed. Dr Waylen also testified that drink 'would probably accelerate an attack of mania'. Mary Ann also stated her father 'used to get depressed and melancholy and fretful, after he had been drinking'. On one occasion he had tried to commit suicide by wading into the Swan River. Mary Ann also claimed her father's depression and melancholy was always made worse with alcohol.

In his final remarks the Chief Justice declared: 'In this case there was nothing to show that the prisoner was not perfectly master of his actions and that he did not know what he was doing when he committed the outrage'. Henry Haynes was found guilty of his wife's murder and executed on Wednesday morning of 23 January 1884 on the grounds of Fremantle Prison. Though he seemed indifferent to his fate while in gaol, the press reported a change in his demeanour as the execution date neared. One of his last requests was to be buried next to his wife.[436]

In the space of a few months from October 1883 to January 1884, Mary Ann Haynes witnessed the brutal bashing of her mother, gave evidence in court for and against her father and then, after his execution in January, was left with two young brothers to support. She had also lost both her parents. It was an horrific ordeal for a teenager to go through. As Mary grew up quickly in the years following the murder, she thought her marriage to

Benjamin Sweetman would ease the pain of the past. Busy with regular pregnancies and the work of bringing up seven children, family life diverted her attention for the time being.

By the first years of the twentieth century, however, she was drinking heavily and increasingly prone to public outbursts. Did she worry that she was like her father? Was her drinking a means to deal with the trauma she had suffered as a teenager? No records can tell us exactly how deeply Mary Ann was affected by her mother's death and her father's execution. Other than the court and press records detailing the trial and describing her as upset during the course of the trial, Mary Ann Sweetman is a silent player in WA's history until she later came to the attention of the authorities for her own criminal conduct. As a young woman, Mary gained the sympathy of the press in the 1880s but by the 1910s she was notorious as a hard drinking woman who fleeted between the streets and prison, leaving her husband to bring up their children.

Mary Sweetman declared in court in December 1918 it was the 'drink that drove her mad'.[437] Over the years she had listened in court to many medical experts declare her a dipsomaniac. By medical definition, her inability control her drinking was also linked to an unbalanced state of mind. It may well be that alcohol affected Mary's mental state but looking into the events of her earlier life, it is hard not to make a connection between a family tragedy and her later drinking.

Standing ready to have her photo taken in Fremantle Prison in March 1911[438], Mary Sweetman must have known this was the course her life would now take. It was a far cry from the unassuming young girl who helped her mother in the front shop. As we will see in a later chapter, once Mary Sweetman was caught in a cycle of drunkenness, disorderly and regular gaol terms, her life took a direct course towards loneliness, marginalisation and an intimate understanding of life on the streets and behind bars. Henry Haynes' moment of anger, rage and violence devastated the life of his eldest child. This is what is not told in the press stories about Mary Sweetman the drunk.

'The worst woman he knew'

Along with Esther Warden and Mary Ann Sweetman, Sarah Jane Mattson completes the trifecta of most notorious females criminalised for public insobriety. In the dozens of convictions listed in the Fremantle Prison Register and details of crimes reported in the local press, Mattson embodies various facets of female deviancy in early twentieth-century Perth. According to one policeman, Corporal Harris, she was 'the worst woman he knew'.[439] While public drunkenness is a minor offence today, as a woman back in the early twentieth century, Mattson was pushing social boundaries. She was an habitual drunk, refused to stay home and look after her family, fought in public with other women and loitered for sex.

Police and magistrates tried unsuccessfully for years to understand Sarah Mattson's public indiscretions. On numerous occasions, Sarah was described in court as an embarrassment to her 'good husband' and neglectful of her four little children.[440] Like Mary Sweetman, the authorities thought drink made Sarah Mattson 'mad'. Magistrate Roe publicly stated he thought there was 'a screw loose somewhere' in her.[441] Yet doctors could find nothing wrong with her beyond the effects of too much alcohol. On another occasion in court, Roe labelled Mattson close to being a dipsomaniac: 'You are perfectly well, but you can't touch drink – it sends you mad'.[442] With heightened concerns about female drinking into the twentieth century, coinciding with temperance movements and efforts to confine women to a domestic identity as wives and mothers, Mattson became an outcast of Perth; demonised then criminalised for her drunkenness and lack of conformity and characterised as a bad mother.

*

Sarah Jane Mattson was born Sarah Power in Yorkshire, England around 1880.[443] She was the only child of William Power, a joiner and his wife, Mary Elizabeth (nee Quinlan).[444] At the time of Sarah's birth, Yorkshire was still largely agricultural, despite the rapid industrialisation of England through the nineteenth century. In the main centre of York, workers were mainly based in small workshops for craftsmen and unskilled workers.[445] Like many other people from the local area, the Power family may have moved to York at some point when Sarah was young. In the years from 1831 to 1881, the population of York doubled as people looked for ongoing work in the town centre.[446] As a popular tourist town from the 1860s, York attracted young families from across the region hoping for more work beyond agriculture.

Opportunities were limited though. As Sarah Power grew up she would have been well aware of the few working opportunities open to her as a female. Most women employed in York were domestic servants, charwomen or washerwomen.[447] Unlike some of the larger industrial centres in other parts of the country, York had no large-scale factories in the late nineteenth century.[448] Sarah's later Fremantle prison record indicates she moved around from Yorkshire in her younger years. Both Scarborough and the larger Northumberland region are listed as previous places of residence.[449] However, as she approached her mid-teens, Sarah Power's sense of opportunity extended well beyond England. She looked to Australia and the gold rich colony of Western Australia.

Sarah Power is first present in Western Australian records in 1898 with her Boxing Day marriage to Ernest Carl Mattson. Like his new wife, Ernest was a foreigner, a Swede, looking for a better life in Western Australia.[450] Ernest and Sarah may well have met at the Fremantle Immigration Office, down at the Wharf. In what was a small Perth population of close to 27,000 people[451], by comparison to the larger city centres of Sydney and Melbourne, a man and woman could pass by one another frequently enough to catch the other's attention.

The ink hardly dried on the Mattson marriage certificate when Sarah conceived their first child. Ernest Oskar was born in Perth on 7 October 1899.[452] The couple waited a little longer for the birth of their next child, another son, John, born in Perth in 1902. By 1903, Sarah and Ernest were living in a small house at 13 Raphael Street, Subiaco. Gazetted as a municipality in 1897, Subiaco rapidly expanded in size over the first decade of the twentieth century. In the ten years from 1901 its population increased four-fold. As the metropolitan area expanded, working-class families moved out of the city centre and into the surrounding suburbs, one of which included the popular Subiaco site.[453] The Mattsons moved into a new area of small weatherboard cottages bustling with young families making a living as best they could. Most were trying to avoid the poverty of shanty life in the inner city and the tents springing up around East Perth.[454]

It was in their weatherboard cottage in Raphael Street that Sarah gave birth to triplets – a boy and two girls – on 5 November 1904. After many hours of delivery, and now realising she was mother to three more children at once, Sarah was dealt a harsh blow. Within a day of the birth, the Mattsons lost all three babies.[455] In an age before supportive health services for new mothers and counselling for the loss of a child, Sarah gave birth to and buried three children in the space of days. It must have been a harrowing time in her life.

Two years later, the Mattsons welcomed twin boys into the family, Frederick G. and William Frederick, born on 16 January 1906.[456] Frederick Mattson ended up in the Surry Hills and Redfern areas of Sydney where he married Dorothy Violet Mosley, a country girl from York, Western Australia, in 1934. He enlisted in World War Two, survived the war and lived into his eighties.[457] Frederick's twin remained in Perth and, as we will see, took to a life on the streets like his mother.

Having suffered the loss of three children, Sarah and Ernest were also trying their best to bring up four young sons in their Subiaco cottage. Sarah was struggling. By 1911, she was making regular appearances in the Perth Police Court, firstly for creating a nuisance while drunk in her street. In an area where cottages were built close to one another and locals talked to each other at the front of houses while children played, Sarah's indiscretions were noted by the neighbours and reported to police. While we don't have any way of knowing why it was that Sarah drank excessively and stayed away from the family home for long periods, the strain on the marriage was starting to show. Then came the deaths of more children. In the space of only a few weeks, Sarah and Ernest buried twin sons. Sydney Mattson, born in January 1913,[458] died on 20 May:

MATTSON- On May 20, 1913, at Children's Hospital, Perth, W.A., Sydney, the dearly beloved infant son of Ernest and Sarah Jane Mattson, of 13 Raphael-street, Subiaco. Aged 4½ months. "Our loved one at rest."[459]

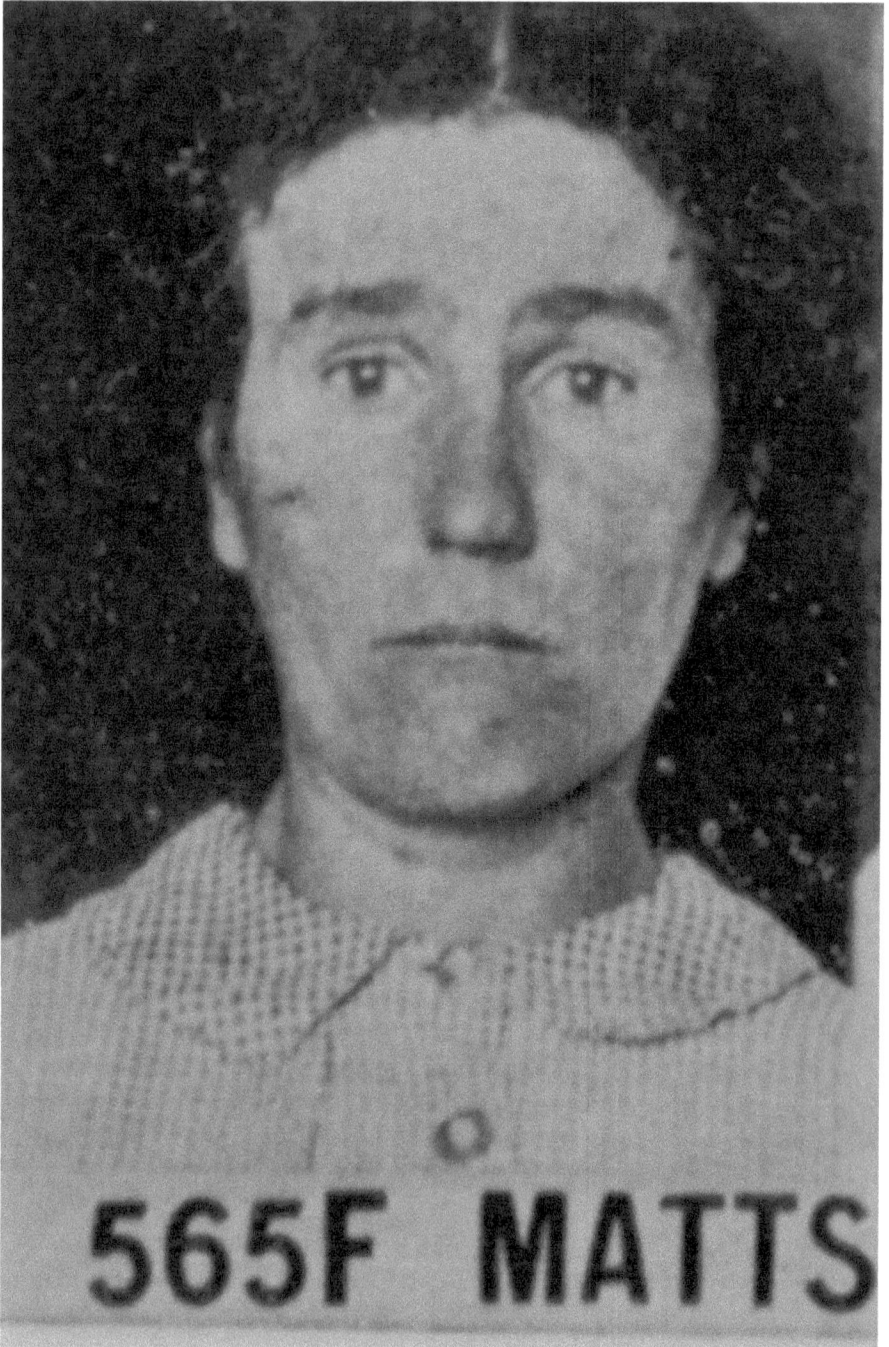

Sarah Mattson, 1916

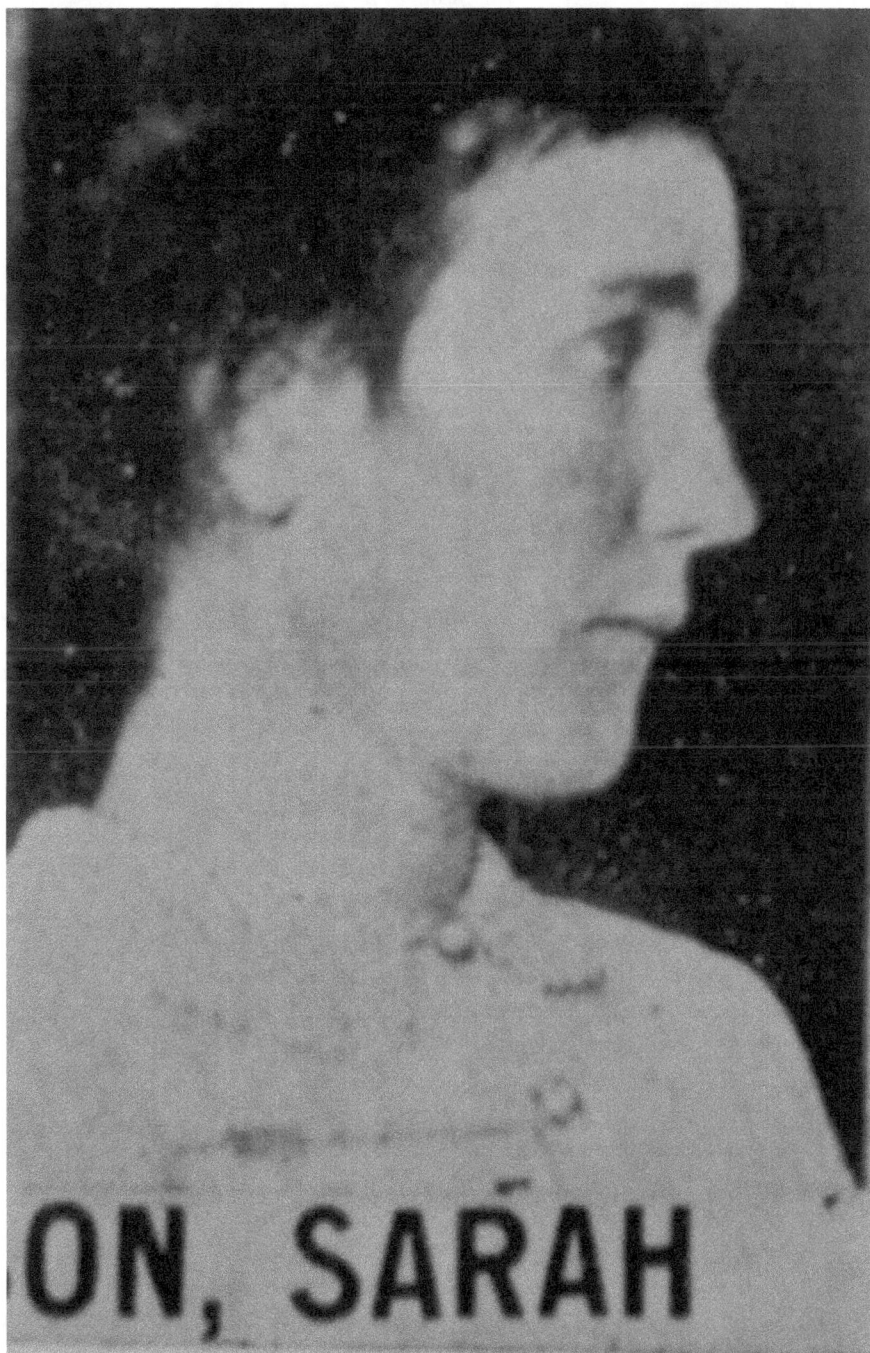

ON, SARAH

Sydney's twin brother, Charles, died only days later on 4 June.[460] Nevertheless, the loss would have been deep for Ernest and Sarah. Five of their children were now buried in Karrakatta Cemetery. Close to 6,000 infant deaths recorded in Perth from 1870 to 1914.[461] Poor living conditions in parts of the metropolitan area and a drastic increase in the state's population after the gold rushes of the late nineteenth century led to outbreaks of gastro-enteritis, tuberculosis and pneumonia. Children under twelve months of age were among the most vulnerable members of society and often succumbed to weaning diarrhoea and complications associated with teething.[462] Lack of vaccinations could be another explanation. Ernest Mattson had in fact been charged and fined with having neglected to get his infant child vaccinated back in June 1902.[463]

The loss of twin sons failed to bring the Mattson couple closer together. Instead, it launched Sarah back into a life on the streets with regular intervals away from her children while serving time in prison. Mattson's drinking and public disorderliness kept her from any semblance of a family life. In February 1914 she was sentenced to six months in gaol as a 'habitual drunkard'.[464] Mattson was the feature of a short article in *The West Australian* early in 1915. Under the heading, 'An Erring Mother', the paper reported Mattson's appearance in court on a disorderly charge. A local constable described having to remove her from Russell Square eight times in one day and could not understand why she acted as she did. She had £100 in the bank and owned two blocks of land. However, it seems by this stage that her husband looked after their children.[465] Publicly shamed, it did little to curb her public drunkenness. Three months later Mattson was again in court and sentenced to seven days in gaol for 'being an habitual drunk'.[466]

By September 1915, and facing another drunkenness charge, Sarah Mattson was sent to the Home of the Good Shepherd.[467] Released early in December, she was again before the courts on a drunkenness charge days later and sent to prison. What the authorities did not know at the time was Sarah was pregnant. In January 1916 she was transferred to the Maternity Home and in March gave birth to another son, Sydney.[468] He died on 11 June 1916. Of their ten children, the Mattsons had buried six as infants.

Ernest Mattson reached breaking point in May 1916. In a notice in *The West Australian* he notified the public he was no longer responsible for any debts incurred by his wife after 1 May.[469] Excluded from their home and refused access to her children, Sarah was arrested in Perth on 29 June 1916 for drunkenness. She was sentenced to fourteen days hard labour for this latest drunkenness charge and a further six months for habitual drunkenness.[470] On her release from gaol later in the year, she was charged with creating a disturbance at the Great Western Hotel in Perth. Drunk on the premises and abusing anyone within reach, Mattson threw a glass at another woman. Only just out of gaol, Sarah went back inside for another two months.[471]

Ernest Carl Mattson died on 1 May 1918, aged forty.[472] Suffering from pulmonary and laryngeal tuberculosis, he passed away at Wooroloo Sanatorium near Northam. Back in the early twentieth century, the Sanatorium served as a place to manage people with tuberculosis around the metropolitan area. It was believed fresh country air would help sufferers. Unfortunately, it did little to cure Ernest Mattson.

Without at least some support from her husband from 1916, and no hope of any after his death two years later, Sarah descended even further into a life on the streets. Her habitual drunkenness now led to charges for the allied offences of vagrancy, idle and disorderly and theft. Sarah Mattson also formed close associations with other women on the streets. Usually numbering between five and ten, these women, including Sarah Mattson, congregated around the inner city parks. Russell Square, Weld Square and Wellington Square were popular gathering points. Here the women met throughout the day and shared their experiences of street and prison life. The reality, however, of such groups is as much as similar experiences provided support, group members were also subjected to the frustrations of other women lashing out at the world around them.

In an incident described in the press in January 1919 as an 'Exceptionally bad case', Sarah Mattson, Alice Brown and Norah White were charged with having engaged in a 'stand-up fight' in Stirling Street, Perth. In a haze of drunken obscenities, they fought with one another in open view of people passing by. Police were called, intervened, and whisked the trio off to the Perth lockup. All three were sentenced to twenty-one days in prison.[473] The papers had a field day with the appearance of the three women in court:

SARAH, ALICE AND NORAH LAPSE INTO LANGUAGE AND DRUNKENNESS

In response to the names Sarah Matson, Alice Brown, and Norah White, at the City Police Court this morning, three battered-looking members of the feminine gender limped up into the dock and said they pleaded guilty to being drunk yesterday in Stirling-street. Prosecuting Sergeant Smith said that although the charge was only drunkenness the case had exceptionally bad features…There was much bad language, and the amateur Amazons had torn nearly all the clothes off one another's backs. They were all nearly naked when brought into the lock up. All had records of an unenviable nature. Their Bacchanalian belligerency was rewarded with 21 days imprisonment.[474]

The use of 'Amazons' is interesting in the above court report. Mattson and her feisty group of women on the streets presented authorities with a different characterisation of females engaging in criminal activities. Unlike the stereotypical portrayals of women as weak or victims, the violent female criminal was characterised as something 'other' to their sex. It was popular in the press in Britain from the early nineteenth century to portray such women as 'Amazonians' and entirely different to respectable women.[475] Sarah Mattson's actions in public, both drunken and violent, allowed the authorities and press to single her out as an unnatural woman.

Without any means of support by the early 1920s, Mattson earned money for food and alcohol through soliciting in the streets. She was charged with loitering for an unlawful purpose in Russell Square in December 1922[476] and months later appeared before the Perth Police Court on an idle and disorderly charge. Detective Sergeant Cameron gave evidence that Mattson was known to 'make the acquaintance of men staying at low-class coffee palaces and while they were asleep to steal their money'. A similar case reported against Mattson a few days before by a lodger at the Duke of York Coffee Palace prompted the magistrate to hand down a sentence of three months in gaol.[477]

> Not Wanted at Christmas— Sarah Matson (41) and Mary Govan (45) belong to the class of women whom the police consider it advisable to have within prison walls during the Christmas season. While they have no visible means of support, it is known that they obtain a livelihood in ways that are dark and can be relied upon to be unusually active when some of our less cautious brethren from the country are in town. This year the two women will partake of the Christmas dinner in the Fremantle Gaol, for they were this morning sentenced to three months' imprisonment on vagrancy charges.[478]

Members of the police closely watched Sarah Mattson's public deviance, something that could well have contributed to her regular charges. Mattson was charged in July 1924 with vagrancy and sent to Home of the Good Shepherd for six months based on evidence from Constable White.[479] The following year, not long after being discharged from gaol, she was charged with having stolen a handbag containing money and imprisoned for thirteen days, unable to pay the fine.[480] By the end of the year, Mattson was again sent back to gaol, this time for six months on an idle and disorderly charge. Constable White again gave evidence that she had done no work for a month, did not have lawful means of support, and 'frequented hotels with men, and was a general nuisance'.[481] It seems, however, that soliciting was the result of a life having spent everything on alcohol. Sarah was trying to make some money and while the authorities listed her as a common prostitute, she used it as a means to survive on the streets.

Sarah Mattson was now living on the streets and barely scraping together enough money for food. She was sentenced to a month in gaol in January 1929 as a vagrant. Plain-clothes police found her 'sleeping in a lavatory on the Esplanade, Fremantle'. She provided police with three different names and addresses and was charged as rogue and vagabond.[482] Another sentence in February 1931 landed her in gaol for five months as an habitual drunk.[483] It was a life now firmly placed between the streets and prison.

Sarah was not the only Mattson coming to the attention of the police. From the late 1920s Sarah's son, William Frederick, was regularly before the courts on charges of damaging property, drunkenness, vagrancy and theft. In court in 1943 he admitted to over thirty prior convictions and attributed his crimes to drink. In this case, however, the charges were more serious than any his mother had faced. He was sentenced to seven years imprisonment for unlawfully dealing a boy under the age of fourteen.[484] William's father died when he was twelve and from his earliest years his mother, Sarah, was in and out of gaol for offences against good order. While instability of family life did not impact negatively on his other four siblings, including his twin Frederick, William Frederick gave the authorities cause to worry about maternal drinking. While Sarah is not mentioned in any of William's appearances in court, William listed his mother as next of kin when he enlisted in World War Two in October 1942.[485] Though we don't know the full nature of their relationship, Sarah and William, mother and son, at similar times, inhabited an underclass world on the streets of Perth in the early twentieth century.

*

Sarah Mattson's battle with alcoholism on the streets of Perth reveals an important connection between the early twentieth century and today. As much as alcohol – its use and misuse – is repeatedly discussed and researched in Australia, 'we are always going back to the drawing board, cataloguing its manifold harms, searching for their causes, and exploring options for eliminating, or at least alleviating, them'.[486] There is some hope that Australians are moving beyond 'national stereotypes of boozers and wowsers toward a new era of social responsibility'.[487] However, one thing that has remained constant in debates in Australia about alcohol since the late nineteenth century is female drinking is understood differently.

Marilyn Lake, looking at drinking history in Australia, argues women were excluded, particularly in pubs, and when they did drink heavily it was mainly to deal with anguish. Lake saw drinking as a 'masculine privilege'.[488] Drunkenness in Australia is linked to a male mateship legend and an ongoing image of drunkenness as a part of masculinity.[489] Not drinking for men is sometimes seen as being 'weak and feminine'.[490] Chris McConville, though recognising the masculine tradition attached to drinking in Australia, uses the example of a Fitzroy pub in Melbourne as evidence working class men and women drank together. According to McConville, it was class that separated drinkers, not necessarily gender.[491] Lake and McConville were, however, writing about different time periods. More women were going to pubs in the 1890s than they had been in the middle of the century, the period of Lake's research. Clare Wright's work on female publicans is inspired by this debate. Wright gives women a place within Australian pubs, as both drinkers and licensees.[492]

The women featured in this book demonstrate another facet of female drinking in Australia. Esther Warden, Mary Sweetman and Sarah Mattson were usually excluded from pubs and hotels. It was not simply their drinking that was questioned; their habitual drunkenness distinguished them as social outcasts. They had pushed the respectable boundaries to breaking point through repeatedly appearing inebriated in public, sometimes with violent consequences. Unable to stay sober or control their drinking, female habitual drunks found they had no place in society and slipped through its cracks. These women, like sixty-two year-old Mary Ryan sentenced to a month in gaol in October 1927 for drunkenly abusing men drinking in a bar,[493] were mainly standing on the outside of pubs looking in. All too often the streets offered them a home of sorts and a place to drink.

Both men and women were targeted in arrests and prosecutions for public drunkenness. However, for women, their drunkenness was seen as a far greater social problem. Current social panics about female drinking are not new. In fact, research going even further back in Britain shows female drinking has been singled out 'as a matter of concern' since at least the fifteenth century in western culture.[494] What we can do with female drinking, in the historical sense, is place it within 'understandings of intoxication and drunkenness...situated in particular historical, social, cultural and political contexts'.[495] At the start of the twentieth century and in the decades of war, depression and social upheaval that followed, drunken underclass women were characterised and marginalised as bad citizens, unable to contribute to Western Australia's future in the newly established Australian nation.

Sarah Mattson's drinking also highlights ongoing discussions about feminine identities. As recent research shows, '[W]hen women, young and old, enter discussions of intoxication and drunkenness it is as if the terms take on new meanings...'[496] Socially, in general, female drinking is looked down upon, women are more embarrassed when drunk and their actions sexualised.[497] This is something Australian women share with women in general in western culture. One young woman in Britain in 2004 argued the press and government 'demand explanations for women's drinking that we don't ask of men's, as if falling over after a few pints were an exclusive male right'.[498] Drunken male football fans wandering the streets after a finals game in Fremantle in 1910 in the early hours of the morning were held accountable for their actions by police but the press portrayed the scenes in an almost humorous way.[499] Female drinking was rarely portrayed as anything close to humorous. When Michael Brennan appeared in Fremantle Court on a drunkenness charge in December 1928, he was described affectionately as a 'well-known character in Fremantle'.[500] Female habitual drunks were also described as characters but usually in the sense of being the 'worst character', as Esther Warden was described in 1917.

Research into historical female drunkenness shows us that media coverage in recent years about an increase in females drunk in public are not new, nor are the panics about young women drinking and using violence.[501] Eva Grace Scolaro featured in news stories through the first months of 2010 for glassing another woman in a club in Northbridge the previous year. Handing down an eighteen-month prison sentence, of which Scolaro served six months, the magistrate described it as a 'cowardly and unprovoked attack'.[502] It echoes other glassing attacks of the early twentieth century, including Sarah Mattson's Anzac Day attack on a friend in Weld Square.

Societal disapproval of female drinking continues to dominate discussions of alcohol and crime. Female vulnerability is still emphasised and connections made between women and their roles in the care of others. In fact, as research on gender and drinking suggests, 'society is unprepared to recognise and deal with such deviance'.[503] Intoxication is more closely tied to masculine identities.[504] Alcohol problems, therefore, must be understood in 'a social context of roles, norms and circumstances of use'.[505]

Police photos of Sarah Mattson reveal a rather desperate-looking woman. In the context of this book, Sarah Mattson's mug shots ask us to think about her life beyond criminal convictions. In doing so we discover a woman who suffered the loss of five children before her worst days of public drunkenness. It leaves us wondering what impact this had on Sarah and her life within the family home. Sarah Mattson's criminal record also serves as a reminder that nearly a century after she first fronted court, society is still trying to understand female drinking and defines it against female respectability and ideals of the good woman.

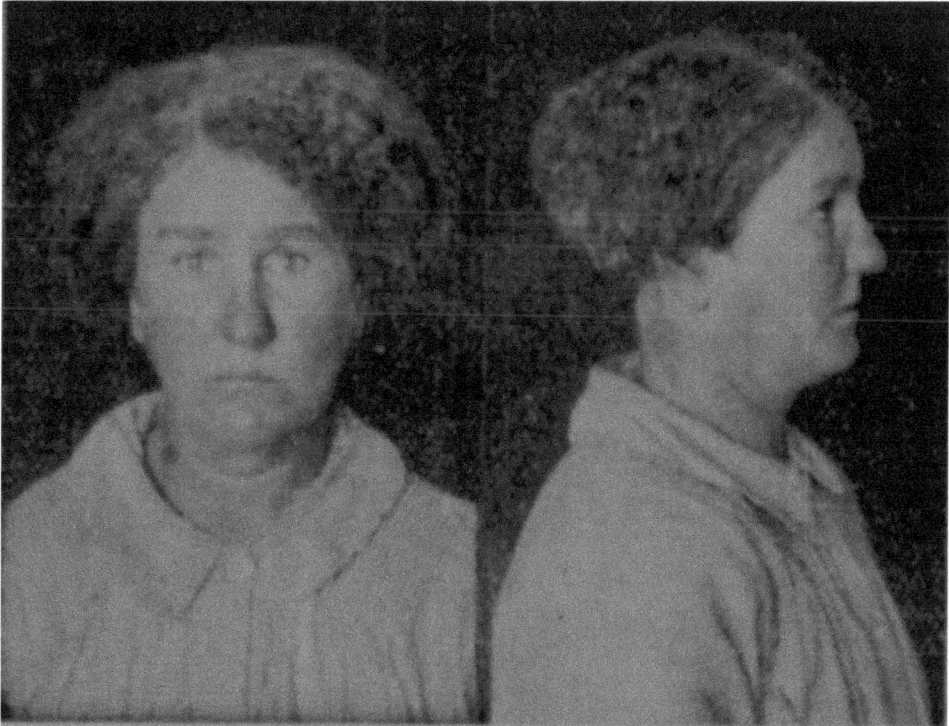

F-289. F 565.—MATSON, Sarah Jane
(Prostitute, etc.)

Sarah Mattson, 1930

4.

The Social Evil

'An Awful Character' – 'we are puzzled really to know what to do with this woman, as she is an awful character, said Sergeant Smith, when prosecuting Esther Miller, aged 28 years, who was charged with being an idle and disorderly person...Mrs Dugdale [of the Women Police], who explained that the arrest was made more for accused's own protection, added: 'This woman's ideas of life are very degraded...'[506]

Esther Miller was a fallen woman; eleven years in and out of the Salvation Army Home in Victoria failed to reform her and in September 1918 she appeared in the Perth Police Court on an idle and disorderly charge. Less than three months later, Esther was again before the courts. She had escaped from the Old Women's Home in Fremantle, was without work and 'in the streets unprotected'.[507] Released in February 1919, she was again charged as an idle and disorderly person later that year and sentenced to six months in gaol.[508] It wasn't just that Esther had no work and was 'unprotected' in public. Esther Miller was a prostitute.

Esther Miller was depicted in court reports as yet another example of bad women on the streets of Perth in the early twentieth century. She was a woman who engaged in sex on the streets and brought down the decency of institutions with her 'degrading conversation'.[509] While the Victorian era officially ended with the death of Queen Victoria in January 1901, it continued to influence into the first decades of the new century. Victoria had set a high standard for women in Britain and the far reaches of the British Empire. Mother to nine children and devoted wife and widow to Albert, she was representative of the good wife, mother and woman. She was not the fearsome, unruly woman, the 'deviant woman' who was 'outcast and despised member of the community'.[510] The prostitute as a 'fallen' woman dominated West Australian discussions about prostitution from the late nineteenth century. Alongside drunken females on the streets, the police, court and newspapers used prostitutes as visible examples of deviant women failing to meet social expectations. At a time when women were expected to be morally superior, Esther Miller's 'fall' was taken very seriously. Prostitution, it was argued in the first years of the twentieth century, had to be contained and regulated. In this context, the street prostitute was criminalised as an idle and disorderly person in an effort to take her off the streets and rescue her femininity. If she could not find work in a brothel – one way in which prostitution was regulated behind closed doors – the street prostitute was placed in institutions or imprisoned for months at a time.

Fallen Women

Representations of the fallen woman date back as far as the Old Testament and in more recent history with John Milton's *Paradise Lost*. The prostitute is depicted in a socio-religious manner as similar to Eve's fall and the corruption of man.[511] With the growth of Evangelical movements in the nineteenth century[512] and increasing discussions about 'morality and progress'[513], the female prostitute needed to be saved to prevent further moral degradation in society. Social purity movements from the 1880s in Britain and United States influenced Australian responses to prostitution and heralded in a era of intervening in the lives of the 'dangerous classes' to purify private and public lives.[514]

Prostitution, labelled the 'great social evil'[515], represented a 'fall from femininity'.[516] Prostitutes failed to live up to the Victorian ideal of the chaste, morally superior woman.[517] The prostitute was characterised as morally corrupt and unnatural within the gender order.[518] As historian Lucy Bland highlights, 'To say that a woman had "fallen" implied that she had lost her modesty and become quite "other"'.[519] Perth's prostitutes, according to *The Sunday Times* in 1908, displayed 'the extreme wantonness of our fallen women, who seem once they take the crooked road, to at once lose all their self-respect'.[520] Rose Skivington and Lizzie Molyneaux were described in the press as 'abandoned women' in 1902 when they were charged as idle and disorderly persons.[521] They were not literally abandoned women but had abandoned the feminine ideal.

In Britain, prostitution was used by social reformers as an example of the ills of modern society. As Paula Bartley writes, 'prostitution commanded attention from the church, the state, the medical profession, philanthropists, feminists and others, each of which offered a range of solutions to control and ultimately to end it'.[522] The social purity movement from the late nineteenth century aimed to create a 'moral climate' in which prostitution would cease to exist.[523] One major impact was the social, medical and legal regulation of the 'fallen' woman.

In Western Australia, either through her own 'folly' or forced into selling sex, the woman on the streets had fallen out of respectable society, as social reformer Grace Ferguson depicts in a letter to *The West Australian* in 1918:

All women "on the streets," as we call it, are not totally depraved and devoid of all shame, by a long way. Some poor girls, from folly and silliness or absolute ignorance have fallen, and failing to gain a footing in respectable society again, have gone under. Others have found the battle of life too hard for them – God help them – and have sold their bodies to sustain life or help their families, but they still retain their sense of shame'.[524]

While Ferguson expressed a view shared by most within the social reform movement, there was also some criticism of the double standards in sexual promiscuousness. In a letter to *The West Australian* in September 1899, as the new century approached, 'Decency' of Perth argued:

This argument of woman's moral superiority, necessitating stern punishment in transgressors and consequent leniency in the case of men, might have been sufficient for the badly educated woman of the last century, but it will scarcely recommend itself to the logical pure-minded woman of to-day, to whom sin is sin whether in man or woman. The chastity of the home is to be supported by our wives and mothers, not by husbands, fathers, or sons; in other words, our brothers and sons may be moral lepers, but our sisters and daughters must be kept pure to be fitting mates for them.[525]

Young girls were, however, viewed as especially vulnerable to the double standard. From the eighteenth century, the good girl was of particular concern in turning to prostitution and then being left destitute and a shadow of her former self.[526] By the nineteenth century there were concerns for girls from respectable families being lured into prostitution. This was sensationalised at a time when prostitution was likened to 'white slavery' and taken up in international crusades against this exploitation. Men were said to decoy

> young girls with bribes of money and toys or else procured them for brothels by pretending that they were to enter domestic service. This white slavery, as it was known, emphasised the innocence of prostitutes at the expense of morally guilty men. Undoubtedly, those involved in the rescue and reform of prostitutes needed to convince themselves, and those whom they asked for financial support, that prostitutes were worth saving'.[527]

It was also a reaction to the changing role of women and rapid urbanisation.[528] Arguments around sexual slavery have endured. As Kathleen Barry argues, 'Female sexual slavery is present in all situations where women or girls cannot change their immediate conditions of their existence; where regardless of how they got into those conditions they cannot get out; and where they are subject to sexual violence and exploitation.'[529] This, however, has been contested as an extreme example of recruiting women into prostitution.[530]

White slavery debates in Western Australia, and across the Australian states into the twentieth century, centred on portrayals of white girls as corrupted by Chinese men who used them in sexual slavery. This coincided with increased restrictions on

Chinese immigration into Australia and the implementation of what has come to be known as the White Australia Policy. The moral degradation of prostitutes provided social reformers with an opportunity to also raise fears about foreigners and the Chinese 'other' within Australian society. White slavery debates 'reinforced the idea that foreigners had designs on the purity of young girls'.[531]

Foreign prostitutes had been used across Australia, particularly in Queensland and on the West Australian goldfields, to satisfy male needs. As the Queensland Police Commissioner argued, the use of foreign workers was 'less revolting and degrading than would be the case were it met by white women'.[532] By the start of the twentieth century, however, the focus was on white girls and slavery, after immigration restrictions decreased the number of foreign sex workers.[533] Police targeted Chinese brothels in their regular raids on the sex industry in Perth and Fremantle. Young women found in these 'dens' were described in court as 'a disgrace to their country and their sex'.[534] The sensationalist paper *Truth* claimed 'Asiatic agents were operating in every Australian city to funnel girls to brothels'.[535]

Outcast from respectable society and working in brothels near Chinese market gardens, prostitutes were forced to live with less 'respectable' people.[536] Women shown to be living with a Chinese man were repeatedly brought before the courts on vagrancy or idle and disorderly charges and were subject to allegations of prostitution by police and magistrates. Women claiming to have visible means of support, by default of their association with a Chinese man, were also charged as vagrants.[537] May Ahern, a woman we will meet in the next chapter, argued in court in 1920 that a Chinese man had been keeping her thus proving she had grounds for lawful means of support. The police and magistrate disagreed and she was sentenced to six months in gaol.[538] Ahern had previously been linked with Chinese establishments. In 1910, details of her immoral lifestyle in a Chinese tenement, along with two other young women, Myrtle Connor and Vera Matson, were publicised in *The Sunday Times*.[539] As Jan Ryan argues, 'White' women who married, lived with Chinese, or acted as their prostitutes, were discriminated against, despite their 'whiteness', and racism shaped these 'white' women's lives'.[540]

Truth claimed in January 1904 that it was forced to publish details of a case of 'monstrous immorality' in the interests 'of the cleanliness of our city'. Three young women appeared in court on idle and disorderly charges and were said to be in company of 'thieves and suspicious characters'. However, their worst digression from respectability was frequenting a 'Chinaman's place in Stirling Street' in the city. There is an interesting twist to the story, however. The court preferred one of the women's associations with a Chinese man to her mother who was said to have been largely responsible for her downfall.[541] Eva Claffey's mother had been sentenced to gaol as an idle and disorderly person on a number of occasions. In 1902 a magistrate, in sentencing mother and daughter, said Mary Claffey was responsible for her 'daughter's degradation'.[542]

White slavery debates at the end of the nineteenth century enforced legislative changes in Australia whereby men living off the proceeds of prostitution could be prosecuted.[543] Western Australia was most radical in its approach. Under a provision in the Justices Act (1902) a person could be labelled as of 'evil fame' based solely on the suspicion they would commit a crime.[544] Nellie Waterman appeared in court in June 1905 charged by her husband with being a person of 'evil fame'. The couple were married the previous November and after only a few weeks, Nellie left her husband and began living at what was described as a house of ill-fame in James Street, Perth. Nellie countered her husband with claims of cruelty to which he responded he simply wanted to give her a home. The case was dismissed but Nellie Waterman was told to find a more respectable place to live.[545] Despite his loss in the case, the 'Evil Fame' section of the Justice Act allowed Waterman to take his wife to court on suspicion she was likely to engage in prostitution. In another case, Violet Fitzpatrick, alias Hyland (her maiden name), was described in court as 'most dissolute in her habits' and charged with being of evil fame. She was let go under a promise that she would leave Fremantle.[546] She didn't leave and spent the next few years appearing on various charges in both the Perth and Fremantle courts.

Containing Prostitution

'Evil fame' legislation was one part of an overall effort in Western Australia to regulate and contain prostitution. From the 1890s prostitution came to be seen as a serious social problem. It coincided with the mining boom dramatically increasing the non-West Australian-born population and rapid urbanisation across the metropolitan area. While the same can be said for other major Australian cities and also Britain and the United States at the time[547], Western Australia's boom was more marked than other places given it had struggled for decades to attract vast numbers of immigrants. The gold rushes changed this, as they had done in Victoria in the 1850s leading to the rapid expansion of urban Melbourne.[548] By March 1901 WA's population had increased dramatically to over 184,000 from 29,708 in April 1881.[549] Breadwinners leaving the eastern states looking to make a fortune in the gold rushes were responsible for some of the population increase. Desertion records in the *Police Gazettes* show the other side of this with wives and children left behind.[550] As a result, Western Australia experienced a boom in prostitution as rapid urbanisation and heightened immigration increased the demand for sexual services. It wasn't just men who contributed to an increase in prostitution. Women looked for better business in the West, some wanting to escape police attention for their soliciting elsewhere in Australia.[551]

Western Australia followed the pattern of other western societies in its efforts dealing with prostitution: suppression, regulation and abolitionist.[552] The social purity movement, influenced by similar movements in Britain, focussed on suppression of prostitution from the late nineteenth century. The West Australian branch of the National Council of Women ran various campaigns throughout the first decades of the twentieth century to ensure prostitution was not legalised and offer educational assistance to prevent against erring young people[553]. The Social Purity section of the WCTU also played a key role in the push to suppress prostitution, as part of its focus on prioritising families as opposed to 'fickle personal relationships'.[554] While WCTU visits to Fremantle Prison focussed on habitual female drinkers, temperance women trying to reform 'degraded' lifestyles also targeted prostitutes. Similar rescue organisations became popular across Australia from the middle of the nineteenth century and were largely run by Christian denominations. Their work rested on the belief that some 'fallen' women could be rescued, given the opportunity for a respectable life.[555] The rescue home, as in the case of the Home of the Good Shepherd in Leederville and Salvation Army homes, was thus used as a means to reform women and regulate and suppress prostitution.

Suppression of brothels, in particular, was one of the main aims of purity movements and was supported by community members.[556] E. Harris, writing to *The West Australian* from Fremantle argued:

> How is it possible for parents rearing families and having the misfortune of living in close proximity to these places to keep their children deaf and blind to their immediate surroundings? Even the atmosphere of a pure home cannot wholly counteract the baneful influences of this steadily increasing evil.[557]

The letter ends by demanding measures to rid the community of brothels that are 'retarding and threatening the progress of morality and purity in the coming generation'.[558] Prostitution was likened to a pollutant in the community and would infect coming generations if nothing were done to stem its flow. *The Sunday Times* likened prostitution to a 'cancerous growth' that was 'eating out both the moral and physical health and strength' of Perth.[559]

From 1895 the West Australian government increasingly favoured a regulatory model. Police and authorities labelled the prostitute as an idle and disorderly person, immorally contributing to society, and a serious social problem at the time. As a result, legal changes were enacted in Western Australia giving police the power to deal with unrespectable women in public. Idle and disorderly charges were brought about through police contact with women in a number of public situations. As was the case across Australia at the time, women labelled as common prostitutes were then subjected to being charged with street offences such as loitering, vagrancy, disorderly conduct and idleness.[560] Not all women charged with an idle and disorderly offence were prostitutes. However, the Idle and Disorderly section of the WA Police Act (1892) allowed for prostitutes to be prosecuted as vagrants if unable to show lawful means of support.[561] Common prostitutes could now be fined £2 or imprisoned for at least a month.[562] Brothel keeping under the Criminal Code was a misdemeanour carrying a three-year gaol sentence with hard labour.[563]

Just how many women the authorities were trying to regulate is interesting. *The Sunday Times* claimed in 1908, 'There is more prostitution amongst us, proportionately speaking, than in any of the other capital cities of the Commonwealth'.[564] Was this true or rather a better reflection of the supposed threat of prostitution? A decline in mining in the first years of the twentieth century saw more movement of people away from the goldfields to Perth and its outlying areas. However, prostitution witnessed a decrease in business with less men flowing through Fremantle port on their way to the goldfields.[565] In 1901, prostitutes in Perth numbered about 140 out of a female population of over 17,000. In Fremantle, 40 prostitutes were identified among a female population of 6,342.[566] According to police evidence in the years leading up to 1914, there were around thirty to forty regular prostitutes listed as having 'no fixed address'.[567] The infrequent nature of prosecutions for soliciting or loitering meant there were some 500 cases against women in the first decades of the twentieth century in Western Australia, as compared with over 10,000 drunkenness cases.[568] *The Sunday Times'* claim Perth had proportionately the highest rate of prostitution in the Commonwealth, is perhaps more reflective of conservative opposition to the regulation of prostitution.

Beyond criminal legislation changes, social reformers, police and the authorities pursued containment of brothels as a way to regulate prostitution. The authorities did not favour an abolitionist approach, though it was debated in some social reform circles. Police in particular were unwilling to completely rid Perth and its surrounds of prostitution. There was a perception within the police that prostitution was a necessary evil and had in fact limited criminal assaults on girls and women, perhaps even protecting respectable women and their families.[569] Prostitution could therefore provide men with an outlet for sexual urges needing instant gratification. However, it raises the issue of whether authorities should tolerate violent attacks on prostitutes as a preventative action protecting respectable women. Again, the good and bad woman divide is employed here.

To limit its wider social impacts, however, prostitution had to be contained. The various churches played their part in decrying the growth of brothels around Perth. Reverend Kench of the Trinity Congregational Church, discussing the social evil of prostitution, argued 'the vicious man should have to go to pains and inconveniences to satisfy his lusts, and that he should be under the ban of the respectable section of the community'.[570] Reverend Moore from the Presbyterian Church also 'did not despair of the evil being entirely overcome eventually'.[571] Church leaders supported the 'suppressive measures' of the amended Police Act in containing the 'growing evil' of prostitution.[572]

Areas of containment were favoured across Australia at the time. Prostitutes could be kept out of respectable areas of Melbourne in the early twentieth century 'if there was one area where the trade was not interfered with'.[573] This is effectively what happened in Perth. While Bannister and Cantonment streets in Fremantle were notorious for brothels, Perth was a more popular brothel site. Elaine McKewon has shown in her historical geography of prostitution in Perth that from the start of the twentieth century the authorities and police were content to allow prostitution to operate in designated zones. A police report in August 1930 revealed:

A close watch is kept over these houses for anything in the nature of soliciting either in the street or from the houses and when found action is taken but so long as they behave themselves and conduct their calling in as quiet a manner as possible the long established custom is followed of not interfering with them.[574]

From 1905, with Annie McKenzie setting up the 'Nera' brothel, Roe Street became a central area for prostitution in Perth. Police raids on brothels in the city centre led to a preference for brothels over the railway lines into the less residential Roe and James Streets.[575] By 1915, fifteen brothels operated on Roe Street, with the number remaining around ten into the 1920s.[576] Josie's Bungalow (Villa), owned by Frenchwoman Marie Louis Monier (better known as Josie de Bray), was the largest in Roe Street, along with another two she owned on the street.[577] Isolated houses were known in East Perth, Victoria Park, West Perth and Leederville but none rivalled the Roe Street businesses.[578] Roe Street, in close proximity to the City Police Station, provided police with an area where prostitution could be contained and closely monitored.

Josie de Bray is an interesting character. She kick-started her career in Kalgoorlie before making a fortune from selling sex during World War One in her establishments in Roe Street, Perth. She also worked up a business in selling alcohol. While the temperance movement was looking to restrict after hours drinking, Josie sold beer at exorbitant prices – sly-grog selling, as it was known - amounting to a day's wages for a soldier.[579] By the 1930s, Josie had three successful brothels in Roe Street. Her rise in the sex industry was rarely without incident however. In September 1919 she appeared in court after shots were fired at one of her brothels. Early one morning four men came calling at the brothel. Josie, using a peephole, formerly a letterbox, refused the men entry. As she backed away from the door, under a torrent of threats, a revolver was pushed through the peephole and two shots were fired. Josie was shot in the elbow. Esther Miller, our fallen woman from the start of this chapter, who had been with de Bray moments before in the kitchen, gave evidence implicating four men in the violent attack.[580]

Containment and close monitoring of brothels failed to restrict all prostitution. Women continued to solicit out in the streets and near residences and this brought them into direct conflict with the police. Had they remained in brothels, their prostitution would have been tolerated, given it did not draw attention from members of the unpaying public. Streetwalkers, referred to as common prostitutes, became in identifiable outcast group.[581] They preferred the main streets where they were more likely to find business. They were also more likely to come to the attention of police and passers-by. Streetwalkers favoured the increasingly business-centred, commercialised main thoroughfares of Murray, Wellington, Queen and Barrack streets and park areas such as The Esplanade in Perth. Down in Fremantle they were busiest in Packenham, Bannister and Cantonment Streets. Prostitutes working the inner streets of Fremantle favoured the streets closest to the port. Bannister Street was notorious for streetwalkers in the first decades of the twentieth century. Close to the port and even closer to the main thoroughfares of High and Market Streets and South Terrace, it was perfectly situated for women to lure clientele coming out of pubs and wandering back to docked ships or local boarding houses.

While street prostitution mainly involved women soliciting around the main streets, it included a group lower down the prostitution hierarchy operating out of back lanes or vacant lots in the city.[582] Alice Sullivan was found 'cuddled up' in a stolen bed with a man in an unoccupied house in John Street, West Perth in August 1919. She was described in court as frequently loitering around Perth streets and slept at night in 'fowl houses'.[583] It was the scattered nature of this street prostitution that caused most concern. As police forced prostitutes into designated brothel areas, street prostitutes unable to gain entry into the brothels basically carried on business wherever they could. They looked for business in outlying streets closer to West Perth, Subiaco and Leederville.

Efforts to contain prostitution in brothels overlooked the difficult recruitment process involved that left some women unable to gain entry into them. As Sharyn Anleu demonstrates, '[be]coming a prostitute entails recruitments and socialisation.'[584] A brothel prostitute has to know someone involved in the business, build up a clientele, serve an apprenticeship and adhere to set standards and practices.[585] One of the difficulties in gaining entry into a brothel is the majority of madams only take trained prostitutes. Newcomers to Perth and Fremantle, particularly from the country areas, didn't know the local business and women who used soliciting as one means in which to gain money, alongside other activities on the streets, were not generally welcomed into the major Roe Street brothels. Esther Warden was never welcomed into any of the Roe Street brothels. Originally from England, and possibly having first lived in Victoria before coming to Western Australia, she was a stranger in Perth and didn't exactly endear herself to women around the city.

Parliamentary debates about the 'social evil', particularly street prostitution, increased police campaigns against streetwalkers into the new century.[586] Attorney General Walter James said in 1902, in relation to the Police Act, that '[A] common prostitute would not necessarily be a notorious prostitute, but a person honestly believed to be a prostitute'.[587] Definition of a 'common prostitute' was therefore left to police discretion. Streetwalkers could be labelled 'common prostitutes' if police argued a woman had a reputation.[588] One police constable told the Perth Police Court in 1919: 'I call a reputed prostitute a woman who goes about with prostitutes, gets drunk, lies down somewhere'.[589] Police evidence often outweighed testimony from the accused herself, as in the case of Maria Savage:

> Social Evil - Maria Savage was charged with loitering in Aberdeen-street for immoral purposes. Mr. Penny appeared for accused. P.c. Douglas said he saw her loitering in the street near the house where she lived, and accosting men. P.c. Smith said she had asked him if he was coming to her house. In defence, accused and a witness, Mrs. Stewart, denied that the former had accosted anyone. Accused added she was waiting for a friend at the time. A fine of 30s with costs, was imposed.[590]

By virtue of their visibility in public, especially in the evening or early hours of the morning, women could find themselves under suspicion of illicit activities. As Jill Matthews argues, home was the proper place for a good woman in the early twentieth century. A good woman would not be on streets late in the evening, certainly not alone.[591]

The public nature of street prostitution made it easy fodder for stories in the press, raising social concerns about unruly women. According to *The Sunday Times*:

> One cannot help noticing the large number of dissolute women who are in the habit of frequenting certain hotels here, and their number seems to be largely on the increase. They are for the most part frowsy, old harridans, and certainly not likely to attract the average Lothario, but they are a source of annoyance to decent men who have occasion to wander into some of the private bars in the back-street hotels for a quick nip. The police have been making attempts during the past few weeks to rid the streets of these pests, and one or two of the 'lydies' have had to face the Bench...[592]

Regulation of street prostitution into the twentieth century saw it increasingly represent a smaller section of the sex industry. By the second decade of the twentieth century, police were largely successful in driving most women off the streets.[593] In Fremantle, 'prostitutes who were too old or dissolute to work in brothels any more could still eke out a living on the waterfront'.[594] However, despite periods of growth - the Depression years of the 1930s, witnessed an increase in 'bolder soliciting' on the streets to make more money during the economic downturn and due to a partner's unemployment[595] - port street prostitution was less favoured due to the concentration of brothels in Bannister Street and the movement of business up to Roe Street, Perth. Port prostitutes did benefit though from a regular market in sailors and wharvies and also soldiers during the First World War.

In general, streetwalkers were shown leniency as long as no complaints were made and they were discreet.[596] Containment within brothels had cut back on some soliciting in public but when streetwalkers became a public problem they were charged.[597] Despite some success in containing prostitution, there were also calls for even greater regulation of it. In the early years of the twentieth century, amid the efforts to contain prostitution, the streetwalker also became a health threat.

The Prostitute as a Health Threat

A battered relic of womanhood... Esther Warden was before the Police Court during the week on the charge of being an idle and disorderly female, "I've never seen the accused in the company of a respectable person," observed an outraged John Hop...A weary bench sent her down for a month, there being no other way of dealing with the frowsy, dreadful females who nightly infest the streets of Perth. Badly wanted - a CD Act.[598]

Esther Warden had a number of convictions against her name by 1909, including assault, drunkenness, theft and creating disturbances.[599] However, Warden also worried the authorities when she engaged in prostitution. She was the first person charged with keeping a house of ill fame under the new Fremantle by-laws in 1900.[600] Brothels were tolerated to an extent but when business got out of hand and neighbours complained, police stepped in and charged owners with keeping a house of ill fame. By 1909 she had been charged on a number of occasions with being idle and disorderly and was sensationalised in the press as one of the 'dreadful females who nightly infect the streets of Perth'. Esther Warden and other women soliciting on the streets of Perth and Fremantle were characterised as posing a serious health threat to the community through the spread of venereal diseases. Prostitutes inhabited a social underworld influenced by ongoing Victorian 'social fears and insecurities [about] filth and hygiene'.[601]

The West Australian's plea in October 1909 for a Contagious Diseases Act was not unique. Only the year before *The Sunday Times* ran a lengthy article on the 'prevalence of diseased women in Perth', prostitutes preying on 'our young manhood'.[602] It was another example of the press singling women out as spreading disease.[603] Taking the high moral ground, the paper argued it had a 'duty to the public' to inform them about the state of the social evil. [604] Using the recent case of four girls appearing in court on a soliciting charge and medically diagnosed as 'suffering from a nameless disease', the paper made the claim 'Perth is exposed to a terrible danger'. The main purpose of the article was to argue for a Contagious Diseases Act, similar to one in Queensland where 'Brisbane is the most moral city in the Commonwealth'.[605] Queensland and Tasmania had passed CD Acts in 1868 and 1879 respectively but NSW and Victoria failed to pass the legislation.[606] Despite the failure of legislative changes in other states, diseased prostitutes were portrayed in the West Australian press as a threat to the community warranting the regulation and containment of prostitution and prevention of fallen women back 'within the fold of respectability'.[607] According to the paper, weekly medical tests under a Contagious Diseases Act would prevent Perth from becoming the 'moral sewer of the Commonwealth'.[608]

While a Contagious Diseases Act was not introduced in Western Australia, debates were similar here to those in Britain from the middle of the nineteenth century. The *Contagious Diseases Acts* passed by the British Government in 1864, with amendments in 1866 and 1869, were largely influenced, firstly, by social concerns about prostitution as a 'social evil' and, secondly, the spread of diseases amongst the armed forces during and after the Crimean War of 1854-56.[609] Yet the Acts were not wholly popular, with more than 17,000 petitions sent to the government between 1870 and 1885.[610] Some opposition came from feminists like Josephine Butler who argued against the Acts as sanctioning prostitution as a necessity.[611] Women's groups were also opposed to the 'curtailment of the civil rights of working-class women', who could be arrested and detained as suspected prostitutes.[612] The CD Act was finally repealed in 1886 but they had served a purpose in outlining the prostitute as a health threat to society.

Some weekly health checks had existed in Perth and Fremantle from the 1890s but from 1904 police and magistrates were exerting more than their allocated authority. If they believed a prostitute was suffering from a venereal disease, police and magistrates often worked together to secure a prison term.[613] An official investigation into police, prostitutes and the work of Government Medical Officer Dr Blanchard – the Blanchard Royal Commission of 1915 – revealed police and Blanchard had influenced prostitutes to get medical checks at their own expense.[614] An amendment to the *Health Act (1911)* was also introduced into the Legislative Assembly in 1915 outlining compulsory treatment for venereal diseases and detainment of prostitutes in hospitals (primarily Perth Public Hospital) or gaol hospitals for an indefinite amount of time.[615] Under Section 310 (2):

> Where a woman who is a prostitute, and while residing in a brothel or in premises reputed to be a brothel has received notice under section 307(1), and after the receipt of such notice continues to reside in a brothel or in premises reputed to be a brothel, such woman shall by reason of such continued residence be deemed knowingly to be doing an act likely to lead to the infection of any other person with venereal disease within the meaning and for the purposes of this section.[616]

World War I heightened concerns about the spread of venereal diseases, particularly after cases were reported among recruits training in Perth in 1914.[617] An increase in demand for prostitution from soldiers communing in Fremantle port combined to raise the attention of the authorities. Convictions for soliciting in Perth and Fremantle in fact doubled from 1914-1915 alone.[618] Madge Layton took advantage of the increase in business in January 1916 but was swiftly arrested:

Loitering-Madge Layton, a young woman, was charged with loitering for immoral purposes, and pleaded not guilty. She had accosted soldiers and drunken men in Wellington Street on Wednesday night, in spite, of warnings from the police. The Bench decided to give the defendant an opportunity to prove that she was in earnest when she said she, was willing to go to Kalgoorlie. She was fined £2, in default 14 days' imprisonment, but the sentence was suspended on the defendant's under taking to leave the town within 24 hours.[619]

Madge Layton was willing to leave Perth but when women refused to conform, the authorities pushed for greater use of Vagrancy laws to gaol possible diseased prostitutes.[620]

In the two years from June 1916 to June 1918, a total of 2,653 new cases of a sexually transmitted disease were reported. This was an annual increase of 0.5 per cent of the population.[621] Those denying treatment for venereal disease were but a small minority, around ten per cent of total cases.[622] *The Sunday Times* claimed these figures showed 'no need for shrieking' but pleaded for greater knowledge about the spread of diseases.[623] The paper also claimed 'medical scaremongers' were using 'sweeping generalisations' to weigh in on the VD scare.[624] It is in fact in the interests of sex workers to remain healthy, especially in the early twentieth century, 'as their occupation entails no compensation for ill health'.[625] A Select Committee Report into the Health Act Bill in 1918 made public findings showing prostitutes had in fact 'given less trouble to the Department of the Public Health than some other members of the community'.[626] Nonetheless, the CD Acts and vagrancy laws across Australia had one major effect of locking some women in as common prostitutes where before they had not completely relied on prostitution.[627] Debates about venereal disease and prostitution also placed the blame squarely with women that overlooked the fact women contracted the disease from men too.

As in Britain, health legislation and treatment plans were not popular within women's organisations in Western Australia. The Woman's Guild, joined my the WCTU, held a number of meetings in Perth to discuss further amendments to the Health Bill early in 1918 as part of their opposition to the regulation of prostitution.[628]

Members argued there was little evidence to show that compulsory health checks around the world had eradicated venereal diseases. The Guild drew attention to the flawed nature of loitering and soliciting charges as dependent on the evidence of one policeman alone. The also criticised the double standard inherent in the amendments that undermined greater equality that had been achieved during the war years. Delegates from the WCTU argued the detention of prisoners clause allowed authorities to operate 'against the poorest and most defenceless women and girls in the community'. [629]

By 1938, concerns still thrived about the spread of venereal disease and the threat from prostitution. Medical testimony at the Royal Commission on Perth Civic Administration claimed regulated treatment of venereal diseases was needed to keep up with a growth in prostitution.[630] Based on this the Royal Commission, 'of the opinion that there is grave danger of the spread of venereal disease from promiscuous sex gratification' recommended 'that in the interest of public health a complete and up-to-date clinic for dealing with this aspect of the subject should be provided in the proposed new Perth Public Hospital'.[631]

*

Historic representations of prostitutes as fallen women, as something less than their sex, directly impacted on the lives of Perth and Fremantle women appearing before the courts on idle and disorderly charges. They were both vulnerable and dangerous, and in need of rescuing. All, it was said, had experienced a fall from femininity. The police, courts and media – influenced by public opinion – promoted an image of prostitution as turning formerly good women into fallen, impoverished wrecks of womanhood. Pushed into brothels or allowed to solicit on the streets, as long as no one saw, prostitutes were depicted as a threat to the health of the state. Women soliciting on the streets in the first decades of the twentieth century faced restriction and exclusion from society in way that prevented understanding of their lives beyond stereotypes.

Regulation and containment of prostitution, and the criminalisation of street prostitution in particular, does not tell us a great deal about the women themselves however. Their life stories reveal women charged with loitering, soliciting or idle and disorderly had varying experiences and expectations of sex on the streets and also came from a variety of backgrounds. They were a mix of vulnerable and dangerous characters but also married women and mothers who for an assortment of reasons were on the streets soliciting for sex. We turn now to May Ahern and other common prostitutes criminalised in these years.

5.

'May and her mugs'

Business was good for May Ahern over the festive season in December 1919, but she pushed her luck too far. Apprehended in Fremantle on Boxing Day, May was brought before the courts the next day. With 'raven locks' and 'clad in a pneumonia blouse, transparent sleeves, white stockings, high-healed and other accessories,' she caught the eye of reporters.[632] Charged with loitering, idle and disorderly conduct and use of foul language, May was arrested for soliciting for sex in public. [633] May was portrayed in the press as tempting 'unaware males from the paths of virtue'.[634] According to *Truth*, 'as far as the provocative lure of sex is concerned, [May] is evidently a firm believer in direct action'.[635] In only a couple of hours working her patch in Phillimore Street, May misled a number of men, her 'mugs', who apparently fell prey to her 'warm, pink, palpitating femininity'.[636] When police intervened on Boxing Day, May kicked up a storm, calling them 'bloody mongrels'.[637] Ahern was sentenced to three months for loitering; a further three months for being idle and disorderly and her foul language gained her another week.[638]

Street prostitution was one major way in which women deviated from general crime trends. While men were reprimanded for paying for sex, and could be charged with living off the proceeds of prostitution, the 'fallen woman'[639] was a greater concern. After drunkenness, prostitution was the next offence for which most women were tried and convicted in the courts. Coinciding with greater regulation and control of prostitution at the time, street prostitution brought women like May Ahern into direct contest with police, courts and public opinion. Historically, prostitution has been 'conspicuously fragmented, individualistic and non-

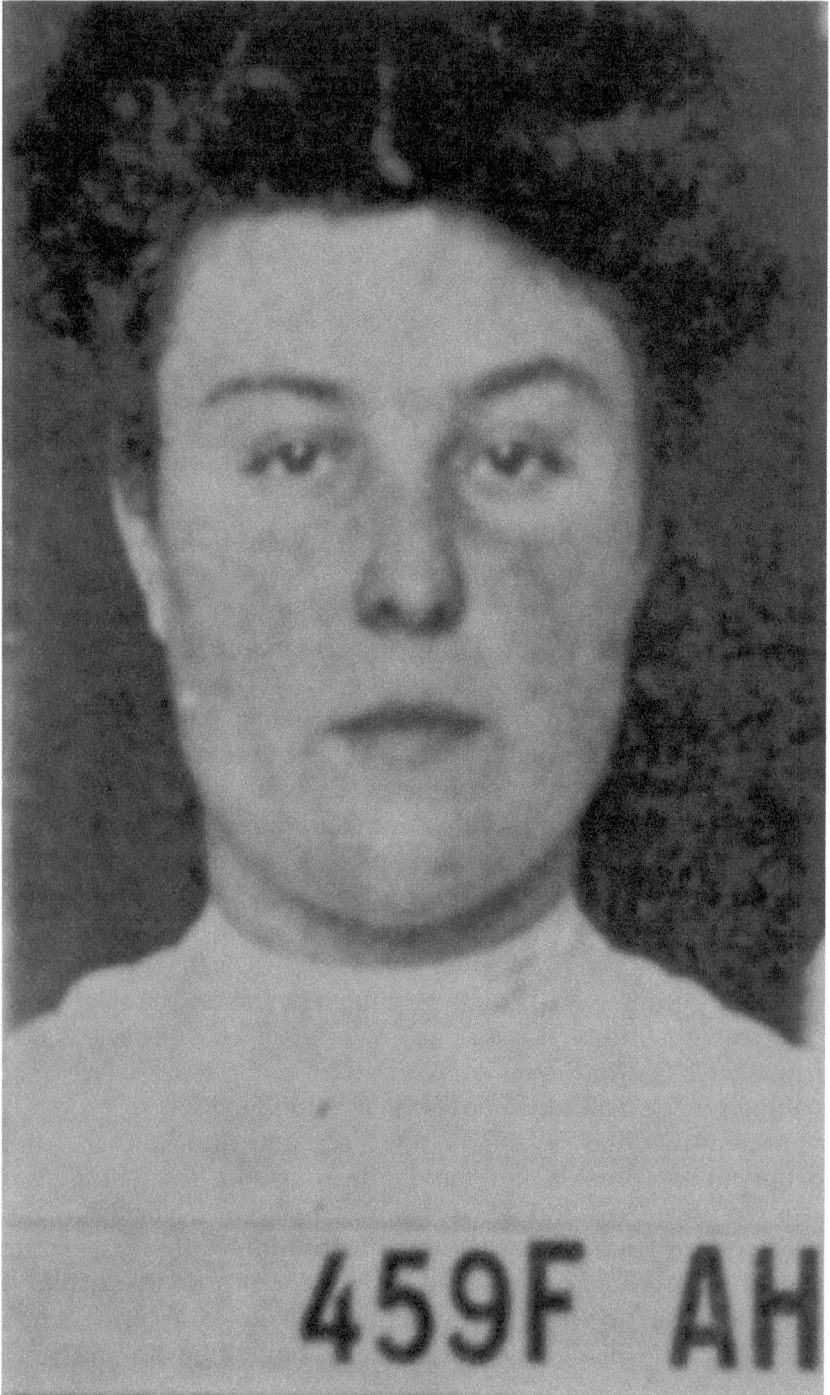

May Ahern, 1916

ERN, MAY

professionalised. It has been widely associated with social and geographical exclusion, stigmatisation and moral indignation'.[640] Females soliciting on the streets were outcast from respectable society. However, in studying the prostitutes, their circumstances and experiences, some history can be given to these women.[641] Their lives show a mix of experiences and their involvement in prostitution provides valuable insights into what was the most public form of deviance for females at the time.

Who were the 'common' prostitutes?

Similar to stratification first described in England from the middle of the nineteenth century, female prostitutes in Perth and Fremantle were classified according to a hierarchy. They included 'kept mistresses; demi-mondains; low lodging house women; sailors and soldiers' women; park women; and thieves' women'.[642] The women featured in this book, soliciting for sex on the streets, were much lower down the hierarchy than 'kept mistresses; demi-mondains; low lodging house women'. While a number of them had worked in brothels at different times, most of the common prostitutes repeatedly fronting the Police Courts as idle and disorderly persons loitered in the streets, parks and along the Fremantle waterfront.

Debate and discussion about prostitutes and the spread of diseases further added to the construction of the 'social underclass as degraded and powerless'.[643] The common prostitute, the woman soliciting for an, 'immoral purpose' in a public place, was of particular concern to police and authorities in the early twentieth century. She was a public example of loose morals and unprotected womanhood on the streets. At a time when women were expected to uphold the sanctity of the home, streetwalkers used their sexuality for business. It is from this form of prostitution that most stereotypes arise and 'draws the most attention from city planners, local residents and business owners, who seek to "clean up" areas where it occurs'.[644]

Police lists of known prostitutes allowed for greater surveillance of female types and the areas they frequented. In one list from 1898, over 100 women were listed as prostitutes alongside houses and streets they frequented.[645] Murray, King and Wellington Streets all featured as main soliciting centres, along with Newcastle, Fitzgerald and Roe Streets across the railway tracks. Women on these lists were generally the most notorious females who came to the attention of police and subsequently appeared in court.[646] Maria Savage was named in the 1898 list and identified as soliciting in Perth streets. She had numerous convictions to her name, including numerous for idle and disorderly and loitering.[647] In the press she was featured under headings like 'The Social Evil'[648]and characterised as a notorious street prostitute. Once on the list, common prostitutes found it hard to avoid police attention.

Backgrounds

Who were these notorious women? Using Raelene Frances' (nee Davidson) analysis of 1,567 prostitutes in Perth, Fremantle and Kalgoorlie from 1895-1939 and my own research of close to 2,000 women detailed in the Fremantle Prison Registers from 1900-1939, along with newspaper reports, it is possible to construct an overview of the backgrounds of common prostitutes in Perth and Fremantle.[649] Around half of all common prostitutes were born in Australia, mainly from Western Australia, New South Wales and Victoria. The gold rushes and increased movement of people into Western Australia into the twentieth century had an impact on background of prostitutes with a large number coming from eastern states. Emily Cresswell, well known to authorities in Perth and Fremantle as an idle and disorderly woman, went by the popular name of 'Sydney Emily' (for her birthplace).[650] French and Japanese women accounted for most of the overseas-born prostitutes, particularly in Kalgoorlie,[651] but Perth and Fremantle attracted more local girls. By the 1920s, however, three-quarters of the prostitutes were Australian-born.[652] This is indicative of the decline in foreign-born residents after the gold rushes and greater immigration restrictions.

English and Irish prostitutes gained a great deal of attention from the authorities and in fact numbered over a third of common prostitutes.[653] Police and authorities in general regarded English prostitutes as the worst, believing them more prone to drunkenness and larceny.[654] Englishwoman Esther Warden is a prime example. In late September 1917 she was arrested and charged using obscene language and being idle and disorderly. She had previous loitering convictions to her name, along with numerous appearances on drunkenness and theft charges. She was described in the press as a 'Dangerous Woman'.[655] Whether or not English prostitutes were more disreputable than other streetwalkers is open to debate. Esther Warden was one of the most visible and publicised bad characters in Perth and Fremantle and she, along with other prominent English prostitutes, may have influenced the stereotype for police and magistrates.

Another Englishwoman, Patricia Roots, also didn't help change stereotypes. Patricia first came to the attention of authorities in 1902 in Leonora when her husband had her placed on the Prohibited List as a prostitute. He believed he could do nothing for her and eventually left her in 1904.[656] That same year, Patricia appeared before the Kalgoorlie Police Court in June 1904 on charges of drunkenness and idle and disorderly. Having promised 'to clear away from the district', she was sentenced to six months in gaol.[657] The *Kalgoorlie Western Argus* called it 'enforced retirement from the busy outside world'.[658]

By March the following year, Roots was notching up a criminal record in Fremantle. Roots headed for Fremantle after her release from prison, but was not long out of trouble. She was charged with loitering in the streets there in March 1905.[659] In October 1908 she was again apprehended in Kalgoorlie during a police crackdown on street walking in the town. Sentenced to a month in prison for soliciting and six months for vagrancy, Roots finally left Kalgoorlie in 1909. It wasn't long before she was again before the authorities, this time in her new hometown of Fremantle. It was here Roots was apprehended in September 1909 for loitering for an immoral purpose and sentenced to four months hard labour.[660] She spent the next few years notching up over fifty convictions in Fremantle.[661]

Research has also shown that prostitutes in Perth and Fremantle were more likely to be Roman Catholics with large numbers from Catholic Ireland, France and Spain.[662] Whether they were churchgoing is difficult to establish with only fragments of their lives left in the records.[663] Prostitutes tended to get older as the decades went on in the twentieth century. Around 1900, most of the prostitutes were between twenty-six and thirty-six to forty years of age. By the 1920s there were more prostitutes over the age of forty.[664] One thing that tended to differentiate street prostitutes from their brothel sisters, however, was age. Street prostitutes across Australia 'were often older than the average sex worker, and more likely to be diseased and heavy drinkers'.[665] This was also the case in Perth and Fremantle.

No one seems to have known just how old Kate Dreardon was over the course of her dozens of idle and disorderly convictions, many for loitering and soliciting. In 1900 she is listed in the Prison Register as twenty-four, in what seems to have been her first prison term. By 1912 she is thirty-six but ages dramatically in the next four years; she is listed as forty-nine in 1916.[666] Kate's mug shot seems to correspond with an older prostitute. She looks to be in her late forties or early fifties in the early 1920s. Dreardon was one of many prostitutes who worked the streets of Perth, unable to secure a position in a brothel.

Allegations were made that prostitutes were mentally unsound, thus contributing to their entry into the world of prostitution. Medical evidence given to the 1938 Royal Commission described prostitutes as varying between being 'below the average in intelligence' and 'absolutely imbecile'.[667] However, of the more than 1,500 prostitutes Raelene Frances researched, only a handful could be classified at the time as 'sub-normal' or 'weak-minded'. She further argues there is 'no evidence to suggest that they were any less intelligent than the rest of the community'.[668] This is probably better understood as being a part of the medicalisation of female criminality and explaining criminal women as inferior based on mental problems.

Previous convictions also reveal internal movement from Kalgoorlie to Perth and Fremantle. From the first years of the twentieth century, police in Kalgoorlie launched a campaign targeting soliciting and loitering on the main streets and basically told women to leave the streets or the town at large.[669] Well-known prostitutes were forced to leave Kalgoorlie if they wanted to escape a conviction and gaol time.[670] They tended to migrate to the coast and continue soliciting in Perth and Fremantle, as was the case with Patricia Roots.

Female recidivists charged with soliciting or loitering between 1900 and 1939[671] reveal similarities with other findings on street prostitution from the Victorian period on. Like street prostitutes in Victorian England,[672] women soliciting for sex in Perth and Fremantle mainly came from unskilled working backgrounds. Their 'trade' was more commonly listed in the Prison Registers as domestic, laundress and seamstress. One-fifth of women convicted as common prostitutes were listed as undertaking 'menial' work.[673] However, as in Victorian Britain, where servants and street sellers dominated, by the late nineteenth century street prostitutes included barmaids, waitresses and shop-girls.[674] One Fremantle barmaid told a *Truth* reporter in 1903 that she spent her nights off in Perth looking for men to entice to a house in West Perth where she and other girls would entertain them. Under the title 'Frolics of a Fremantle Flossie', the reporter publicised details of these evenings and how the barmaid – 'one of the finest girls in the seaside town' – enjoyed her nights in Perth while the bar work offered her 'suitable employment'.[675]This young woman demonstrates the fluidity of prostitution for some women who were able to fleet between socially constructed respectable and immoral lifestyles.

One thing all common prostitutes shared was their 'fall' into prostitution. May Ahern, alias May Petersen, was seventeen when she was first charged with idle and disorderly. She had experienced what society at the time termed a *fall*. Historically, entry into prostitution has been explained in a variety of ways. According to Michael Ryan, writing about prostitution in London in the 1830s, the many causes included:

> seduction; neglect of parents; idleness; the low price of needle and other female work; the employment of young men milliners and drapers in shops in place of women; the facilities of prostitution; prevalence of intemperance; music and dancing in public houses, saloons and theatres; the impression that males are not equally culpable as females; female love of dress and of superior society; the seductive promises of men; the idea that prostitution is indispensable; poverty; want of education; ignorance; misery; innate licentiousness; improper prints, books and obscene weekly publications; and the profligacy of modern civilisation.[676]

Prostitution was thus entered into through a variety of circumstances including: seduction, neglect, poor pay, drunkenness, public house entertainments, double standards, female fancy, lack of education, corrupting literature and modern times. Conventional assumptions about prostitution from the middle of the nineteenth century portrayed the prostitute as entrapped in 'white slavery'.[677] However, there were women whose entry into prostitution was voluntary and gradual.[678]

Explanations offered for entry into prostitution from the Victorian period on mainly related to working-class women. As Paula Bartley shows, 'Born into the lowest stratum of society, without decent family values, working-class girls were thought to develop bad habits and be without the virtues associated with gentility'.[679] Working-class households were characterised as socialising young women into deviant home backgrounds that set up a 'fall' into prostitution.[680] Havelock Ellis, writing *The Criminal* in 1890, proclaimed:

> The prostitute lives on the borderland of crime…in those families in which the brothers become criminals, the sisters with considerable regularity join the less outcast class of prostitutes.[681]

Eva Claffey, previously mentioned in a Chinese den in January 1904, fit this image. Eva, it was reported, had suffered at the hands of her brother who ran a low-class brothel in Highgate and forced her to 'sell her body to Chinese men'.[682] By 1916 she had over twenty convictions for loitering for prostitution.[683]

By the end of the nineteenth century, 'reformers were generally unanimous that prostitution was founded on the poverty of working-class women and saw a direct causal relationship between the low level of women's wages and the recruitment of prostitutes.'[684] Prostitutes were the 'archetypal victims of industrialisation'.[685] In Australia, '[p]overty, lack of education, unemployment, minority group membership and labour market exploitation' dominated recruitment into prostitution from the early twentieth century.[686] A woman's economic position was often blamed for entry into prostitution.[687] Very poor women were driven to prostitution if they were single, homeless and without sufficient economic support. For some, the economic benefits of prostitution outweighed any other work available to women at the time. As one witness to the 1938 Perth City Royal Commission stated:

> I have been all sorts of things. First of all I worked in an office as a bookkeeper, then I had a business of my own, and I finished up as a barmaid. It was from the bar that I went to Roe Street. I found that at the occupation I was following I could not earn a decent wage to keep myself properly...[688]

The 'economic motive' dominated discussions about the causes of entry into prostitution in Western Australia.[689] Low wages, it was argued, made prostitution an attractive alternative. *Truth* ran a story in July 1904 in which it asked the question of whether or not factory work led to poverty that in turn led to prostitution.[690] Using the case of young women working twelve to sixteen hours a day for little pay, the paper declared it was in some respects 'easier to live by sin, and so the life goes on'.[691] One Victoria Park resident wrote to the papers in 1914 arguing 'the economic condition of numbers of women and girls' contributed to prostitution in the metropolitan area.[692] The majority of women listed in Fremantle Prison records came from poor, unskilled working backgrounds.[693]

Marriage, or at least a stable partner, was believed in the late Victorian period to be 'effective protection against prostitution' since a male wage was thought to be enough to keep families.[694] This view denied some realities, however. Sadie Bonner's appearance in court in April 1923 is evidence of the influence of husbands in the solicitation of their wives. Both appeared in court but Henry came off worse for wear. Charged as a rogue and vagabond, Sadie's husband was held responsible for his wife having 'gone wrong'.[695] Henry didn't do any work and sent his wife out onto the streets to support them. While she argued her husband was 'a good man and a decorated soldier', he was sent to prison for six months. Sadie did the odd month in prison in the late 1920s but seems to have had a limited prostitution record, or else managed to dodge arrest.[696]

As a social construction, prostitution was portrayed in early twentieth-century Australia as 'opposite both of marriage and work'.[697] This was a belief rather than a reality in some respects, given married women in both Britain and Australia also numbered amongst the common prostitutes. Over a third of common prostitutes listed in Perth and Fremantle were married. Soliciting on the streets did not prevent some women from finding marital partners. Rose Jones, listed in prison records as working menial tasks and identified as a prostitute, was first convicted as a single woman in July 1899 but later married, according to gaol details.[698] Emily Cresswell also married over the course of her lengthy prison record.[699] May Ahern, one of the most notorious prostitutes in Perth and Fremantle, was single when first recorded in prison records in 1908 but had married sometime during her many convictions for soliciting, loitering and vagrancy.[700]

Desertion played a part in some female lives on the streets. It is difficult to fully catalogue how many women soliciting on the streets were doing so after being deserted by a partner, due to a lack of evidence stating abandonment. Esther Warden seems to have been deserted by her husband early in the twentieth century and Sarah Jane Mattson was barred entry from her home, something likened to a form of desertion. Desertion was certainly treated as a serious crime at the time. The *Police Gazette* regularly featured details and sometimes photographs of men who had left wives and children.[701] Widowhood also kept some women on the streets but of these cases, all had originally entered the Prison system as married women.[702] Mary Warnock's married life did little to stop her soliciting on the streets. Found sleeping in Perth Esplanade in 1902, police described Mary Warnock as having 'at one time been in a good position' but was now beyond reform.[703] This was despite the fact she was married. By 1913 she had a long record:

> A Woman's Record - Mary Louisa Warnock made her 142nd appearance in the Perth Police Court yesterday, when she was charged with loitering. This record was exclusive of numerous visits to the Fremantle Court. She was sentenced to three months' imprisonment, with hard labour.[704]

Born in Dublin, Ireland and unable to read and write, Warnock lacked familial support and basic communication skills that may have helped keep in her better paid work and supported by relatives.[705] Labelled a 'complete nuisance about the city' in July 1903,[706] Warnock regularly loitered in Wellington and Murray Streets[707] and was in and out of gaol on idle and disorderly charges.[708] Mary Warnock was embattled by a life on the streets where drunkenness, poverty and isolation dominated. As an 'unfortunate Magdalene' she featured in a local press story in January 1913 detailing her cycle of street and gaol life which by that stage included around 150 appearances in court, many for soliciting in public.[709] Over the course of her life, Warnock served over 100 prison terms, ranging from days to months.[710] Marriage as security from the streets was quite different in reality.

Alcoholism was another factor linked to a woman's 'fall'. At least half of the women repeatedly convicted as idle and disorderly persons also had repeat convictions for drunkenness and habitual drunkenness.[711] However, most women started drinking to excess after taking up prostitution.[712] Yet it was also not always the case that alcoholism made women more susceptible to prostitution. Mary Ann Sweetman, an habitual drunk and public nuisance, did not loiter for sex in her two decades or so of life on the streets.[713]

The Female Decoy: Knocking about with prostitutes and thieves

Alice Lawson presents us with an interesting case in looking at common prostitutes. She was one of the most notorious prostitutes in Perth in the early twentieth century and defied any construction as a vulnerable, weak woman. Characterised as a 'bad character' and one of the many disreputable women inhabiting the inner city streets, Lawson was in many ways closer to the archetypal female of the criminal underworld popularised from the middle of the nineteenth century in Britain and across Australia. Lawson highlights the tendency for authorities to equate female involvement with gangs with a sexual role. Alice Lawson was a female decoy.

Lawson had a well-established reputation as a criminal woman in Kalgoorlie and, for a brief time, Bunbury, before settling more permanently in Perth. By 1930 she had notched up well over fifty convictions; her last in November 1930 was for drunkenness and 'wilfully damaging a window'.[714] It doesn't seem much to end a criminal career but this was a woman with a criminal record including using obscene language, damaging property, drunkenness, idle and disorderly, vagrancy, loitering, soliciting, stealing and assault. In a criminal career spanning more than thirty years, Alice Lawson gained a reputation as a woman who socialised with thieves and prostitutes and needed removing from public life. Lawson spent close to ten years in prison, one-fifth of her life, and mainly for offences against good order.[715]

Alice Lawson's photograph in the Fremantle Prison Register is unique. Unlike the other women photographed and registered as female prisoners, Alice Lawson is smiling. Much could be read into Lawson's self-assured smile in the mug shot. Is she smiling in defiance? Is she amused that she is once again in prison? Has the person taking the photograph said something humorous to her and captured her reaction? She is a pretty woman with thick, curly hair and for whatever reason, is smiling out from the archives. This is a woman labelled by police as a pest who made her 'presence unbearable wherever she had lived'.[716] From the Prison Register she smiles and beckons interest.

Lawson was born in New South Wales around 1872. She is listed in the prison registers as a married woman, Roman Catholic and involved in menial work. Most prostitutes used menial work as their work status. She could read and write and also used aliases such as Alice Davis and Alice Leeder. With a prison record dating back to January 1898 when he received three months for larceny, Lawson seems to have come to Western Australia and settled first in the coastal of Bunbury before moving to the city. She was mentioned in court in May 1899 when a man appearing on an idle and disorderly charge gave evidence he had spent time with Lawson in Bunbury before they were ordered to leave the town. He was said to be living off women and the 'fruits of their misfortune'.[717]

Alice was also charged and sentenced to fourteen days in Prison in April 1901 for using obscene language and creating a disturbance in Perth. Police described her as an old offender, though she was a young woman. She was arrested hiding out with two 'notorious criminals' but claimed the police had treated her badly, giving her a black eye.[718] Two years later, in court on one of her many idle and disorderly charges, she was described by police as 'always knocking about with a lot of prostitutes and thieves' and sentenced to a month in prison.[719]

Alice Lawson tried her luck in Kalgoorlie but was charged with being disorderly in January 1903. She abused the arresting officer but claimed she was drunk at the time and 'knew nothing of what had occurred'. She spent another six months in prison.[720] The following year she was part of a police investigation of a house in Hannan Street, Kalgoorlie. The man accused of having no lawful means of support was said to live in a 'reputed brothel' and kept company with thieves and prostitutes. The house was the 'resort of people of bad repute'. Alice Lawson was one of them, along with Patricia Roots:[721] two notorious women associating with one another.

Described in 1902 as a 'violent female' and 'no stranger to the Court',[722] Lawson's identity as a female decoy provides another characterisation of the common prostitute. In January 1900, the papers reported a case where:

> It was stated in evidence that the woman had lured a man to a vacant piece of ground where the victim of her wiles was set upon and robbed by two men who took from him £1 and a watch valued at £10.[723]

The thieves' woman figures prominently in characterisations of common prostitutes and in this way is linked to thieving gangs on the streets of Perth and Fremantle. The underclass inner city streets were contested grounds in the first years of the twentieth century. Criminals saw the streets at their territory while the police saw it as their duty to protect the public from crime and criminals on the streets. Geoffrey Pearson's work on hooliganism in Britain identifies persistent 'respectable fears' about street violence and disorder. Such fears became part of the social landscape, as did those labelled 'hooligans'.[724]

Female decoys were known to work for 'push' gangs. These gangs were notorious in the Australian cities from the late nineteenth century. Mainly made up of young males characterised as larrikins, street rowdies,[725] push gangs roamed the streets looking to mug people passing by and in general made a nuisance of themselves on the streets. Some of the most notorious push gangs resided in Sydney and Melbourne, particularly The Rocks Push and the Surry Hills's Forty Thieves and Big Seven in East Sydney.[726] In Perth and Fremantle hooligans and hoodlums, as they were also termed, were organised around clear social spaces. Their territories, both real and sensationalised, created an urban geography deeply concerning for the more respectable members of society. One resident, in a letter to editor of *The West Australian* in May 1925 referred to 'city roughs and hooligans…supported by a host of hysterical flappers'.[727] They were a 'disorderly mob' that daily disrupted business and social life. In Perth the most notorious push gangs staked out their territory along Murray and Wellington streets. The Murray street gang were regularly seen 'loafing in the vicinity of public houses' and numbered among some of the most 'hardened ruffians'.[728] Made up of a dozen or so men, they were allegedly responsible for a series of garrotting attacks on Murray Street where passers-by were set upon, held firm around the neck and their pockets emptied.[729] In Fremantle the push threat was so severe at the turn of the twentieth century that it had taken considerable efforts from police and authorities to bring the culprits to justice and restore some order to the streets.[730]

The push gangs also threatened the increasingly respectable areas of the city too. The press declared a state of lawlessness in West Perth at the turn of the twentieth century when a gang threatened respectable residents. Members of a 'gang of criminals and hooligans known as the West Perth push' appeared in court in January 1904 and added fodder to news stories about the push pest in the city.[731] Ringleaders Patrick Callaghan and William Gildersleeves were said to have prowled Russell Square looking for unsuspecting members of the public to attack. In the papers they were characterised in a literary way:

> At this stage A RUDE VOICE BROKE in upon the scene, and Bottle-oh 'Skinny' McNamara, the Esplanade orator, rushed into court and asked to be allowed to clear his character.[732]

The female larrikin and member of push gangs was of particular concern at the time. Female gang members, according to the press, 'drank, stayed out late, hiked up their skirts, got into fights, and generally dared each other to act rebelliously'.[733] This ran contrary to the feminine ideal of the proper young woman who was largely seen and not heard. While young men were largely apprehended and convicted for gang-related crimes, across Britain and Australia from the late nineteenth century, women actively participated in gangs and further pushed the social boundaries.[734]

The 'female decoy' played a key role in some gang activities. Similar to gangs in Victorian England at the time,[735] the female decoy lured men into dark alleyways where the male members of the gang set upon them. This female member of the group was often likened to a prostitute. Prostitutes, it was said by Havelock Ellis writing in the 1890s, corresponded 'more closely to the class of instinctive criminals'.[736] In this way, the female decoy was regarded as more criminal than the regular common prostitutes.

Along with Alice Lawson, New Zealand-born, Minnie Forrester, was another well-known 'evil fame' decoy in Perth. Her criminal record over two decades included habitual drunkenness, vagrancy, idle and disorderly and soliciting.[737] Yet she was most notorious for keeping company with thieves and bad characters on the streets of Perth and Fremantle. According to police, she was 'the biggest decoy in Perth'.[738] In one of her many appearances before the authorities, Forrester was in court on April Fools' Day 1903. Constable Strapp gave evidence she made a 'habit of taking drunken men down dark alleys, when thieves would rob the men'.[739] For this she was sentenced to two months in gaol and publicly declared the worst of the female decoys. In an earlier case in December 1901, Forrester was implicated in a gang attack on a young man in Perth. James Thorpe gave evidence in court that he visited many hotels one evening with Minnie. In one hotel, he and Minnie were watched by a group of men before they continued on to another place to drink. When they parted company, the men followed Thorpe, knocked him out and stole his wallet.[740] Minnie Forrester had successfully got Thorpe drunk enough for the gang to attack.

Marriage did little to alter Minnie Forrester's criminal record. She married William Regan in Geraldton in 1905 but soon after was back thieving on the streets. It was a violent marriage by all accounts. William Regan appeared in court in 1908 charged with assaulting Minnie who gave evidence of what the press called her 'husband's brutality'.[741] While William Regan gave evidence that he had hit his wife, he claimed her addiction to alcohol was the real issue along with her habit of bringing strange men home with her. The court did not agree and sentenced William to two months' imprisonment.[742] By 1914, after several appearances in court, the Regans were described as an, 'undesirable couple' by the papers, listing the 'usual evidence of no work and bad company'.[743]

One of the problems associated with police, press and public labelling of female gang members as decoys is any girl or woman associated with a gang was depicted as a prostitute.[744] By virtue of their keeping company with young male larrikins, 'the girls' morals were so self-evidently loose that it was all one and the same'.[745] Minnie Forrester was sexualised by police and the press as a loose woman who 'lured men down alleys' to assist gangs of thieves. Perth's 'biggest decoy', however, was also a young woman battling a drink problem and caught in a cycle of associations with abusive men. The gang also provided young women an outlet to socialise with other women and form friendships on the streets. They were nevertheless used as examples of 'bad' women on the streets who fought with each other, used obscene language and created a public nuisance. What we don't know about Minnie Forrester is the extent to which she actively made choices about her life on the streets. There is an element of the victim in her story but perhaps she was also a woman who used her 'decoy' work as a means to establish an identity on the streets.

Reforming the 'wretched and sinful'[746]

Criminal women, particularly idle and disorderly women, most commonly faced weeks or months behind bars for their offences against good order. However, other measures were used to keep deviant women off the streets and reform their characters. Female offenders like May Ahern could also be ordered to the Salvation Army Home, Home of the Good Shepherd in Leederville or, if found to be of unsound mind, to the Lunatic Asylum in Fremantle and, later, the Claremont Asylum. These 'carceral'[747] institutions were used as part of a broader effort to reform women outside of prison terms. Such measures did not mean criminal women were dealt with any more leniently than they were in Fremantle Prison. Off the streets and out of public view, female offenders were kept behind closed doors in Asylums and Homes to further control and regulate their social transgressions. Resistance and resignation each played a part in how women understood and reacted to attempts to make them conform to a societal feminine ideal of how they should live their lives. For common prostitutes, the Homes in particular were part of a larger network controlling deviants.[748] Here I want to look at the Home of the Good Shepherd in Leederville as it offers a prime example of attempts to reform common prostitutes.

Female offenders faced a penal system in Western Australia, similar to other western nations, whereby punishment was sanctioned by a legal system giving the state the authority to punish people committing offences deemed illegal and morally wrong.[749] From the eighteenth century, the modern penal system developed away from different systems of punishment towards imprisonment as the main form of punishment. By the nineteenth century, though transportation was still applicable to the Australian and British penal system until 1868, imprisonment was the generalised response to crime.[750] The state controlled the prison system and thus centralised state control of crime.

Punishment and reform from the nineteenth century was also closely linked to class and society. Punishment, ideology and class control theories from British social historians Douglas Hay and E. P. Thompson emphasise 'ideological legitimation and class coercion'.[751] For Thompson, the law is an 'arena for class struggle'.[752] Most of the women committing crime regularly in Perth and Fremantle in the early twentieth century were from poor backgrounds. In this way, criminal women were a part of a larger system of punishment responding to crime but also managing society and those lower down the social scale.[753] Further to this, in line with some of French philosopher Michel Foucault's theories, the prison operated as a form of disciplinary power held over the very poor in society.[754]

Twentieth-century West Australian debates about prisons and punishment arose from nineteenth-century discussions of reform within the penal system, initiated to a great extent by British investigations. By the early twentieth-century, treatment and therapy were increasingly being applied to discussions of reforming criminals. Across the Australian states, '[I]ndividual offenders were encouraged to feel they had not been banished from society, but that they still belonged to a larger collective to which they would return'.[755] Following Federation in 1901 and the creation of an Australian nation, social ordering and citizenship discussions influenced how male and female offenders were viewed within society. Rather than having a proportion of the population shut away in prison and banished from society, such people could be made to contribute to society and thus improve the character of the nation.

In this reforming environment, women were caught in a 'hybridity between penal and welfare regimes'.[756]Female experiences of punishment and reform have historically been, and continue to be, different to men. Recent feminist criminology studies argue women face transcarceration, meaning their lives are regulated through a variety of social controls including the penal system, social welfare and mental health. Women are more likely to be controlled by psychiatry and social work than regular incarceration.[757] In fact, European feminist scholarship indicates women have long been treated differently to men in terms of to use of separate institutions beyond the prison. As early as the sixteenth and seventeenth centuries, female offenders were subjected to penitence, religious instruction and reformative labour in reformatory houses before any discussion of this in general was applied to reforming criminals in general in the nineteenth century.[758] Historically, women have suffered 'institutional exclusion, segregation and control' for a longer period than men, something that indicates different experiences of crime and deviancy.

Similar to the experiences of women in Europe, female offenders in Perth and Fremantle were confined in institutions on a greater scale than their male counterparts. While women were predominantly incarcerated for crimes against good order and prisons continued to be seen as a deterrent in the first decades of the twentieth century, the option of being sent to a Home or Reformatory was applied to female offenders more than it was to men committing similar offences. Public discourse argued young women needed to be rescued from being corrupted in prison. In a July 1912 article, *The West Australian* argued the 'fallen' female was handicapped in prison by that fact habitual offenders outnumber first offenders six to one. Young women committing their first offence were supposedly being subjected to greater criminality in prison that they were outside its walls. According to the paper, it was a 'disgrace' and something more had to be done for the 'fallen sisters'.[759] Amidst these public concerns about prison and its lack of reform, women were increasingly being sent to reformatory institutions and homes as a means to curb their supposed 'fall' from femininity.

Many of the women arrested for offences against good order were at one point sent to the Home of the Good Shepherd in Leederville. Common prostitutes were even more likely to face time away in the Home. Like other religious Homes in Australia from the late nineteenth century, the Home of the Good Shepherd focused on the 'spiritual and moral regeneration' of female occupants as a means to reform them back into society.[760] The common prostitute was of particular concern. As one Perth local wrote to *The Sunday Times* in 1904, the Home of the Good Shepherd provided an opportunity for the 'debased of the female sex' to 'rise from the depths' of misfortune.[761]

The work of the Home of the Good Shepherd in 'rescuing women' was based on a centuries of dealing with fallen women in society. The convent or asylum– as reformatory, school and boarding house – has a long history of treating and housing women stretching back to the early modern period in Europe. Italy, though city-states and not unified until the later nineteenth century, features in these histories. It is here, particularly with the establishment of women's institutions in Florence, that the authorities and religious philanthropy created a Catholic reform movement targeting 'problematic women' and brought about the creation of the Magdalene house.[762] As the popularity of women's institutions extended across Europe from the sixteenth century, a network of asylums was created that continued to influence later reformatories in the nineteenth and twentieth centuries. It signals a long history whereby deviant women have been institutionalised and 'measured, judged and corrected'.[763] Since the early modern period in western society, prostitution has featured as a prominent symbol of the 'rescue' work of the asylums.[764]

In Australia, 'rescue' organisations began springing up across the colonies from the middle of the nineteenth century and were established by the main Christian denominations. Cheaper than gaols, the Homes were mainly concerned with rescuing prostitutes and 'at risk' girls.[765] The main goal behind the refuges in Australia was to remove women from corrupting influences, allow them to repent and return to a moralistic life.[766] They would thus progress from 'fallen' to 'penitent' women.[767] Political motives of reformers were clear in terms of their intent in reforming women and re-constructing their lives along respectable guidelines. The key focus on 'feminine propriety and social usefulness' was utilised in the Catholic Homes across Australia from the late nineteenth century.[768]

A number of explanations were offered for a woman's 'fall' in society and her need for reform. Refuges referred to the 'sin of the cities' as in part responsible for corrupting women.[769] Bad company was another explanation for women's 'fall' in society, whether from neighbours, friends or people on the streets.[770] In Western Australia, Catholic Bishops worried about the impact the gold rushes had on the population and an increase in depravity.[771] Refuges were publicised as also protecting society by removing immoral women from the streets.[772]Eighteen year-old Ethel Cregan was sent to the Home of the Good Shepherd in 1912 after police arrested her for creating a disturbance and stealing from a man in Fremantle. Documenting her 'fall' in court shortly afterwards, police advised the magistrate to consider placing her in the Home to keep her away from 'loafing about the streets in company with the worst characters in town'.[773]

In this climate of concern about prostitution and fallen women, the Western Australian community welcomed the arrival of Good Shepherd sisters to Perth in 1899 to rescue abandoned women.[774] The Magdalene Home operated in Adelaide Terrace, Perth from 1902 with help from Home of the Good Shepherd staff in France and Victoria. In 1904, it moved to a Leederville site in Ruislip Street, with twenty women and four sisters first housed in the new premises.[775] From the first moments of its establishment, the work of the Home was clearly communicated to the West Australian public. Reporting the Home's opening late in 1904, *The West Australian* highlighted the task ahead for the sisters who had devoted their 'lives and energies...to fallen women'.[776] In his opening address, the Reverend L. J. Smythe outlined the mission of the Home to provide charity for fallen women and rescue their souls: 'The inmates of the home may be wretched and sinful in the eyes of the world, yet they were the children of Jesus Christ'.[777]

The women housed in the Home of the Good Shepherd were expected to commit to a routine of 'prayer, example and kindness' and domestic training.[778] They worked hard in the laundry – work that provided revenue for the Home – and were encouraged to value hard work. The Sisters were determined to keep idle women from idle thoughts and used domestic work as a means to keep them occupied in the hope this work ethic could transfer beyond the convent.[779] In the first years of operation up to 1909, a total of 613 women passed through the Home, of which one-fifth arrived straight from court or on release from prison.[780]

Kellie Louise Toole's research into Catholic refuges in Australia has found that while the refuges intruded into women's lives and their sense of identity, there were enough pleas to be taken to the refuge to also show how some women viewed them exactly as they were established, as a place of *refuge*.[781] Nellie Davenport, a well-known offender, pleaded with a magistrate in Fremantle Police Court in 1912 to send her to the Home of the Good Shepherd. For Davenport, the Home was a place of refuge by comparison to prison.[782] As Toole argues, there was a 'genuine sense of charity and humanitarianism' in the work of the refuges.[783] Historically, this humanitarian basis dates back to the first magdalen homes in early modern Europe.[784] Sisters at the Home of the Good Shepherd often provided help for repeat offender Vera Pearce. In March 1907 Pearce was charged with attempted suicide. She was found in Russell Square, barely alive.[785] Pearce was admitted to hospital in an excited, drunken manner and said she was 'rough on rats'.[786] Doctors believed her symptoms were consistent with taking poison; Vera confirmed this saying she had taken sulphate of zinc. At her trial the following month, a representative from the Home of the Good Shepherd said she would take Pearce into the Home. For this idle woman, the Home really was a source of refuge.[787]

In Australia in the first decades of the twentieth century, the majority of penitents entered the Australian institutions of their own free will and could leave when they wanted. At the Leederville Home, close to seventy per cent of women admitted in the first decade of the twentieth century left voluntarily.[788] However, there were a minority of women who were sent to the Homes by the courts and could be legally detained there.[789] It is in this that we find a different experience for women criminalised at the time. The common prostitute or drunken woman, criminalised for good order offences, did not enter the Home of her own free will. Female offenders were free of the prison walls but they were nevertheless serving a sentence handed down to them by the courts in the time spent at the Homes. Often these women reacted by trying to run away from the home. Sent to the Home after caught soliciting on the streets, Helena Adams ran away soon after. When police found her, she was once again selling sex.[790] As Rae Frances argues, the Homes 'made a common assumption that some prostitutes, at least, would chose to live a respectable life if given the opportunity'.[791] As Helena Adams shows, this assumption did not carry for all women.

The case of Emily Cresswell also raises questions about the extent to which the Homes provided refuge and looked after the females housed within. Women with a criminal record seem to have experienced less charity than other women living in the refuges. Cresswell claimed in December 1903 that staff at the Home of the Good Shepherd had burned her on the arm with an iron as punishment for talking.[792] Taken to the Home as a woman of 'evil fame', Cresswell had a long list of convictions. 'Sydney' Emily rarely served any less than a few weeks in prison for soliciting, using obscene language and vagrancy.[793] However, six months after her allegations against the Home, Emily wrote a letter of repentance to the staff and 'promised to reform'.[794] Despite Emily's retraction of the allegation, it still casts some doubt on the conduct of the staff.[795]

The dichotomy between help and control is not an easy one, however. In fact, it is more beneficial to see the Homes as humanitarians and also purveyors of social control.[796] This was especially true of the experiences of common prostitutes. Staff at The Home of the Good Shepherd wanted to rescue women from prostitution as well as reform their deviant identities. As Ellen Bowen was told in court in 1922, after she had asked to be taken to the Home, she was taken off the streets for the 'protection of the public'.[797] Common prostitutes had to be reformed and the best place to do it was behind closed doors and away from the public. Their isolation was a key part of reform.

The Home of the Good Shepherd, along with similar refuges across Australia, aimed to show society that it could reform common prostitutes. Through repenting their former life, 'fallen' women could again contribute to society and live respectable lives. The problem facing the women, however, is the public was not so forgiving. Many women were denied work based on their former convictions and were ostracised.[798] Another difficulty facing the women inmates was the reality that the Homes created an 'isolated colony of women hidden away in the inner suburbs, forgotten by all except those confined there'[799] Women also tended to be, 'passed around between institutions that really did not want them'.[800]The key difference here in this story, too, is prostitution represents another gendered aspect of punishment and reform: only women were institutionalised and punished for prostitution.

*

May Ahern was one of the many fallen women about the streets of Perth and Fremantle in the first decades of the twentieth century. Described by a magistrate in 1923 as 'one of the worst female cases of this class',[801] Ahern was a woman who defied any attempts at reform. May was regularly sent off to Fremantle Prison as a way to keep her off the streets. When this didn't work she was sent to the Home of the Good Shepherd in an effort to reform her through strict religious guidance, work and moral reform. Magistrates were not convinced reform was possible for May. When Magistrate Roe sent three of May's female friends to the Home in January 1908, he told May 'she was the leading spirit in seducing other young girls onto the streets'.[802] Ahern's last stint in Fremantle Prison was a month's imprisonment in April 1945.[803]

While common prostitutes were outcast from society, May Ahern's life shows how small groups of prostitutes, through similar working areas and regular appearances in court together, formed close friendships on the streets. They lived a precarious life but their shared community is an important part of accounting for experiences of prostitution on the streets of Perth and Fremantle.[804] Streetwalking brought with it female support networks. Bertha Connor, Myrtle Connor, May Ahern and Vera Matson were arrested in Perth in January 1908 as idle and disorderly persons without visible means of support.[805] They appeared together again in 1910, part of an investigation into a house of ill repute owned with a Chinese man. Described in the press as 'frail pieces of femininity',[806] they nevertheless relied on each other for friendship and support.

In May Ahern and other women soliciting for sex on the streets, we find a variety of experiences. Common prostitutes worked the streets for a number of reasons from economic hardship (Sadie Bonner), the thrill of underworld life (Alice Lawson and Minnie Forrester), and often were caught in a cycle of soliciting that persistent gaol terms could not break. Mary Warnock, an Irish migrant, shows us the difficulties of trying to make a living in a city far from the help of relatives and friends. There are the silences too. What led to Patricia Roots engaging in sex work, so opposed by her husband? In all, however, we find *women* working the streets. What all these women share is a collective identity as immoral women having 'fallen as low as a woman could fall'.[807] Their identities as women were debased by public discourse singling them out as something 'other' to their sex. The Victorian England world Patricia Roots left as a young woman continued to influence a feminine ideal in Western Australia well into the twentieth century. The common prostitute, the streetwalker, was at the forefront of social perceptions of bad and immoral women. She remains there even today.

6.

'A City Pest' [808]

They were rogues and vagabonds, incorrigibles, nuisances and pests. Women repeatedly committing offences against good order in the first decades of the twentieth century were convicted for collective offences including drunkenness, idle and disorderly, loitering, obscene language, damaging property, and vagrancy. Such female recidivists were labelled a 'complete nuisance', as in the case of Rose Skivington:

> A City Pest - Rose Skivington, a woman well known to the police, whose appearances in Court are very frequent, was again brought up on charges of using obscene language, and with having damaged the property of Patrick Cleary, the licensee of No Place Inn. After the evidence of the licensee and P.C. Murphy had been given, Sergeant McCarthy made a statement, showing that the woman spent most of her time in gaol, and the moment she was set free was a complete nuisance. On the first charge the accused was sentenced to 14 days' imprisonment, and on the second was ordered to pay £3, the amount of the damage, or in default one month's imprisonment, the sentences to be cumulative. [809]

Skivington first came to the attention of the police and courts in 1898. Charged with disorderly conduct in Perth, she was sentenced to twenty-one days hard labour unless she could pay the fine. As would happen throughout Rose's criminal life, she couldn't afford the fine and ended up in gaol. Originally from Newcastle, a rural area to the east of Perth, Skivington knew few people in the city and spent most of her time drinking, loitering and creating public disturbances. By 1924, and in her sixties, Rose was a 'rogue and vagabond' with no hope of reform and regularly living on the streets. Women like Rose Skivington committing collective offences against good order were criminalised as vagrants and publicly demeaned as a nuisance. Their street lives existed beyond the boundaries of female respectability and served as examples of the threat errant women posed to the social order.

Accounts of women criminalised for a variety of public offences, particularly vagrancy, offer an opportunity to see beyond the stereotype of the vagrant as a man. As recent Canadian research demonstrates, the lives of women on the streets challenge such notions.[810] Scholarship in Australia since the 1970s has increasingly contributed to what we know about women on the streets, including Anne O'Brien's work on the poor in New South Wales from 1880 to 1918 and Christina Twomey's *Deserted and Destitute: Motherhood, Wife Desertion and Colonial Welfare*.[811] What the experiences of female vagrants show us is women are treated differently. Unlike male vagrants, females were characterised as drunken, loose, mentally unstable and keeping bad company. Even when not soliciting on the streets, a direct connection was drawn between public offences, vagrancy and a fall from femininity. Men on the other hand were queried about their lack of employment but never sexualised in the same way as women. Females, it was argued, must have been doing something improper to attract the attention of police.[812] In Perth and Fremantle, the female all-rounder committing a variety of offences against good order was characterised as a city pest. Their vagrancy was a problem but a far greater social crime was their inability to conform.

The Public Nuisance

A prominent picture that emerges in going through the criminal records for women arrested on the streets of Perth and Fremantle is female recidivists were rarely charged and convicted with one offence only over the course of criminal records that averaged around two or three decades. They were all rounders' in terms of committing a variety of offences against good order and did so at a time when there was considerable council, press and public discussion about creating a healthy, sanitary, respectable metropolitan centre. The public nuisance was at odds with efforts to maintain respectability in the city centre and down to the port city of Fremantle. People regularly wandering about the streets and creating a nuisance were characterised as casualties of urban living, while equally being seen as a threat to respectable communities.

Urban planning regularly featured in government, press and public discussions from the late nineteenth century in Western Australia. Perth expanded in size with the population influx from the mining boom and entered into the twentieth century as an emergent metropolitan centre. One of the main goals of urban planning is to foster a healthy, respectable lifestyle for residents in good communities[813] and government and planning officials aimed to achieve this in Perth and Fremantle. From the 1880s, the Perth City Council was tasked with expanding roads, public facilities, parks, recreation areas and ensuring residents could enjoy pure water and good sanitary conditions.[814] Council discussions focussed on filthy living conditions in the poorer parts of the city, which in turn created a Central Board of Health.[815] In 1904, *The West Australian*, informed by the City Council, ran an editorial applauding the progress of Perth into a burgeoning city.[816]

Metropolitan expansion from the late nineteenth century led to closer scrutiny of city life and people on the streets. At the time, men and women regularly conducted business and socialised about the streets. Public space was used by a variety of people. Farmers walked their stock down main streets, even into the twentieth century, on their way to slaughter yards. Market gardeners sold goods around the streets and vied for attention with young boys selling papers and small publications from wheelbarrow stalls. Elegant women in the latest finery walked carefully along St Georges Terrace on their way to a leisurely stroll along the Esplanade, sometimes joined by husbands on a break from work in the one of the offices. In the back streets of inner Fremantle, children played games outside of school hours and mothers walked on while they caught up on the local gossip. Some children waited outside pubs while their father had a quick drink with the lads after work. In an age without social media, the streets were the life of local areas and where friends, neighbours and businessmen crossed paths regularly.

Public spaces were also closely regulated, particularly working-class and underclass areas. Heather Shore, writing about the youth crime in nineteenth-century London, argues the very poor 'came to be regarded as incapable of innocence.'[817] Poor, urban street life came to be associated with vice and crime. People regularly wandering about the streets and creating a nuisance were characterised as disreputable. They were a public face of urban life that either needed to be dealt with or suppressed from view. Police 'clean ups' dominated the first years of the twentieth century. In their efforts to maintain good communities as part of their daily work, police regularly took to the streets to rid them of the city's 'undesirables'. These undesirables were mainly arrested and charged with being disorderly. While drunkenness featured prominently in criminal statistics for men and women, the disorderly offence was next highest in court sentences.[818]

City officials were particularly interested in disorderly women knocking about and living on the streets. Any deviance from respectable behaviour was quickly noted and police were sent in to deal with a number of female public nuisances. They included the likes of Mary Ryan, arrested in October 1927 for creating a disturbance in Pier Street, Perth. She was arrested and charged with drunk and disorderly after standing 'outside a hotel abusing men in the bar'.[819] Mary Hearnder, too, was described in court in July 1905 as a '"thorough nuisance" about the town'.[820] These women regularly featured in police clean ups.

Clean ups were conducted throughout the year but a more concerted effort was made in the weeks leading up to Christmas. Public nuisances could not interfere with respectable festive life. Esther Warden found herself a part of a police clean up close to Christmas in 1915. Warden had been brandishing a hairpin as a weapon at people passing her in the city and was a nuisance around the local pubs before police found her asleep in a Chinese den.[821] Martha Potter also found herself targeted in a police clean up before Christmas in 1908. Fined for using obscene language in Coolgardie Street, police evidence labelled her a public nuisance and 'in consequence of her language people had to leave the neighbourhood'.[822] In November 1920, *The West Australian* reported the round up of a group of female vagrants. All were repeat offenders and knew one another well on the streets:

Vagrants - With the approach of the Christmas police are evidently endeavouring to clear the streets of a number of undesirables. Three women, Kate Dreardon (37), Annie McConochie (40) and Patricia Roots, were presented on charges of having been idle and disorderly persons having insufficient or no visible means of support. All the accused admitted their guilt and expressed the desire to be sent to an institution. Roots and Drearden were ordered to go to the Home of the Good Shepherd for three months, but McConochie was denied the privilege, as she had been many times at the institutions and had left before the expiration of her time. She was sentenced to one month's imprisonment.[823]

Arrests in public allowed for an open display of the regulation of deviant femininities. Unlike their male counterparts, female offenders were categorised as something 'other' to their sex, as in the case of Nellie Davenport. Ellen's repeated run-ins with the law were used in the papers as an example of the social problems associated with women who overstepped the boundaries. More than committing offences against good order, Pirie was characterised as something 'other' to her sex; an immoral, corrupted female:

A Degenerate Woman - Nellie Devonport (28) was charged with obscenity, and, further, with being an idle and disorderly person. The woman was said to be a most degenerate character and a town nuisance. In April last she was sentenced to six months' imprisonment on a similar charge, and this was her twenty-sixth appearance. The Bench sent her back to gaol for six months.[824]

Ellen, more commonly known by her street identity of Nellie Davenport, was first imprisoned for vagrancy in December 1897. She served three months with hard labour based on her three previous vagrancy convictions. Around thirty at turn of the century she was a married, Roman Catholic laundress who could read and write. She appears to have been widowed during the course of her convictions.[825] Born in New Zealand around 1870, at some point she moved to Sydney and from there came to Western Australia, though her nationality is given as Australian. Ellen Pirie has one of the longest criminal records in the Fremantle Female Prison Register. It is over three foolscap pages.[826] Her greatest crime, however, was being a 'degenerate woman'.

Pirie's criminal record shows gaol terms for a variety of public offences including habitual drunkenness, using threatening and obscene language, disorderly, soliciting prostitution and damaging property. By 1909 she had forty-eight convictions to her name, the last in 1938, with sentences ranging from days to months. By this stage she had close to 150 convictions and was in her late sixties.[827]

Ellen Pirie was regularly in and out of gaol. As an example, she was released from gaol on 26 August 1901 on a drunkenness charge and apprehended only three days later in Fremantle as an idle and disorderly person. Unable to stay out of trouble longer than three days, she was sentenced to three months back in Fremantle Prison.[828]

There is much we simply can't know about Ellen Pirie beyond offence details in the papers and basic information in the Registers. Who was her husband and how was she expected to support herself after his death? None of this is taken into account in offering explanations for her actions. To what extent did the lack of family support, having originally come from New Zealand, impact on Ellen's ability to find work and stay off the streets? What did Ellen think about characterisations of her as a 'degenerate woman'? The difficulty for Ellen Pirie and other women charged as public nuisances is marginalisation from mainstream society ensured female offenders remained in a cycle of offending and were unable to find support to keep them off the streets. Without means of support, they were also further outcast and criminalised as vagrants.

Criminal Vagrants

Perth-born Elizabeth Caroline Davey first came to the attention of authorities in 1913 when she was charged as a 'rogue and vagabond' for loitering for prostitution. Identified in the papers as one of the many 'undesirables' on the streets of Perth, she was sentenced to three months' hard labour in Fremantle Prison.[829] It was but one of dozens of convictions she would serve over close to forty years. Davey was in her late thirties when she started to rack up her long record of convictions and by the time of her death in 1950 and in her mid-seventies, she was a well-known female offender.

Davey was another of the 'all-rounder' criminal women when it came to being a nuisance in public. Also going by the name Caroline Hewitt, she was notorious for loitering for prostitution around the inner streets of Perth and Fremantle and was repeatedly charged for drunkenness and idle and disorderly. In August 1915, Davey pleaded for a chance to correct her ways but was sentenced to over two months in prison for having no home and wandering drunk around 'the streets and byways of the city'.[830] Four years later, after numerous convictions for drunkenness and idle and disorderly, Davey was described in court as an, 'eccentric inebriate' with an, 'insatiable craving for alcohol'.[831] By the 1920s she was recognised on sight by police and keeping 'bad company'.[832]

Elizabeth Davey was not always on the receiving end of court convictions. In March 1918, she appeared in court as a complainant in a case against Herbert Hart. The two came to the attention of police one Friday evening when Hart began hitting and kicking Davey in Pier Street, Perth. Elizabeth was assisted by a man passing by and taken to the hospital fearing for her life. Davey's mother also appeared in court and gave evidence about the physical nature of the assault. For his part, Hart claimed Davey was drunk that evening and had actually fallen in a gutter whereby she sustained the bruises on her body. He gave evidence she had been imprisoned three times recently for drunkenness. Hart had served in the war and was trying to set up a life for himself again by putting all his money into a house. The magistrate, though clear in telling Hart to stay away from Davey, sentenced him to a fine and if he failed to pay it he would have to serve one month in prison.[833]

The assault case is an interesting one. Herbert Hart physically assaulted Elizabeth Davey leaving her with wounds that needed medical attention and yet he was given a fine or a month in prison in default of payment. Davey had regularly spent anywhere from one month to six months in gaol for offences against good order. As a repeat offender, her convictions were harsher based on her record. However, none of the charges were for violence or assault.

The main problem for authorities was Elizabeth Davey was not just drunk and loitering in public. She was a nuisance vagrant who spent most of her time on the streets of Perth and Fremantle, outside of prison terms and stints in the Women's Home. She kept company with 'thieves and rogues'[834] and visibly defied the gender and social order of the time as a female vagrant.

Vagrants, like Elizabeth Davey, were among the many 'undesirables' targeted by police using new legislation to shift idle persons off the streets and out of public view. Under the West Australian Police Act of 1892 (with amendments in 1902), people without lawful work and 'no fixed abode' were charged as vagrants and liable to weeks or months in gaol depending on their criminal record. The new legislation allowed police to use the term 'vagrancy' loosely and arrest habitual drunks, common prostitutes and those behaving indecently as vagrants. The criminalisation of the vagrant in Western Australia, as was the case across Australia, dated back to English laws passed in the fourteenth century aiming to control the movement of unemployed workers.[835]

While the WA *Police Act* did not use the terms 'vagrancy' or 'vagrant', it set out a short list of those who would be convicted as vagrants in the general sense. The Police Act allowed police officers to charge men and women as 'idle and disorderly', 'rogues and vagabonds' and incorrigibles'. People could be charged as idle if they were shown to have no lawful means of support; begging; frequenting places with thieves and common prostitutes; or acting in a riotous or indecent manner. Those charged as 'rogues and vagabonds' already had previous idle and disorderly convictions and 'incorrigibles' had also been charged as 'rogues'. [836] It was a clear delineation between the deserving and undeserving poor and those with previous convictions and committing a public nuisance were most susceptible. So it was that Emily Cresswell was convicted as a rogue and vagabond in 1905 and Mary Paltridge was also imprisoned for the same offence in 1927 for sleeping in empty houses.[837]

Varying social, economic and political contexts over the first decades of the twentieth century impacted on the lives of the very poor in Perth and Fremantle. In particular, the recessions of 1897-1898 and 1908-1910 hit the poorest hard.[838] There was also a spike in the number of disorderly and vagrancy prosecutions in 1915 amid fears of venereal disease outbreaks and the absence of men in the war. War also disrupted family life and raised concerns about gender roles in Australia. Later, the Great Depression of the 1930s is perhaps a prime example of economic downturn impacting harshly on the already struggling members of society. Shoplifting offences and petty fraud increased during the Depression, with imprisonment numbers increasing over the years from 1930-1934.[839]

Historically, concern about the plight of the poor has focussed on men's employment due to societal expectations of men as breadwinners.[840] In Western Australia, female poverty was linked to dependency on men.[841] Women were characterised by their 'social and economic vulnerability'.[842] Regardless of whether they were men or women, poor relief was always more readily given to the aged, infirm and sick, as long as they were regarded as the deserving poor and free from engaging in criminal activities.

At the Female Poorhouse in Goderich Street, Perth, greater emphasis was given to care for aged, infirm or sick women but applications for admittance show women at various stages of their lives. The Home also took in poor single women, as was the Old Women's Home in Fremantle (part of the Fremantle Lunatic Asylum). An interesting aspect of poor relief in these times is women were generally constructed in a non-working identity within the home but poor relief showed an expectation on women to work.[843] It has much to do also with expectations on working-class women.

The debate over relief for the deserving and undeserving poor was prominent in conceptions of those caught in the poverty of underclass life. In the early twentieth century in Britain and Australia there existed a fear this residuum would 'contaminate and subsume the respectable working class'.[844] The very poor in society became a nuisance by the end of the nineteenth century,[845] with the unemployable increasingly understood as a social problem group.[846] Literature from the late nineteenth century in Britain influenced the perception of the unemployable as different to those temporarily out of work. The unemployable included children, old people and women around childbearing years but also 'lunatics', the sick, criminals and those simply unable to keep down a job.[847]

The work of Henry Mayhew in nineteenth-century London impacted on understandings of the poor, underclass and criminal class. *London Labour and the London Poor* singles out the non-workers and 'Dangerous Classes of the Metropolis'.[848] Here we have the distinction between the underclass and those within it who were characterised as criminal and dangerous.

The West Australian ran a story in January 1929 on what it called derelicts and beggars. Within this article there is much that resonates with the work of. Outlining the long history of the vagabond – the vagrant – the writer claimed Western Australia 'has yet a fair quota of derelicts'. In this sensationalist piece, the 'tramp' is characterised as the 'bum' hanging around hotels but is less of a nuisance than the beggars and street vendors. The story, however, also portrays the vagrant as a romantic figure. The romanticism of *The West Australian* article is invoked in the passage:

> There is a joy in the wayward vagabond, who can escape from restraint and levy toll on his more fortunate fellows, loving, as he does, the freedom of the streets and the luck of the beggar who asks for alms.[849]

Studies in England from the start of the twentieth century looked to secondary causes of poverty such as drinking and gambling. In this case, poverty was not beyond the control of the individual.[850] Arguments arose that poverty should be explained beyond the personal and moral to a focus on industry and environment.[851] Through their persistent unemployment, the vagrant deviated from standard social mores; they were 'disruptive to the social order'.[852] Vagrancy laws have historically been used to control idle people not contributing to society through their own labour and 'seemingly unfettered by traditional domestic life'.[853] Vagrancy laws were used in Australia to clear out public nuisances.[854]

In modern Australian history, vagrancy was penalised at times of labour shortages in order to encourage more people to work and increase productivity.[855] In Melbourne in the late nineteenth century, vagrants were said to threaten good order and progress.[856] This is similar to attitudes from the eighteenth century in Britain where vagrants were linked to crime and subversive elements of slum life.[857] Nineteenth-century literary, social, political and legal thinking was influential into the twentieth century in Britain, Europe, the United States and Australia with vagrants continuing to be connected to dangerous criminal underworlds.

Women who transgressed the boundaries between the private and public spheres were denounced for their behaviour and charged as vagrants. Public complaints about nuisance women was one major way in which women on the streets found themselves under police surveillance and appearing before the courts. Vagrancy legislation allowed the authorities to deal with nuisance women, regardless of whether or not they actually were vagrants. In the United States from the nineteenth century, young women arriving in the cities were seen as able to be saved from a vagrant life if they could be married and settled into family life.[858]

Female vagrants were generally characterised in Perth and Fremantle as lacking virtues and more likely to enter into prostitution. They were beyond the bounds of the home and family life.[859] Mary E. Collins was arrested in Pier Street in September 1919 and subsequently convicted of drunkenness and vagrancy. Evidence was given in court that she had spent the last three weeks in a drunken state and 'roaming the streets in the company of women of very low repute'.[860] Martha Geeson was charged with vagrancy in August 1900 as a means to get her off the streets and out of public establishments as a public nuisance.' Bar staff gave evidence of her taking two or three men to the back of the Imperial Hotel in Perth and for this identified her as having 'dirty and immoral habits'.[861]

There also existed genuine concern about women living on the streets, particularly in the work of those within the Salvation Army Homes spread about the city. In July 1899, Mrs Shaw, wife of the Captain of the Salvation Army, gave evidence in court that she was prepared to take Marion Curedale into the Home to prevent any more arrests for drunkenness. Mrs Shaw offered to take Marion into her family home if it would help to reform her as a mother.[862] Public discussions such as these about reforming domestic family life often persuaded the authorities to opt to for treatment of criminals outside of prison walls. In this way, gender and the 'well-being' of family life in Australia was prioritised in improving the character of the nation.[863] This was particularly the case in what has been called the 'Familist' era in Australia from

World War One to the 1970s where the nuclear family dominated ideas about the family 'type'.[864] If a Home or refuge could offer better support to an offender and help reconnect them with their family, this was favoured over imprisonment for minor crimes.

In some cases, as with Marion Curedale, the Home was a place of refuge. Born in England in 1847, Marion/Mary Ann Hardman[865] married George Curedale in Perth in 1863.[866] George, originally from Lancashire in England, was charged with forgery, found guilty and sentenced to transportation in August 1856. Within three months of receiving his pardon in March 1863, he married Mary Ann.[867] She was the daughter of the man who had employed George as his clerk. William Hardman, also a Lancashire man, was a gunner in the Royal Artillery and retired a sergeant. Widowed twice before 1847, he then married Elizabeth Spry.[868] By the middle of the century he was lured by the opportunity to immigrate to Western Australia and create a new life for his wife and five children (four of whom, including Mary Ann, were from his first two marriages). The family arrived in the colony aboard the *Minden* in 1851 with William listed as an Enrolled Pensioner Guard. Mary Ann's father was later credited with having fought at the Battle of Waterloo in 1815. Given he was born in 1808, it was quite a feat, though a tad untrue, for a seven year-old boy.[869]

George ran a wholesale fruit and vegetable business in Fremantle, part-financed by Mary Ann's brother, Richard. He rented a vacant lot at the rear of the business in Leake Street where he kept his horse and cart. It was here that the couple's first child, Ellen, was run over by a neighbour's cart and killed in June 1866. After this ill-fated venture George established a market garden nearby but it did not last beyond 1875.[870] More hardships faced the Curedale. Mary Ann's father died in September 1878 and her stepmother, Elizabeth, died less than a decade later in June 1886.[871] George's health started to fail from 1886 when he suffered a near-fatal heart attack. The following year he suffered another attack and it was at this point that he arranged for his Grosvenor vineyard and quarries to be taken over by his friend and associate, Alfred Davies. Upon George's death, Mary Ann was to be given one hundred pounds and allowed to live rent-free in the house on the property.[872] George died on 28 May 1887 leaving Mary Ann with six children under the age of fourteen to look after (her eldest was eighteen).[873] Family history tells of a loving partnership, with George's last act before his death being a kiss and embrace for his wife.[874]

When George died, Marion lost her main source of support and at the age of forty was left in desperate need of assistance.[875] She applied to the government for assistance in 1887 but was denied any money after having received two hundred pounds and a rent-free residence after her husband's death. Evidence from the Welfare Department also cast a shadow on her use of the money, singling her out as an alcoholic.[876] The money from her husband's death was not enough to maintain her large family and pay for alcohol on a regular basis. She soon found herself falling into poverty.[877]

Family history once held that Mary Ann had given birth to thirty children.[878] In fact, the press also corroborated this large family, listing Mary Ann as the mother of twenty-two children in 1903.[879] Just as her father was said to have served at the Battle of Waterloo, Mary Ann did not give birth to a record number of children. She did, however, still have a large family of thirteen children.[880]

Marion Curedale's main failing was alcohol and too much of it regularly. While she had a large family around Fremantle whom the court thought should come forward to look after her, Marion Curedale was a lonely figure on the streets of Perth and Fremantle. Before her December 1900 appearance she had been wandering about the streets for at least three or four weeks.[881] Aware of the difficulties her court appearances created for her family, she often used her maiden name as an alias when arrested on the streets of Perth and Fremantle.[882] Over the course of her convictions from 1897 to 1909, Curedale was imprisoned for over nine of these twelve years. Knowing her family history and wanting to genuinely help her off the streets, Mrs Shaw's plea in court in 1899 shows the extent to which some people wanted to break the cycle of offending for women in this period.

Policing the female 'pests'

Preventative measures were also instituted to tackle the problem of women on the streets at all hours of the day, either drunk, soliciting or with nowhere else to live. One major way in which the government, through the police, tried to deal with idle and disorderly, vagrant women was the introduction of the Women's Police in 1917. It was established at a time when there was greater surveillance of female lives across Australia due to fears of venereal disease contamination during World War One and the backlash against feminist promotion of the 'new woman'.[883] The Women's Police in Western Australia played an important role in the control of women's identities. As Leonie Stella states, '[t]heir primary function was to control the sexuality of women and children, especially young women'.[884] Another side of this was their efforts to protect women from abuse, given women were more vulnerable than men on the streets.[885] Most of these women were caught between seeing women on the streets as 'fallen' contaminators - through sexualisation of their activities – and victims of a system that criminalised them for their lack of conformity.[886] The work of the Women's Police was contradictory: female officers both protected and controlled women.[887]

The Women's Police was instituted after campaigning from the early years of the twentieth century for greater control of women on the streets. Moralistic arguments raised by women's organisations, including the Women's Guild and WCTU, centred on the need to protect women's social mores. Regulation of prostitution on the streets of Perth and Fremantle also boosted efforts to introduce women into the police force. By 1915, proposals for the appointment of women police highlighted the threat from venereal disease sensationalised in the press.[888] The words of one WCTU spokeswoman summed up the moralistic arguments for introducing female police officers:

> There is a great probability that women police patrols would greatly help in the protection of the weak, and the punishment of those who deliberately plan their destruction. In Great Britain, woman police are said of be a 'walking conscience'.[889]

Edith Cowan, the first female Parliamentarian, also believed policewomen would save young women from 'social degradation and from disease'.[890]

The Colonial Secretary announced the appointment of two women police to the press in July 1917.[891] Helen Dugdale and

Laura Chipper would each work under the Inspector of Police at the Metropolitan Branch, but their work was listed as a 'minor' branch. They were at all times to wear plain clothes to enable greater trust with women on the streets.[892] Both women had experience in social welfare and charity organisations and were keen to 'rescue' and reform women on the streets. Female police numbers were limited in the first decades of operation. From 1917 to 1939, the Women's Police consisted of, on average, around five females and never exceeded ten across the state.[893]

The female officers were appointed to prevent crime, not to prosecute it. In their day-to-day duties, these women were expected to: keep children off the streets; prevent truancy; patrol public entertainment areas to protect women and children in these parts; patrol slum areas and look after drunk women and neglected children; observe brothels, public houses, wine shops and hotels frequented by prostitutes in order to prevent young women from being lured into this life and business. The Women's Police were also expected to assist women generally in public and keep a record of all their interactions with fallen and criminal women about the streets. In the end it was hoped they would be successful in reforming women but there is also mention in the statement of duties that they would list the 'incorrigibles' so that male police making arrests would know the women unable to be reformed by the Women's Police.[894]

In the early years of their work, Dugdale and Chipper kept detailed records of their work with women and children on the streets of Perth and Fremantle. In one annual report in June 1921, Constable Dugdale recorded her work in following up inquiries into female misconduct, neglected or destitute children, and cautioned women for drunkenness, immorality and vagrancy. Dugdale interviewed close to 400 women in her office and cautioned a further 171 girls and women. One of her main duties listed was helping women home who were under the influence of drink.[895] The Women's Police were very clearly there to prevent crime and keep women off the streets as best they could. Interviewing and meeting with women was another way in which they could exert their police authority and control women, without having to resort to imprisonment. Where possible, the Women's Police recommended women on the streets be sent to Homes, including the Salvation Army Home and the Home of the Good Shepherd.

Female officers also played an important role in giving evidence in court against female offenders. These were the women who could not be appropriately reformed and were thus listed as incorrigibles by the Women's Police. When Elizabeth Davey, a well-known vagrant, appeared in court in February 1931, policewoman Dugdale gave evidence that she had been watching Davey for some time and recorded her frequent accosting of men and living on the streets.[896] Policewoman Chipper gave evidence against a young woman in a theft case in 1927 in which she described the accused as dishonourable and unable to keep a good position in society.[897] Evidence from a female police officer in court was almost tantamount to a conviction. In their role as moral upholders, the Women's Police carried great weight in how they characterised women on the streets. Policewoman Dunlop described an aged offender, Catherine Clark, as disgusting, filthy and the source of many complaints about the city streets.[898] It was a damning character reference. In this way, the Women's Police acted as another form of surveillance of female lives on the streets of Perth and Fremantle. Female officers upheld the dominant view of the time of women as society's moral guardians. When women failed to uphold this ideal, they were singled out by the Women's Police, interviewed and if not sent home or, if without a place to live, to reformatory institutions, they were brought to the attention of male police officers who would then arrest the women for offences against good order.

A Vagrant Identity: Lilly Doyle

If they maintained a presence about the streets, racking up numerous convictions and repeatedly named in the press reports of their court appearances, street women became local identities. One prominent case is Lilly Doyle, characterised in police and court records as a well-known public nuisance and vagrant in Fremantle. Her criminal record is one of the most extensive in the Fremantle Female Prison Register. From 1898 to the early 1930s, Doyle notched up over 100 convictions.[899] She is portrayed in court as a woman who had been given 'plenty of chances' and 'every opportunity to live a respectable life'.[900] In the end she could not be reformed and lived most of her days on the streets or in prison.

Elizabeth Doyle was born in Fremantle somewhere between 1868 and 1870; her age differs across court, prison and newspaper records. She is listed in the Prison Register as a single, literate, Roman Catholic woman. Her work - trade – is given as menial tasks but the word prostitute has been added later in the prison record.[901] Doyle was first recorded in Fremantle Prison in October 1898, serving three months for indecent behaviour in Fremantle.[902] Her criminal record, however, stretches back to 1895 when she was fined for disorderly conduct.[903] Over the course of the next forty years, Lilly Doyle was charged with a variety of offences including: idle and disorderly, vagrancy, drunkenness, loitering, soliciting prostitution, unlawful possession, creating a disturbance, damaging a car and obscene language.[904]

Lilly was not alone in some of her convictions. In December 1895 she was charged along with her sister, Alice:

> FEMALE DEPRAVITY - Two young girls named Lily and Alice Doyle were charged with being loose, idle and disorderly persons. Constable Jones stated that for the past 12 months the accused had been a source of annoyance to the police and the public. From 6 o'clock in the evening till 12 and 1 o'clock in the morning they roamed the streets, going from one hotel to another in company with men whom they induced to " shout" for them. Lily, who had a worse record than her sister, was sentenced to three months imprisonment, and Alice received a term of one month.[905]

Not much is known about Lilly's family other than mention of a couple of family members in court records. When she was charged and fined in April 1900 for using bad language in Fremantle, a William Doyle tried to rescue her from police and was also fined.[906] He may have been a brother. Looking through birth, death and marriage records, the most likely candidates for Elizabeth's parents were John and Hannah Doyle. In 1874, Hannah gave birth to a daughter, Alice. By this stage they also had a son, Thomas, born in 1872.[907] When Lilly died Thomas Doyle was listed as a grantee.[908]

The authorities seem to have had enough of Lilly by the first years of the twentieth century. She was charged again with vagrancy in Fremantle in February 1902 and sentenced to four months with hard labour.[909] From there on she regularly served lengthy sentences in Fremantle Prison. She had notched up seventy-five drunkenness convictions alone by 1918. By the 1920s, any petty offence landed her a long stint in gaol. She was imprisoned for three months in November 1923 for using obscene language in High Street, Fremantle.[910]

Lilly Doyle's inability or unwillingness to conform to feminine ideals at the time played havoc on the life she led in Fremantle. Again, we don't know much about her family or any support that may have been available, but from all accounts she mainly lived on the streets or in shanties. Her heavy drinking, loose mouth and tendency to be seen and loudly heard in public meant she was regularly on the police radar and singled out as a public nuisance living the life of a vagrant.

Public perceptions are important here in looking at the life of Lilly Doyle. Characterised in court newspaper reports as a nuisance vagrant about Perth and Fremantle, she was outcast from mainstream society. One court case in particular demonstrates her low regard. Doyle was knocked down by a horse and cab in January 1910, as she was about to enter the Hotel Australia on the corner of Beach and Parry Street, Fremantle (now the International Backpackers). She suffered injuries to her head and legs and the papers reported 'every tooth in her head' was loosened.[911] The driver, F. Willis, appeared in court in February charged with having driven a horse endangering the public. Evidence was given by a waitress at the pub to the effect that she heard a speeding vehicle and then the cries of Lilly Doyle. Another witness, a local mariner, contradicted this evidence saying he thought the cart was travelling at a normal speed. When he was told, once inside the pub, that a woman had been hit, he had a drink first before going out to check. This evidence drew some laughter from the public crowd in court. The case was dismissed, partially through a no-show from other key witnesses.[912] It is an interesting case in that police gave evidence that Doyle was not intoxicated. Added to this, a male witness recounting having a drink before checking on the injured women drew laughter in the courtroom. Had Lilly Doyle been a middle-class mother and wife, rather than a well-known drunk, idle and disorderly person in Fremantle, would the reaction have been the same? Not likely.

Some locals in South Fremantle knew Lilly Doyle in a different way. For Bill Marks, himself a popular Fremantle identity as bookmaker, racing identity and two-up operator, Lilly Doyle was one of a few street people he remembered from his younger years in South Fremantle. In his autobiography he recalls:

> Lily Doyle, a middle aged woman who lived in a humpy in the sand hills between South Beach and Robbs Jetty, would regularly come past our house about 9.30 at night and we could always hear her before she got to our home, walking in the middle of the tramline singing 'Wedding Bells' at the top of her voice, heading for the shanty town known by the locals as 'Hollywood', usually with a bottle of methylated spirits in her hand. When I look back I can but feel pity for her and the rest of them who lived in squalor in those humpies.[913]

Lilly Doyle certainly lived in squalor but she was not completely alone in the world. As Julie Kimber, accounting for experiences in Orange, New South Wales, argues, comradeship developed amongst vagrant women:

> What might appear to be lonely lives are, on closer examination, something quite different. By looking at dates of imprisonment we can surmise that on occasion the police conducted ' round ups' of local 'vagrants'. Thus, it seems plausible to assume either that comradeship increased the risk of arrest or that criminality itself forged comradeship.[914]

Lonely as she may have seemed to Bill Marks on those walks to the Fremantle shanties, Lilly Doyle associated with other women sleeping rough on the streets of Perth and Fremantle. Whether they first knew of one another on the streets, when charged in court or on arrival in prison, some vagrant women came to closely associate with each other. Doyle appeared in court in December 1915 with Lillian Morris, Sarah Gundry and Rose Jones. The four women were arrested together and sent to Fremantle Prison. It was Doyle's 99th appearance in court.[915]

Ellen Pirie/Nellie Davenport was also linked with various women on the streets. She and her friend, Marion Curedale, appeared in court in 1901 on charges of drunkenness and vagrancy. With over twenty previous convictions, they were portrayed in the press as a couple of old offenders and sentenced to three months in prison for being drunk and living on the streets.[916] Davenport also appeared in court in 1908 with Lena Farrell, both charged with being persons without visible means of support. Police evidence supported an image of the women as 'associates with persons of bad repute'.[917]

*

Female habitual criminals in the first decades of the twentieth century in Perth and Fremantle were far more likely to commit offences against good order than they were serious indictable offences such as fraud, sexual crimes, wounding or murder. At a time when West Australian society was trying to create social cohesion around turbulent decades of boom, war, recovery, depression and the onset of another world war, people committing a variety of offences against good order were criminalised as a threat to the social order. That their crimes were committed in public is important. Police, courts and a public culture intolerant of recalcitrant behaviour used good order laws to morally punish women drunk, loud, disorderly and soliciting on the streets. When they were found to be living a life on the streets, vagrancy laws were used to punish them further for having no means of support.

Efforts to regulate public space brought women on the streets into direct view of the police, courts and press. Female use of the streets became problematic. Women engaging in a variety of offences against good order were treated differently than their male counterparts. Regularly sexualised in police, court and press reports, they were depicted as a greater threat to the social order not so much as criminals but as women who could not be controlled. They were the public face of uncontrollable womanhood. As we will see in the next chapter, the gendered dimensions to press reports of court appearances helped to depict female offenders as social outcasts.

Rose Skivington, Ellen Pirie, Elizabeth Davey, Lilly Doyle and other women charged with collective public offences, all share similar experiences as women caught in a cycle of offending. They were marginalised from society through regular, lengthy gaol terms. On release from prison after three to six months and with little or no family support, these women were left to fend for themselves. Labelled as part of an undeserving poor based on their criminal records, most women lived in cheap (temporary) accommodation, back alleys, parks, in shanties along the beaches, or sometimes resorted to selling sex in low-class brothels. Prison was more stable than the life they faced on release. Caught in this cycle of offending and named and shamed in the papers, they faced few options in life.

With the passage of time, we might well look at these stories and see the progress made in the decades since in reforming offenders and aiming to avoid lengthy prison terms for lesser public order offences. It is now generally accepted that the cycle of offending needs to be broken and offenders need greater opportunities for reintegration in society after gaol terms. It is comforting in a way to trace a progression towards a more just system that takes into greater account the need to use prison as a last resort. Had Esther Warden lived today, she might be recommended for counselling for alcoholism, anger management and offered opportunities for volunteer work in community projects.

While men and women are no longer imprisoned for months at a time for vagrancy, there is something timeless in the stories of women caught in a cycle of offending and confined to the streets. The homeless continue to sleep rough every night in Perth and Fremantle. One organisation, *Homeless Connect Perth*, holds regular events in Russell Square, Perth, close to where many of the women in this book spent most of her time and died alone. An initiative of the Council of Capital City Lord Mayors, *Homeless Connect* offers access to a wide range of essential and ongoing services to help people get out of homelessness. Despite such projects, however, Western Australia continues to have one of the highest levels of homelessness in Australia. In data collected from the 2006 Census, homeless people in WA numbered just over 68 per 10,000 of the population. In New South Wales, Victoria and South Australia, the rate of homeless people was between 41 and 52 per 10,000 of the population.[918] As recent reports indicate, despite improvement in the economy, the homeless rate is one constant in Australian society.[919] While the homeless are no longer named and shamed in the press and portrayed as a 'city pest', as in the case of Rose

Skivington, they remain a presence on our streets and remind community members that the very poor are still being left behind, despite improvements in the economy. The vagrant is no longer criminalised but do we really, in our daily lives, stop to wonder why it is that a person has found themselves on the streets? Much of what has been put forward in this book in terms of personal histories is done with a view to humanising the person on the streets.

7.

Court Identities

Lilly Doyle appeared in Fremantle Court in March 1920, facing another charge of creating a disturbance, this time in High and Market Streets. Inside the business of the Petty Courts, Doyle was well known to magistrates, police and court workers. For her regular offences against good order, these were the people she faced before prison. It could have remained this way. Outside of perhaps a few bystanders or audience members in court, knowledge of Lilly Doyle's many criminal convictions could have largely remained behind closed doors. The presence of court reporters prevented this. In the news report that followed her appearance and subsequent conviction in March 1920, Lilly was sensationalised in the press and labelled 'A Police Court Identity'.[920]

Within the business of the Perth and Fremantle Petty Courts (Police Courts) we can identify particular characterisations of women appearing for offences against good order. It was a regular business. Cases were heard before the Police Courts six days a week, with individuals rushed through one after the other. From 1915-39 alone, over 40,000 female cases were heard before the Petty Sessions. This was just under nine per cent of all cases.[921] While a large number of the cases were repeat offenders, such evidence provides a good overview of offences, particularly those against good order.

The regular business conducted in the Petty Sessions and combination of police, public and magisterial evidence led to a construction of female criminality that saw women committing offences against good order stereotyped as dangerous types who threatened the social order. In the Supreme Court, by contrast, female offenders were seen as tragedies.[922] Therefore, 'a woman's appearance at police court was a "staged event", a social drama largely manipulated by police and judicial authorities'.[923] Female offenders were repeatedly singled out in court as for their female identities and magisterial comments reinforced a stereotype of the bad woman.

Petty Court Sessions provided ample opportunities for news reporters to focus on scandalous cases and the repeat appearances of individuals committing offences again good order. Women regularly appearing in court became household names through the frequent reporting of their appearances in the press. *The West Australian,* and other papers reporting Lilly's many appearances, contributed to turning her into a criminal identity in Perth and Fremantle. As a repeat offender, and by virtue of her deviance as a *female* offender, Lilly Doyle regularly provided tales of drunkenness, debauchery and idleness for the papers to use to full effect in entertaining and educating their readers about the bad women of the inner streets of Perth and Fremantle. In doing so, newspapers turned female offenders into court identities.

*

People mainly learn about crime and criminals through media narratives. It remains the case today that most people understand crime through what they read and see in the media, though social media is increasingly gaining prominence in everyday communication of news. Mass media thus plays an important role in disseminating knowledge about crime in society. Back in the first decades of the twentieth century, West Australians primarily knew learned about crime from the newspapers. Named and shamed in the local press for successive years, Lilly Doyle and other women committing offences against good order provided sensational material for newspapers looking to educate and entertain readers. Much of what we can know about women appearing the Petty courts, in terms of available public sources, comes from newspaper reports. Court evidence books, for example, only cover the years from 1915 onwards, whereas press reports are available from 1900. They include evidence from police, witnesses and sometimes the accused, along with police and magisterial evidence. News reports offer valuable insights into police and court business.

News stories are shaped by news values whereby 'editors and journalists will select, produce and present news according to a range of professional criteria that are used as benchmarks to determine a story's "newsworthiness"'[924]. Women committing offences against good order faced constructions in the newspapers conforming to particular news values. Their offences in public were deemed to have public appeal and public interest as far as the news values of the journalists and editors were concerned. Ultimately, newspapers use sensationalist headlines to accompany 'stories about crime designed to shock, frighten, titillate and entertain'.[925]

Newspaper history in Western Australia dates back to the first newspaper, *The Fremantle Journal and General Advertiser*, handwritten in the colony in 1830. *The Perth Gazette and Western Australian Journal*, one of the first printed newspapers, is the forerunner of today's *West Australian* and came into business in 1833, four years after the establishment of the Swan River Colony.[926] In the first decades of the colony, newspapers were produced on a weekly basis until *The West Australian* began its daily run.[927] In these first decades, crime was mainly presented in terms of overall statistics, outside of prominent manslaughter, murder or fraud cases. Regular crime reporting, using daily court appearances for information, did not become popular until the second half of the nineteenth century, due in large part to the convict transportation period from 1850-1868 and the population increase associated with the late-century gold rushes. Throughout the nineteenth century, serious crimes gained greater attention than the lesser crimes of drunkenness and theft. By the end of the nineteenth century, three newspapers - *The West Australian*, *The Sunday Times*, *The Daily News* - dominated in Perth and Fremantle, along with another popular paper, *Truth*. As it was across Australia, *Truth* was Western Australia's 'scandalsheet' from 1903-1931. By the turn of the twentieth century, crime and court reports appeared on the first pages of the papers, signifying their popularity.

Regular court reports in the leading newspapers in Perth and Fremantle offer insights into characterisations of criminal women. The sensationalism of the stories is obvious but they are nevertheless useful in gauging what people thought was most scandalous in these years. All four papers were consistent in their objectification of female criminals as 'bad' women and rarely employed humour in dealing with their offences against good order. As crime historian Michael Sturma argues, newspapers are complicit in detailing and also shaping community perceptions of crime.[928] Media institutionalise crime through regular reporting for a mix of information and entertainment.[929]

Using evidence from regular court sessions, mainly police evidence, newspapers affirmed a negative stereotype already conferred on women by the law, police and courts. Stereotyped as drunks, bad mothers, loose women and public nuisances, the activities of criminal women were publicised in regular crime stories by reporters aiming to titivate and condemn at the same time.[930] Women who committed offences against good order were marginalised through weekly and sometimes daily crime reports.[931] While they only committed ten per cent of the crimes against good order, women were over-represented in court reports because they were not *expected* to engage in criminal activities. Stories about women committing crimes make for good, sensationalist reading. Criminal women are thus fascinating for their novelty value.[932]

Individual crime reports about women appearing before the Perth and Fremantle Police Courts ranged anywhere from thirty to a hundred words in length, depending on the evidence given in court and general interest around the case. A key part of my analysis of female offenders and the press is how they were constructed in court reports. It is in part informed by Ulrike Tabbert's research considering the linguistic construction of offenders in the press. Corpus Linguistics – the interpretation of language for its perpetuation of ideologies[933] - can be used to reveal the frequency of words and phrases in press depictions of female offenders. Negative associations with crime are transferred to the offender in a manner that separates them from society. Language enables the press to construct offenders within the context of current ideologies.[934] In the case of the criminal women in Perth and Fremantle, newspaper reports constructed female offenders as something 'other' to their sex and challenging dominant ideologies of femininity.

Using a sample size of 1,000 newspaper court reports for both men and women – and compared with evidence gathered from court evidence books (1915-1940) – I have been able to identify the words most frequently used to describe women appearing in court for offences against good order. Narrative analysis of recurring themes[935] in the portrayal of women in court reports reveals all leading newspapers employed key terms as sub-headings for individual cases involving women in the courts. At least a third of all court reports for women featured sensational headings employing key terms to distinguish the gender basis of the report. Story titles included: 'A Violent Female'[936], 'Her Century'[937] (in relation to number of convictions) 'A Female Vagrant',[938] 'A Drunken Woman,'[939] a 'negligent mother'[940] and 'A Dangerous Woman'[941]. *Truth* tended to be more creative with its titles at times, as in the case of 'May and Her Mugs', describing a soliciting case in January 1920.[942] The media was juxtaposing terms that were not socially expected of women. By comparison, men were generally not singled out in this way.

A third of all court reports featuring women used the standard form of providing the offender's name, the offence committed, and punishment details. Aside from the use of names, no other language identifiers were used to distinguish the gender of the offender. By comparison, non-gender specific language was applied to over two-thirds of crime reports for male appearances in court. The most common words used to describe repeat female offenders were 'dissolute women' and 'pests'[943], 'female nuisance' or a 'notorious female'[944]. Nellie Davenport, habitual drunk and idle and disorderly person, was described as both a 'degenerate woman' and 'town nuisance' in the one report in 1902.[945] Comparatively, men portrayed as actively committing offences whereas women a public nuisance simply by their presence in the city streets. Such characterisations, through the use of specific language, demonstrate the ways in which the media allows society to measure itself against the outsider.[946] Female offending is seen in the media as something different and inherently deviant.[947]

Newspaper reports repeatedly used moralistic language when describing the character of female offenders. More than men, women were singled out in reports as 'immoral', refused to take a warning, and disregarding chances offered to live a respectable life. Even when the language employed takes on a harsher tone, it contains moralistic undertones. Criminal women were portrayed as morally bankrupt. When Lilly Doyle appeared in court in July

1912, one sergeant gave evidence, subsequently reported in *The West Australian*, that she had been given 'every opportunity to live a respectable life' and yet she still continued to live about the streets and loiter for an immoral purpose.[948]

While some women like Esther Warden and Alice Lawson were depicted as dangerous, nasty, terrors, most women were described in reports as troublesome, annoying, riotous, frowsy, dreadful, rowdy pests. It was their vocal and visible presence in public that was most worrying within the press stories than any criminal activities. Elizabeth Davey, used by the press as a key example of the vagrant nuisance, is portrayed in one report as frustrating to the police for her inability to stay off the streets. According to police she was always in about the streets and in bad company.[949]

One-third of all Petty Session court reports for male and female appearances singled out previous convictions as a way to construct offenders, particularly recidivists. Apposition is employed in these court reports to set up less debate about the background of the accused. By naming the individual and depicting them as 'an old offender' or 'no stranger to the court', the offender is characterised as a known criminal. Their appearance in court is, then, one in a list of many such appearances. For the reader, the language allows them to construct the offender as something of a court identity, as in the case of Cecilia Reilly (Riley) in 1910:

> Her Seventieth Appearance-In tattered and much-soiled raiment, Cecilia Riley, an elderly woman, made another appearance in the dock of the Police Court, Fremantle, yesterday morning. It was not a new role for her, the "records" setting out that she had looked over the dock rails on 69 other occasions. It was said against her yesterday that she had no fixed place of abode, no lawful means of support, was idle and disorderly, and further had committed an unmentionable offence.[950]

Habitual female criminals like Cecilia Reilly, Esther Warden, Mary Sweetman and Sarah Mattson were also singled out more often than men by demeaning language. They are referred to in reports as 'undesirables', 'riotous', 'notorious', 'detested', dreadful' and the worst cases of women brought before the magistrates.

Court reports also demonstrate the extent to which social order was maintained in the Petty Sessions by evidence from the arresting police officers. Police evidence was paramount in court decisions, particularly where they ran the prosecution. Attorney General Walter James said in 1902, in relation to the *Police Act*, that '[A] common prostitute would not necessarily be a notorious prostitute, but a person honestly believed to be a prostitute'.[951] Definition of a 'common prostitute' was therefore left to police discretion. Streetwalkers could be labelled 'common prostitutes' if police argued a woman had a reputation.[952] According to one Perth police constable in 1919: 'I call a reputed prostitute a woman who goes about with prostitutes, gets drunk, lies down somewhere'.[953] Police evidence often outweighed testimony from the accused, as in the case of Maria Savage charged in October 1901 with loitering for immoral purposes in Aberdeen Street, Perth. One officer gave evidence he saw her loitering and accosting men, while another stated Savage invited him to her house. In her defence, supported by a Mrs Stewart, Maria claimed she was merely waiting for a friend. She was found guilty and fined.[954]

Police evidence was crucial in court proceedings due in large part to the nature of police work. Responsible for maintaining the social order through close surveillance of the inner city and port streets, police came to know repeat offenders well. There is an element in their court evidence of characterising women in particular ways after knowing them as regular offenders for a number of years. A third of all crime reports in the press featured specific police evidence. When habitual drunk Mary Ann Sweetman appeared in court in December 1914 on a charge of vagrancy, P. C Ford deposed that she was a 'menace to the East Perth neighbourhood'. Sergeant Smythe also gave evidence that he had known Sweetman for eight years and in that time had been 'eight weeks out of prison'.[955] Female offenders also came under the scrutiny of other women in court. Evidence given by female police workers aided the characterisation of bad women, as in the case of Esther Miller, convicted for idle and disorderly largely based on evidence from 'Mrs Dugdale [of the Women Police], who explained...'This woman's ideas of life are very degraded...'[956]

Newspapers often employed the words of an 'authority figure' as a means to convey opinions the papers were looking to publicise but showed greater clout with expert testimony.[957] Police evidence and statements and magisterial comments were utilised in a third of all reports for men and women. The press was able to use authoritative statements as evidence for the need to control women. Repetitive use of police evidence and magisterial comments allowed the leading newspapers to make judgements about women committing offences in a way readers felt was qualified by official views. When Esther Warden was arrested in January 1917 for vagrancy, *The West Australian* used police evidence to characterise her as 'one of the most dangerous women in Western Australia'.[958] Another woman, Blanche Williams, was labelled the 'Worst Woman in Perth' in 1903 through use of a quote from a magistrate.[959] Much of what we know about Lizzie Molyneaux comes from the words of magistrate and police, as quoted by the press in efforts to comment on deviant women. Once the magistrates and police had made up their mind about a particular offender, the press used court characterisations to maintain the image of the bad woman for public consumption. When Molyneaux appeared in court in January 1899 she was identified under the court report heading: 'A Tearful Vagrant'.[960] Magistrate Roe was not convinced by her tears, however, and called them 'idle tears'.[961] Having been convicted with idle and disorderly, vagrancy and drunkenness on numerous occasions, magistrates rarely gave her anything less than at least a month in prison for good order offences. Six months later, in June 1899, *The West Australian* used magisterial comments to show Molyneaux had a 'good home in Leederville' but shunned respectability to misbehave about the streets.[962] In March 1908, press reports again quoted police and magisterial evidence to maintain the image of Lizzie as a 'general nuisance in the streets'.[963]

Characterisations of women in court news stories reveal unique representations of criminals when the offender is a female. The female criminal is depicted as the 'Other' in society. She transgresses a 'metaphoric womanhood, making her the lightning rod of social and cultural tensions of the period.'[964] Newspapers encouraged the celebrated criminality of female offenders to legitimise 'the practices and conventions of both domestic and public life'.[965] Celebrated criminality arises from a connection between the criminal and the public. Members of the public need to be able to relate in some way to the criminal – through fear, disgust, rebellion or sympathy – in order for the offender to resonate.[966] Resonance is effective when it stimulates a response or interaction.[967] A clear indication of this in Perth and Fremantle in the early decades of the twentieth century was the letters written to the papers by members of the public reacting to the regular news stories about criminal women. In one letter, a 'subscriber' to *The Sunday Times* wrote of their disgust at the vice and crime visible in the city and singled out women as the worst offenders:

> It would give me very great pleasure to see a drunken woman bundled away into safety the moment she set foot into our public thorough-fares, instead of being allowed to spend the day lounging about the streets to the deep degradation of her sex.[968]

The regularity of reports about criminal women, and the naming and shaming evidenced in characterisations of females in court, created a public distinction between the good and bad woman.

Female Voices

Newspapers framed stories about female offenders in particular ways to educate and entertain readers. However, my research reveals another aspect of newspaper reporting that can contribute to humanising female offenders. While most court reports used magisterial and police evidence to establish the details of the crime(s) committed, some reports included testimony from the accused. In these snippets of information – compared for their accuracy with the Court Evidence Books – we can hear the voices of the women appearing in court. In the absence of personal records for some of the most prominent female recidivists, quoted remarks from court sessions provide some insight into how the women understood their circumstances and whether or not they agreed with the negative stereotyping placed on them by the courts, police and press.

Some female offenders affirmed a bad woman identity in the evidence they gave in court and detailed their own fall from a good woman ideal. Charged with vagrancy in August 1908, Mabel Gilday told the magistrate: 'It is only two years ago since I was a good woman.' She then pleaded a case to be allowed to leave the city claiming 'it's hard to turn over a new leaf if one is kept constantly in prison for not getting work. I am no one's enemy but my own'.[969] She was given a few days to get out of Perth but months later was back in court on an idle and disorderly charge.[970] Mary Warnock pleaded with a magistrate to give her one more chance in April 1910. At her previous appearances she had declared how sorry she was to both the magistrate and police. However, this time the magistrate was having none of it. He sentenced Mary to over six months in prison. As the papers reported, she became hysterical and had to have first aid administered to her outside of court.[971] Mary Ann Martin also conferred a bad female identity on herself. In March 1911, she told the magistrate:

> Your Worship, I am so bad now. Yesterday morning I was making for the hospital, and I was too late. I went down the street and met some of my friends, and I don't remember any more. I am bad.[972]

A greater number of women, two-thirds of cases where responses were recorded, challenged the institutional sexism of the time and negative police characterisation of their activities. Some responses show open resistance in the courtroom. One woman in the Perth Police Court in April 1920 shouted at Policewoman Dugdale that she was 'as good a bloody woman as any bloody woman around here'.[973] Susan Long contested police characterisations of her as a female drunk in August 1907. Long claimed she was not in the least bit drunk, saying it took 'two bottles of whisky, a dozen bottles of lager, and a drop of vermouth, to get her "going."'[974] Mary Sweetman, appearing on a charge of using obscene language in August 1910, blamed both the police and her husband:

> Accused: Yes - Them records have got me seven years in gaol. As soon as I get out the police get me agin, an' I get no chance. It's all -me 'usband's doin'; 'e won't keep me children; it breaks me 'eart, and I takes to a drop of drink, yer Washup! I gets a job, then the police go an' tell me' missus that I've been in gaol an' I'm done agin![975]

Sweetman also asked the magistrate in court in January 1914: 'During the last twelve months I have been only four weeks out of gaol, so how can I be an habitual?'[976] Sweetman's response demonstrates her mindset in relation to negative characterisations. Despite being regularly arrested for drunkenness when on release from prison, Mary Ann did not think of herself as an habitual drunk. For Sweetman, her previous convictions worked against her, rather than any habitual acts of drunkenness: 'Do give me a chance. 'This is the first time for the New Year. Two hours at Fremantle yesterday did it'.[977]

Alice Lawson, a tough young woman with a criminal record in Kalgoorlie, Perth and Fremantle, provided interesting evidence in court in Kalgoorlie two days before Christmas in 1906. Lawson appeared as a witness in a case against William Taylor. Charged as a rogue and vagabond, Taylor was arrested for living off the proceeds of prostitution and without lawful means of support. When the prosecuting officer asked Lawson, 'What are you?' she sarcastically replied: 'A woman'.[978] Lawson then went on to tell of how the accused had been living with her and had been living off the money she made from prostitution. She pleaded with the magistrate to take into account that Taylor was abusive and had assaulted her at the Shamrock Hotel. Taylor interjected and tried to place more blame on Lawson, telling the Magistrate: 'Your Worship, you can see it is only a prostitute trying to swear an honest man's life away. This woman has a lot of convictions against her'. While Taylor was sentenced to three months in prison and the magistrate allowed Lawson's evidence, the judgement was then placed firmly on Taylor to 'keep away from women of bad character'.[979]

One of the best examples of open defiance in the courtroom comes from Cecilia Reilly. In the fifteen years that followed Reilly's first conviction in 1898, she notched up over seventy convictions for neglect, drunkenness, loitering and soliciting. Born in either Victoria or New South Wales – her birthplace is given as both in the Prison Register – Cecilia became a known court identity through the reporting of her many appearances. She was not one to take sentencing lightly, however. When charged with leaving her child in a perambulator (pram) in the streets while she went drinking around Fremantle in August 1898, Reilly objected in court and argued she had only gone off to run a short errand.[980] She spent the next month in prison, depicted as a 'negligent mother' in the press.

Over the course of the next decade, Reilly made frequent appearances in court. On one occasion she asked to bring in a witness to support her assertion that she was not a vagrant. In October 1903, Joseph Williamson testified that he had been keeping Cecilia for the last seven years and provided her with means of support. For his part, however, Williamson was negatively characterised as 'untidy, unwashed and unshaven'.[981] He did little to help Cecilia's case.

By 1910, much of the fight was gone in Cecilia Reilly. In January she appeared in court with an infant in her arms and was charged with drunkenness and neglect.[982] Sent off to prison for another six months and her child placed in state care, Reilly had now spent many years in and out of prison. For the most part, when on release, she lived on the streets and drank away the days. Charged with vagrancy in November 1910, Reilly pleaded with the magistrate to let her down lightly. According to the news story following her appearance, she broke down and said 'everybody in the world had taken sides against her. No sooner would she finish one sentence before she was "run in again" by the police.'[983]

The best evidence of Reilly's defiance comes from her appearance in Fremantle Police Court in 1903 when using Williamson as her witness. By the stage, Cecilia had dozens of convictions and was well known to Magistrate Fairbairn. Charged with vagrancy and depicted as a woman who liked to drink 'a drop too much', Reilly was sentenced to six months in prison. Before she could be led away, Riley addressed the magistrate: 'Thank you, your Worship. May you be stiff dead when I come out.'[984]

Other women shared Cecilia Reilly's brazenness in court. Edith Barber, appearing in Fremantle Police Court in 1907, was charged with being idle and disorderly and using obscene language. Charged and convicted only months earlier as an idle and disorderly person, and in the habit of frequenting Chinese dens, Barber was sentenced to three months in prison. As she left the dock, Edith turned to the magistrate and thanked him: 'Good: I thought you'd make it a sixer.'[985]

Vera Pearce openly challenged the judgement of police on several occasions in court. Regarded an 'old offender' for her many appearances in court, Pearce was known to police and magistrates for her long list of good order offences including drunkenness, idle and disorderly, and public disturbances. Charged with creating a disturbance in Charles Street in August 1910, Pearce claimed she was well within her right to abuse the arresting police officer. P.C Robinson stated in court that he arrested Pearce for abusing him while he cycled by her on the street. Off-duty and not looking to make an arrest, Robinson claimed Pearce made a scene and continued to hurl abuse at him. When a crowd started to gather close to the offender, Robinson made his arrest as her antics were now in full public view. In court, Vera Pearce defended her actions: 'I should just think I would. You took my child from my breast and gave it to the murderers to be murdered'. Robinson confirmed this had in fact happened but claimed the child was sent to the Children's Home, where it died, to protect it from being carted about the streets by a drunken Vera Pearce. To the very last moment in this case, Pearce resisted the power of the authorities. When the magistrate told her she was 'not fit to have a child', Vera decided to take a gaol term over a fine, saying, 'I wouldn't pay a fine to you'.[986] In this one exchange we can see Vera Pearce contesting police and magisterial authority. For her repeated objections in court, Pearce earned the title 'Police Court Identity' one month later in September 1910.[987]

*

Perth and Fremantle newspaper editors used regular sessions from the Police Courts to tell readers what happened when people broke the law. Within this reporting, newspapers were also complicit in creating moral panics about female engagement in illicit activities, particularly public drinking. Regular reporting of female appearances in court for on drunkenness charges played into anxieties about the social order. Newspapers used cases of female habitual drunkenness as a form of social control, targeting a public world where 'intoxication and drunkenness are firmly located in social spaces'.[988] While the press could not control society as such, it could nevertheless play its part in commenting upon society at the time, generating ideas about conformity within Perth and Fremantle and entering into debates about crime. This was particularly poignant in the first three decades of the twentieth century following on from the introduction of the *Police Act* of 1892.[989]

Deviance is created by society and impacts on how criminals are perceived. Crime reports inform people about individuals within society who are acting outside the bounds of social expectations.[990] When female offenders challenged the courts, they were not praised in the press for acts of defiance, as the women may well have seen it. They were used as examples of the limited life chances available to a woman who fell from respectability. Readers were encouraged to place themselves in opposition to the crew of wicked, bad and immoral women imprisoned in Fremantle or sent off to a Home.

Offenders are 'packaged' in particular ways in the press. Newspapers create images of offenders that allow readers to construct them as something different and 'other' to mainstream society. In reading about deviant women about the streets of Perth and Fremantle, readers were able to form an image of the women through use of particular language in the news stories. They were ragged, filthy, offensive and degenerate. If they were recidivists, press reports created images of female offenders as conniving, overtly sexual and dangerous. It helps the reading public identify deviant women not necessarily as criminal types but as bad women. It was less a criminal lesson than a moralistic education to maintain the social order. To use Simon Adams' argument on press reporting of female murderer Martha Rendell in 1909, female offenders seemed to represent an 'inversion of everything a woman was supposed to be'.[991]

Despite their role in maintaining social order and efforts to titillate readers and sensationalise crime, when placed together, court reports spanning the course of each criminal life are important in telling the larger story of the effects of life on the streets. Brief moments of reporting the words of a female offender are important in tracing individual reactions to crime and punishment. It is in the court reports that we hear Blanche Williams, charged with idle and disorderly in April 1903, contest police evidence on the grounds they were 'storytellers'.[992] Courtroom testimonies provide subtle examples of the ways in which female offenders negotiated and understood their circumstances. While they reveal examples of women affirming the public stereotype of the bad woman, a larger number of women in fact rejected deviant characterisations. As Melissa Bellanta states in recent scholarship, 'we still know comparatively little about the politics of *un*respectability'.[993] Female offenders demonstrate that the distinction between women's own understandings of their subjectivity and public representations needs to be considered more in what we know about the negotiations of female identity in the early twentieth century. Esther Warden, Cecilia Reilly and other women fronting the Police Courts for offences against good order were all sensationalised as bad women. However, with little or no personal records available for female offenders, snippets of testimony in the newspapers help to humanise female experiences outside of crime statistics and prison records.

8. Endings

'Found dead in Russell Square'

A post-mortem examination of the body of Mary Jane Paltridge (66), of no fixed address, who was found dead in Russell Square, Perth, on Saturday morning, revealed that she died from suffocation. It is believed that blood dripped from abrasions on her face, ran into her mouth and choked her. She is known to have received the abrasions recently and it is thought that she fell in the park and started then bleeding.[994]

Mary Jane Smith, originally from the small country town of Newcastle (later renamed Toodyay), travelled down to the city sometime in the early twentieth century. She married Fremantle man, Frederick Paltridge, in 1911 but he deserted her sometime in the next ten years.[995] Unable to keep down a job or somewhere to live due to regular stints in gaol, Mary frequented the streets of Perth and Fremantle, sleeping wherever she could find a bench or some cover for the night. Paltridge was well known to the police and magistrates and had served dozens of sentences in Fremantle Prison since the 1920s, mainly for drunkenness and vagrancy. She was a vagrant local identity in the inner streets of Perth. In October 1949, and in her sixties, Paltridge died alone on a park bench and her body was discovered the next morning. It was a lonely death and symbolic of the lives of women cast out on the streets of Perth and Fremantle for offences against good order. Regularly drunk, soliciting, loud, obscene or sleeping rough, their sense of loneliness is audible in the discovery of Mary Paltridge's bloodied body. Of the hundred or so female recidivists informing much of the content of this book, few overcame the troubles that dogged their lives on the streets. This chapter charts the last years of prominent female recidivists criminalised for offences against good order and characterised as the most notorious women on the streets.

*

Sarah Jane Mattson failed to heed Magistrate Roe's words in 1911. In court on a drunkenness charge, Mattson was told to stay away from alcohol. It almost always led to a stint in prison and many weeks away from her husband and small children. By the 1930s, with her husband dead and all her children grown up, Sarah was living a hard life on the streets. She was arrested on Anzac Day 1933 for assaulting her friend, Elizabeth Collins, in Weld Square. Collins received fourteen wounds to the face and scalp, allegedly from Mattson striking her with a drinking glass.[996] Mattson appeared in court on Monday 8 May and was sentenced to six months' gaol. Lucille Skinner gave evidence that Mattson was drinking with Collins and a man during the day before a fight broke out. Mattson broke a drinking glass on a seat and attacked Collins with it, then walked away. A male companion poured water over Collins' face but it was left to Skinner to take her to the hospital. In court the magistrate told Sarah he did not believe the consumption of methylated spirits was mitigating circumstances and she was fortunate she did not do further damage to Collins.[997] Mattson's drinking was now harmful to anyone who associated with her.

Little hope remained for Sarah Mattson by the late 1930s. She appeared in court in June 1937 on a rogue and vagabond charge. Police found her sleeping in a stable off a lane between Pier and Moore Street with two men. She was sentenced to fourteen days in gaol.[998] In December 1938 she was knocked down on Wellington Street. Though she suffered concussion and lacerations, the driver claimed she stepped out in front of his car in a drunken state.[999]

Sarah Mattson was charged numerous times as an habitual drunk from the late 1930s until September 1950.[1000] She died a year after her last conviction, on 19 September 1951. Listed as late of 45 Charles Street, West Perth, she was buried in the Anglican section of Karrakatta Cemetery[1001] Despite a hard life on the streets, Sarah was over seventy at the time of her death. She had shown resilience on the streets that few could compare with. Yet, her last years were marked by the loneliness of a woman living out her days without family or close friends for support.

It seemed for a short period that Patricia Roots might find happiness in her final years. Well known for loitering in the streets of Perth and Fremantle, deserted years before by her husband, Roots re-married in 1929 after serving her last conviction in 1927. It did not last, however. Patricia's husband, Frank Aulmich, died two years later in Fremantle leaving her lost about the inner city streets. She moved into a lodging house in William Street, Perth but was said to walk the streets alone. In one reported case, Martha Aulmich (previously Patricia Roots) was reported missing by family in *The West Australian* in January 1939. [1002] Family attributed her wandering to loss of memory. Eventually found, Martha died in August 1939,[1003] only weeks before Australia entered World War Two. She left behind a long record of convictions for loitering, soliciting and vagrancy.[1004] Martha Aulmich wandered the streets due to dementia later in life, but they were streets she knew well and may have provided some comfort through familiarity.

Elizabeth Davey lived through major events in West Australian history from the gold rushes of the late nineteenth century to Federation, two world wars and the Great Depression. Her life story, however, is confined to what we know of the portrayal of her as a troublesome vagrant. Despite her protestations in court in 1921 that she had a home, sewing machine and was willing to sell it all and escape to the country if she was only given a chance, Elizabeth Davey was sentenced to three months' imprisonment for vagrancy.[1005] Police evidence condemned her as a public nuisance and 'always on the streets'.[1006] No sooner was she chased out of one street than police would find her in another street nearby.

By the late 1930s Elizabeth Davey was largely confined to a life on the streets where she 'frequented hotels and wine saloons' with other members of the criminal underclass.[1007] She slept in parks and byways where she hoped police would not find her, including a railway seat at East Perth Railway Station.[1008] During the day she begged on Barrack and Wellington Streets. The streets she inhabited for so many years also took her life. Elizabeth Davey was struck by a car in William Street on 6 September 1950 and died the following day aged seventy-five[1009] According to the coroner, it seemed she had walked onto the road oblivious to the traffic.[1010] Her death was recorded in the Fremantle Prison Register shortly after, bringing to an end a long criminal record.

Cecilia Reilly appeared in court in November 1910 on a charge of idle and disorderly and vagrancy. Described in the press as dressed in tattered and soiled clothing, it was Cecilia's seventieth appearance in court. By this stage she really felt everyone was against her and was unable to keep up the tough exterior she had shown on previous occasions. Only a few years before, Cecilia had cheekily remarked that she could do a two-month stint in prison 'on her head' and was removed from the court 'vowing vengeance on the constable who had arrested her'.[1011] Now almost four year later, when the magistrate sent her to prison for three months, she broke down in court and pleaded for leniency.[1012] After this charge, Reilly was rarely out of gaol.

Cecilia's record came to an end in March 1913. She was arrested for public drunkenness on Tuesday 25 March and taken to the Fremantle lockup. Once there, she was placed in a cell awaiting an appearance in court the next day. Unlike today where inmates are regularly checked on, particularly with ongoing rallies against Deaths in Custody, Cecilia was left alone in the cell and unattended. Police found her dead in the cell the next morning. Sometime before 10am she had died, a doctor later testified, from a heart attack complicated by a bout of pneumonia.[1013] At the end of Reilly's prison record, in red ink, prison staff entered the word 'dead' and included a cut out of the newspaper story about her sudden death.[1014] Only death could end Cecilia's repeated run-ins with the law.

For much of her adult life, Mary Ann Sweetman worried that she was her father's daughter. An ex-convict who suffered from bouts of depression and showed an increasing addiction to alcohol later in life, Henry Haynes left a difficult legacy for his eldest child. Not only did his killing of her mother severely traumatise Mary; the circumstances only further reinforced the deep concerns she held for her father for many years. When, as an adult herself, Mary Sweetman was diagnosed as a dipsomaniac in 1905 – what doctors described as an uncontrollable craving for alcohol – her fears seemed realised. Mary Ann Sweetman was unable to maintain her family life through alcoholism. Mary's frequent bouts of drunkenness on the streets of Perth and Fremantle (East Perth was a favourite area) placed her in direct reach of local police looking for the usual suspects in their efforts to keep public nuisances off the streets.

By November 1916, Mary Sweetman reportedly had 200 convictions to her name, the majority for drunkenness, along with creating a disturbance and using obscene language. Described by police in December 1914 as a 'menace to the East Perth neighbourhood',[1015] she was well known in inner city streets for her public deviations from being a respectable wife, mother and woman. On one occasion in April 1914, she was apprehended for behaving in 'an erratic manner' and throwing bottles of beer at people passing by in Barrack Street.[1016] In another incident, police arresting her on Adelaide Terrace for chasing boys with a pint glass in her hand, likened Mary to a 'wild animal'.[1017]

Despite the efforts of police and authorities to treat her alcohol problem by imprisoning her away from access to alcohol, Mary Sweetman could not be reformed. In evidence before the court in December 1914, Sergeant Smythe stated: 'I have known her for eight years; during that time she hasn't been eight weeks out of prison'.[1018] Things were little better the following year. Sweetman appeared in court on Saturday 13 November 1915 for creating a drunken disturbance in Barrack Street. Evidence was given she was seen 'pulling soldiers about', 'hit a civilian in the face' and threw her arms around a returned soldier. When he pushed her away she fell in the road, got up and struck another person passing. Mary Ann had been before the court on eight previous occasions that year for disorderly conduct, along with numerous appearances for drunkenness. She was sentenced to two months in gaol with hard labour.[1019]

By 1920, Mary Ann Sweetman had little fight left in her. In her fifties and having been in and out of gaol for nearly twenty years, she pleaded with a magistrate to dismiss her latest charge of drunkenness. Sweetman told the court she had missed Christmas Day with her family for the last sixteen years due to gaol terms for drunkenness each festive season. This year she wanted to spend Christmas with her children. The magistrate discharged her with a warning but she had a lot of time to make up for with her family.[1020] We don't know if Mary Ann spent that Christmas with her family. As court and newspaper records indicate from January 1905, Benjamin Sweetman did not want his wife at home and refused to let her in the house.[1021]

Mary Ann Sweetman died at Royal Perth Hospital in February 1922, eulogised in the papers as the 'dearly beloved wife of Benjamin T. Sweetman' and 'mother of Robert, Franklin, Eunice, Percy, Ernest, Cecil, and Clarence Sweetman'.[1022] She is buried in Fremantle Cemetery with her husband and daughter. It is likely the Sweetman family bowed to convention in acknowledging Mary Ann's death and burying her in a family plot where her husband would join her in 1935.[1023] When Benjamin Sweetman died in 1935, his obituary outlined all his major achievements and prominence in the Fremantle community. No mention is made of his wife Mary Ann. She is named in the brief death notice but not the lengthier, obituary written for public remembrance.

Mary's brother, Charles Henry Haynes, was with her at Perth Hospital when she died.[1024] He had not abandoned his sister. Despite her notoriety in the courts and press reports, Mary Ann Sweetman was not just 'a confessed inebriate'.[1025] She was lost inside the demons of her past. Sweetman's story is an important reminder that as much as female lives were sensationalised in the press for habitual drunkenness, they were real people who deserve some understanding beyond merely being recognised as a drunk on the street.

By the 1930s Esther Warden was almost completely alone in the world. She had survived the so-called 'Roaring Twenties' but much in the same way she spent every other decade: in and out of gaol. Caught in a cycle of offending and isolated from the rest of the community through the criminalisation of her anti-social behaviour, Esther understood all too well what R. E. N. Twopenny meant on a visit to Perth in 1883 when he said: 'you feel yourself more out of the world in Perth than in Siberia'.[1026]

Charged with trying to obtain illicit liquor from a house in Roe Street, Perth in July 1933, and sentenced to three weeks in prison,[1027] Esther decided it was time for a change of scenery and moved to Kalgoorlie but her notoriety followed her there. Esther was charged with drunkenness and vagrancy in 1934. Police described her as a nuisance about the hotels, stealing money from patrons and abusing the public. She claimed her move to Kalgoorlie was to find some work away from the stigma attached to her in Perth and Fremantle. The only trouble was she could not give up the bottle. She was imprisoned back in Fremantle for six months from July 1934.[1028]

By September 1935, old Esther was not only drunk; she was armed with a weapon too. The press had a field day labelling her a drunken, armed pensioner threatening local people in pubs. She was arrested one evening at the Victoria Hotel (now Rosie O'Grady's in Northbridge) in possession of a revolver. Intoxicated and unable to walk out of the lounge bar, Esther was escorted to the lock up by the arresting officers. Esther claimed to have found the revolver outside the front door of a house she visited earlier in the day.[1029] After many years spent on the streets, targeted by both police and ex-lovers, Warden may well have thought the find a lucky one. While she had no plans to use it, a revolver may have given her some comfort as a drunken pensioner on the streets. No shrinking violent in her younger years, we can only wonder why Esther armed herself in her old age on the streets. Perhaps she worried age made her vulnerable to attack.

In the months and years following the gun incident, Esther Warden was regularly arrested for drunkenness on the streets of Perth and Fremantle. Each time she was imprisoned for days or months and returned to the cells soon after release from the previous stint in prison.[1030] Esther Warden had spent too many years between the streets, lockup and prison to be able to break her cycle of offending. She still had plenty of fight left in her though.

In an interesting damages case in January 1935, Esther Warden was charged with knocking a camera out of man's hand in a public park and kicking it numerous times on the ground. The photographer made a living out of taking photos of people and then sending the images to the newspapers for use. Esther approached the photographer and objected to his statement that he could take a photo of her and use it in *The Western Mail*. As she told the magistrate in court, Esther didn't want her image in the papers. For a woman whose name had graced the papers for over thirty years of crime reports, she no doubt didn't want the general public knowing what she looked like. Or, possibly, she simply wanted to maintain her privacy, to the extent that she could. Unable the pay for the damages cost, she was sent away to prison for two months.[1031]

Esther Warden died at the age of sixty-nine on 3 November 1942 and was buried in the Roman Catholic section of Karrakatta Cemetery. With over 200 convictions to her name,[1032] Esther was one of the most notorious female offenders in Western Australia. But there was no lamenting in the press about her passing. Like other women criminalised for offences against good order, their endings largely went largely unnoticed, unless they suffered a violent end like Marion Curedale. Without family or friends to maintain the grave, or request its extension of the lease on the plot, no marker remains for Esther's last resting place. The loneliness of a life on the streets followed Esther to the grave.

Like Esther Warden, other women on the streets of Perth and Fremantle remained in a cycle of offending well into their fifties and sixties. For these women, old age and/or death combined to end their convictions. Alice Lawson's convictions continued up until late in 1930 when she was arrested and imprisoned for being drunk and wilfully damaging a window.[1033] By this stage she was well into her fifties. Though she claimed to have work as a domestic, she was well known about the streets of Perth and Fremantle as a public nuisance. Up to the 1920s, Alice was mentioned in reports alongside her husband, Robert Leeder. [1034] The two were known to lurk about the streets and associate with thieves and women on ill-fame.[1035] However, by 1930, when she was charged with the broken window offence, Alice seems to be alone on the streets. Alice used the surnames Lawson, Leeder and Davis interchangeably throughout her criminal career as aliases to throw the authorities off tracing her long record. Also like Esther Warden, Alice never lost the fight in her spirit right up to her last conviction. However, this is where the record of her life ends: over a month in prison for drunkenness and property damage.[1036]

With over 130 appearances in court by March 1920, Lilly Doyle's last years followed a similar pattern to other women on the streets. She was repeatedly arrested and imprisoned for drunkenness, idle and disorderly and using obscene language.[1037] Doyle was caught in a cycle of offending that, like Warden and Lawson, only death could end. Her last conviction for obscene language in January 1932 landed her only three days in prison but it was indicative of the view of the authorities at the time: nothing could break Doyle's life on the streets, drinking and socialising with other vagrants about Fremantle and South Fremantle. Unlike Esther Warden, however, Lilly Doyle was more a threat to herself than anyone else; violence is not a part of her long list of offences. This explains the leniency shown towards her into the 1920s and 1930s, when she was in her fifties and sixties. Lilly died in Fremantle on 21 June 1940 and was buried in the Roman Catholic section of Karrakatta Cemetery.[1038]

Irishwoman, Mary Warnock, used by the police and press as an example of what awaits a woman who 'falls' from a good position, was in dire straits by the 1920s. What hope was there for Warnock when in 1910 a magistrate declared that while he would not do it, the best thing for her would be imprisonment 'for the rest of your natural life'?[1039] The papers claimed in 1920 that she had been before the courts over 200 times.[1040] With many convictions listed in the Prison Register for soliciting, idle and disorderly, drunkenness and vagrancy, Warnock was in and out of prison on such a regular basis that she hardly had time to consider work or a place to live. In October 1924 she was charged with vagrancy but promised to be better in the future. She was sent to the Salvation Army Home for three months.[1041] By 1933, and in her sixties, she was arrested for begging in Barrack Street. [1042] From there the record is silent on the life of Mary Warnock.

'A Diabolical Murder'

Marion Curedale's ending is the most violent of all the women in this book. Charged with being a 'loose, idle and disorderly character' in Fremantle Police Court March 1888, Marion Curedale began wandering about the streets and was often picked up by local police. At her first appearance in court, and aware of her personal circumstances, Magistrate Fairbairn gave her a caution rather than a prison sentence, but told her if she appeared in court again she would be dealt with severely.[1043] It was not the last time Marion saw the inside of the Police Court. Described in court in February 1897 as a 'disreputable-looking woman',[1044] she was sentenced to six months in prison for vagrancy. Marion made her thirtieth appearance in court in December 1900 for loitering about the streets for the last few weeks in a drunken state. Curedale testified to having a large family that she maintained through working work while she was off the drink. A member of the bench said he knew the Curedale family and thought it was partly up to them to help Mary Ann. As reported in the press: 'The Bench said it was necessary that the woman should be protected in some way, and there was no option but to put her under the care of the State for three months'.[1045] State care, even in the form of imprisonment, failed to protect Marion from the dangers on the streets.

By the first years of the twentieth century, an elderly Marion Curedale was portrayed in the press as beyond reform. Aged sixty-eight in 1902 and charged with vagrancy after being found asleep on the Esplanade in Fremantle, Marion Curedale was sent away for seven days in prison.[1046] In February 1903 *The West Australian* singled her out as one of the many disreputable women about the streets:

> Degenerate Woman--Marion Curedale, a wretched-looking old woman, was charged, under that section of the Police Act which renders a person found sleeping out liable to be charged as a rogue and vagabond. Constable Mann arrested the woman in the Fremantle Park, at about half-past 3 o'clock on Sunday morning. The present was her 30[th]appearance at Fremantle, for various offences. Mr. Fairbairn commenced her to gaol for six months.[1047]

Despite her efforts to stay off the streets, Marion's drinking frequently brought her to the attention of local police. By the end of the first decade of the twentieth century, police and magistrates had had enough. Yet, in a sad twist, had the magistrate enforced a gaol term on Curedale in December 1909, she would not have been murdered.

The West Australian public woke on Christmas Day 1909 to news of a horrific murder that had taken place on a yacht anchored near Mill Point, South Perth. *The West Australian* called it a 'diabolical murder' similar to the crimes of Jack the Ripper.[1048] The murderer was a sailor by the name of Thomas James Thomas. Police attending the homicide were scarred by what they saw, describing it as sickening and gruesome.

The yacht, *Banshee*, belonged to a member of the Kalgoorlie Legislative Assembly who used it to holiday along the waters around Perth and Fremantle. This year he was looking to spend Christmas in Perth and frequented the Royal Perth Yacht Club, anchoring the yacht at Mill Point. Representative Keenan had hired Thomas J. Thomas to work on the boat as the caretaker. Keenan asked Thomas to meet him at the Yacht Club on the morning of 24 December. He became concerned when Thomas has not shown up after midday. He hopped on a boat and rowed out to the yacht. It was there in the cabin he found the body of Curedale; she had been killed within the last hour or two.

One witness arriving at the scene moments later described it at the inquest as a terrible scene. Finding a body under a blanket, when he uncovered it he was 'horrified to see the mutilated body of a woman'.[1049] It was then he and Mr Keenan found the suicide note. It was written with lead pencil on a piece of paper and left on a seat in the boat:

> I committed this rash act in a moment of frenzy whilst under the influence of drink, and you will find my body in the river just under the yacht with a small cable attached. Please don't look on me as a criminal for truly I was unconscious. (Signed) Thos. J. Thomas.[1050]

Thomas Thomas murdered Marion Curedale in a drunken frenzy. Keenan found it out of character for the young man. In evidence given to police, he described a well-mannered young man you had spent time on the east coast of Africa.[1051] The papers tried to play on the stories being related that Thomas feared the fever from his recent bout of malaria was returning. Perhaps it was a way of reassuring the reading public that the frenzy could be explained beyond straight-out violence.

Despite good references from his employer, there was no denying the violent nature of the murder. In the press reports afterwards, the frenzy was detailed. Witnesses and police described how a 'long gash extended right over and above the abdomen, exposing the intestines, and the throat was also deeply gashed, the windpipe being severed'.[1052] It was horrific. Those who came into contact with the murder scene told of being unable to eat for sometime after viewing the mutilated body.[1053]

A number of questions remained around the murder case. Why was a thirty year-old man on a yacht with a sixty-two year-old woman? How did Marion get to the yacht? Was she hoping to sleep there for the evening and had drunkenly fought with Thomas whereupon he murdered her? Regardless of the circumstances of their decision to drink together and row out to the boat, it was one of the most shocking crimes known to have occurred in Perth in the many decades since colonisation in 1829.

Marion Curedale was buried in Karrakatta Cemetery soon after the investigations over Christmas 1909. Curedale's murder is an extreme example of the end of a life on the streets. However, in Marion's brutal death we see the same characterisations in place that outcast her from society in the first place, all perhaps leading to that moment on the boat with a stranger. In its reporting of the murder, *The West Australian* singled Marion out as a woman of the 'unfortunate class with a long record in the Perth and Fremantle Courts'.[1054] Curedale's 'unenviable record' was again mentioned in the story's closing lines. Despite the fact she was the murder victim, her criminal record is used to qualify the type of woman who would be out in public in the early hours of the morning. Curedale's lifestyle, it can be inferred from the press reports, contributed to her death. Even in her last moments, Marion Curedale is a 'fallen' woman, outcast from society. Her brutal death failed to curb public discourse about her life on the streets. It speaks for most of the women criminalised in the first decades of the twentieth century.

Epilogue:

Reflecting on the 'bad' women of Perth and Fremantle

When Cecilia Reilly was arrested on Fremantle Esplanade in October 1910 she was asleep on the grass, holding a beer bottle and sporting a black eye. With no means of support or a place to live, police charged her as a rogue and vagabond and the magistrate sentenced her to one month in prison. Like other men and women frequently coming to the attention of the police for drunkenness, idle and disorderly and vagrancy, Cecilia's actions that evening came under the WA *Police Act* and made her a criminal. Unlike her male counterparts, however, police targeted Reilly because she was alone in the park and unchaperoned.[1055] It was no place for a woman. Cecilia Reilly was out of place for most of her life and criminalised for her lack of conformity.

Cecilia Reilly's lot in life is she lived during a period of Western Australian history when offences against good order resulted in lengthy prison terms. The drunk, idle, loitering, abusive, or homeless person was seen then as a direct threat to the social order. In the context of their times, they were criminal types who wandered the streets of Perth and Fremantle and were directly targeted by the police and perceived as a public menace. In the years leading up to World War Two, public transgressions were criminalised as a means to maintain the social order. For offences against good order, men and women were sentenced to anywhere between a week and six months in prison. Repeat offenders were rarely given anything less than three months. The harshness of convictions at the time gave offenders little chance at a different life.

Women committing offences against good order were punished as a means to take them off the streets and out of public view. Yet there is more to this story. While the WA *Police Act* was legislated as a means by which to monitor and punish criminal behaviour, it was also used to control female behaviour and single out deviant women not conforming to the feminine ideal. This ideal, as fraught with difficulties as it was in the lived realities of everyday life, presented an image of the passive, chaste, moralistic woman best contributing to society through respectable paid work or upholding a domestic identity as a good wife and mother. Such constructions of femininity meant female offenders were judged differently in the early decades of the twentieth century. When Magistrate Roe sent Clara Bull off to the Salvation Army Home in 1902 and told her it was a 'chance to be a better woman',[1056] his words echoed dominant public discourse about women charged with offences against good order. It wasn't so much that they were criminals as much as they were bad women supposedly in need of moral re-programming.

Imprisoned for lengthy periods, or sometimes sent to one of the Reformatory Homes, women were denied any stability beyond the prison or Home walls. On release, they couldn't get work because of their criminal record and were 'forever marked... as a recidivist'.[1057] Caught in a cycle of offending, Vera Pearce tried to end her life in 1907 by taking poison. While she claimed she was drunk at the time and did not know what she was doing, the authorities saw it differently and women from the Home of the Good Shepherd asked to take her into their care.[1058] Perhaps Pearce was reacting to the public profile the police, magistrates and papers conferred on her as a bad woman.

Institutionalised sexism in the courts, police work and in the press had a debilitating effect on female offenders in Perth and Fremantle from 1900-1939. By virtue of their presence on the streets and engagement in activities criminalised under the *Police Act*, women charged with good order offences faced a dominant public discourse that characterised them as 'the worst female character',[1059] as in the case of Esther Warden. Deserted by her husband, then her lover and left without support, Warden drank too much and could turn violent and attack strangers. She was a pest about the city streets but her opportunities in life were severely limited. Police closely watched her every time she came out of prison and press stories made her into a local criminal identity, depicting her as the 'worst woman in Western Australia'.

She was so well known about the city streets that is may have seemed to Esther that everyone was watching her, waiting for the next public disturbance.

Negatively stereotyped in public, female offenders were thus largely confined to a cycle of offending, incarceration and marginalisation by a public discourse of respectability. Some within the Perth and Fremantle communities recognised the difficulties associated with trying to break the cycle of offending. In a Perth Police Court in 1917, policewoman Dugdale said: 'The trouble is, once they are down nobody will give them a chance'.[1060] She was referring to prostitutes but might as well have been talking about most women charged with offences against good order. Even *The Sunday Times*, a paper known for sensationalising female appearances in court, took stock of Mary Warnock's situation in 1913:

> A poor unfortunate human derelict is Mary Warnock, who has drunk so deeply of the cup of life's bitterness that this world can possess very few attractions for her. From the streets to the gaol and from the gaol back again to the streets, buffeted from pillar to post, the butt of ridicule and contempt alike of the virtuous and of those sinners who have not yet been found out, where is the helping hand for this unfortunate Magdalene? Whom shall she turn to when no one will have her?[1061]

The reality of society at the time is Mary Warnock, Cecilia Reilly, Esther Warden and other women criminalised for offences against good order were not expected to engage in crime. Crime statistics, historically, tell us that more men engage in crime than women. Within the broader criminal justice system in Australia even today, male offenders far outnumber females.[1062] Women, therefore, are not expected to commit crimes so when they do their appearance in court creates a sensation. It was a gendered experience. The female in court was judged as in need to greater social control to reform her deviant behaviour. Men who engage in criminal activities are rarely questioned about the extent to which this represents a 'fall' from masculinity. Men never suffered a 'fall' from masculinity; they entered into crime.

Female experiences of crime and punishment reveal the ways in which social and gender transgressions overlap to create a double punishment for women. Female offenders are equally criminal and deviant women, suffering strict sentences for moral offences and a lack of conformity to ideals of female sexuality. They are punished with stringent sentences and also socially marginalised outside the judicial system.[1063] When men engage in crime, their presence is largely understood in criminal terms. They have committed a crime and face punishment for that offence. When women commit crimes, they are singled out as *females* who have failed in their moral obligations to society. Women are punished for criminal activities as well as a supposed 'fall' from femininity.

While men and women are no longer imprisoned in Western Australia for months on end for offences against good order, female offenders continue to suffer a double standard in how their offences are understood within society. Social control continues to affect the lives of women in the myriad of ways in which feminine norms are used to construct deviant women. Whereas male offenders experience extreme social control if they are 'less than adult, psychopaths, have inadequate personalities', crime researchers argue that in the case of women 'it is sufficient justification that they are women.'[1064] By virtue of their identity as a *female* offender, women continue to suffer greater social control than men. Therefore, while the sentences have been reduced and rehabilitation implemented to a much greater extent, perceptions of female crime remain the same. Women are publicly demeaned for criminal activities in ways men are not. Men rarely suffer questioning of their sexuality as women do when they engage in crime.

There is another side to this story too. Close socio-biographical investigation into the lives of women staring out from mug shots in police and prison records, enables greater understanding of different personal experiences that in some way contributed to a life on the streets. *Drunks, Pests and Harlots* humanises the women named and shamed in the press reports and captured for posterity in police mug shots. It uncovers personal histories of women cast out from society. With Mary Sweetman, for example, we see beyond depictions of her an habitual drunk criticised in court for her inability to conform to the ideal of the good wife and mother. In Sweetman's story, the girl who witnessed her mother's violent death at the age of seventeen also stares out from the mug shot. She asks us to consider the many and varied experiences of women criminalised in the early twentieth century for offences against good order.

We started this story with Esther Warden - the 'worst female character' – and her long list of convictions from 1900-1939. It was Esther who drew me into the lives of the women detailed in this book. In many respects she embodies their different experiences. Esther Warden was charged with all major offences against good order. She was a drunk, idle and disorderly, obscene, offensive, loitering vagrant. She was an abandoned, 'fallen' woman who spent most of each year in prison or sent around the various Homes and refuges. Esther recognised the cycle of offending that confined her to a life between the prison and the streets. Yet she was no shrinking violet when reflecting on it. When she was arrested in 1911 she told the magistrate the 'police are all against me'.[1065] In 1918 she told the court how hard it was to get off the streets and get work when she had spent so much time in gaol.[1066]

From the lost and lonely to the vulnerable and violent, female offenders were a mix of victims and instigators. They were women caught in a cycle of offending by a society that confined them to an identity as 'bad' women unable to conform to social expectations of the good, moralistic, domestic, maternal woman. They were criminalised for offences against good order but in the double standards of the time it was their inability to conform to ideals of female respectability that stigmatised them further still.

The point of the story being told in this book is not to like or dislike the female offenders but to understand the world into which they found themselves in the first decades of the twentieth century and the circumstances leading to their extensive criminal records. I hope their stories also encourage some thinking about the similar ways in which women, though not criminalised in the same way, are still more likely than men to be stigmatised for public behaviour that doesn't conform to social expectations. We might like to think that we have progressed since the early years of the twentieth century. Repeat cases of public drunkenness, for example, no longer carry a long prison sentence of up to six months. The justice system now looks to rehabilitation over incarceration. However, I'm not convinced that if Esther Warden showed up on the streets of Perth and Fremantle today – drunk, loud and creating a disturbance – that society would not single her out as a deviant woman. Men and women regularly making a public spectacle will gain some attention, whether from bystanders, police or the media, but the gaze is longer and more critical when directed towards a woman.

Notes

Introduction

1 Magistrate's comments when sentencing an elderly female offender to a term in prison for drunkenness. See: *The West Australian*, Monday 15 January 1923, p. 7.

2 *The Sunday Times*, 17 April 1904, p. 8.

3 'PERTH POLICE COURT', *The West Australian*, Thursday 4 April 1918, p. 6.

4 Esther Warden's record in the Fremantle Prison Register runs over four pages from the turn of the century to 1939. See: Gaol Department Western Australia, 'F209 Warden, Esther Muriel', *Register of Local Prisoners (Female)*, State Records Office of Western Australia (herein SROWA), Perth, Series 678, Consignment 4186/1.

5 Raelene Davidson, 'Prostitution in Perth and Fremantle and on the Eastern Goldfields, 1895-September 1939', MA thesis, University of Western Australia, 1980, p. 51.

6 Ibid, pp. 94-95.

7 'HIGH LIFE IN KING STREET: A PESTILENT SPOT', *West Australian*, Wednesday 4 July 1900, p. 2.

8 *West Australian*, Saturday 3 January 1903.

9 *The Sunday Times*, 17 April 1904, p. 8.

10 Statistics compiled from annual registers covering the years 1900-1939. See: Government Statistician's Office, *Statistical Register of Western Australia*, Perth, 1903-1939.

11 Adam Graycar and Peter Grabosky, 'Trends in Australian Crime and Criminal Justice' in Graycar and Grabosky (ed), *The Cambridge Handbook of Australian Criminology*, Cambridge University Press, Cambridge, 2009 digitally printed version, p. 15.

12 Clive Emsley, *Crime and Society in England, 1750-1900*, Pearson Longman, Harlow, 2005 (third edition), p. 24.

13 'PERTH POLICE COURT', *The West Australian*, Monday 6 June 1921, p. 6.

14 Graycar and Grabosky, 'Trends in Australian Crime and Criminal Justice', p. 9.

15 Quoted in Emsley, *Crime and Society in England*, p. 30.

16 Emsley, *Crime and Society in England*, pp. 26-32.

17 Ibid, p. 32

18 Statistics compiled from annual registers covering the years 1900-1939.

See: Government Statistician's Office, *Statistical Register of Western Australia,* Perth, 1903-1939.

19   Ibid.
20   Jill Julius Matthews, *Good & Mad Women: The Historical Construction of Femininity in Twentieth-Century Australia,* Allen & Unwin, North Sydney, 1984, (1992 edition), p. 125.
21   'THE DRUNKARD AS CRIMINAL' in *West Australian,* Monday 18 January 1915, p. 6.
22   Raelene Davidson, 'Dealing with the "Social Evil": Prostitution and the police in Perth and on the Eastern goldfields, 1895-1924 in Kay Daniels (ed) *So Much Hard Work: Women and Prostitution in Australian History,* Fontana Books, Sydney, 1984, pp. 165-166.
23   Matthews, *Good & Mad Women,* pp. 111-112.
24   Ibid, p. 122.
25   Martha Vicinus, 'Introduction: The perfect Victorian Lady' in Martha Vicinus (ed), *Suffer and Be Still: Women in the Victorian Age,* Indiana University Press, Bloomington and Indianapolis, 1973 edition, p. xiv.
26   'May and Her Mugs', *Truth,* 3 January 1920.
27   Matthews, *Good & Mad Women,* pp. 175-176
28   'CITY POLICE COURT', *The West Australian,* 1 August 1900, p. 3.
29   'POLICE COURTS', *The West Australian,* Tuesday 17 June 1902, p. 2.
30   'Women in Policing Exhibit', *Journal for Women and Policing,* no. 11 (2002): 43.
31   'POLICE COURTS', *The West Australian,* Tuesday 1 July 1902, p. 7.
32   Barry Godfrey, Paul Lawrence and Chris A. Williams, *History & Crime,* Sage Publication, London, 2008, chapter 8: Linda Mahood, *Policing gender, class and family, Britain 1840-1940,* UCL Press, London, 1995, pp. 5-6.
33   Margaret Tennent, '"Magdalens and moral imbeciles": Women's homes in nineteenth-century New Zealand', *Women's Studies International Forum,* Vol. 9, Issues 5-6 (1986): 491-502.
34   Fremantle Arts Centre, *Absence of Evidence: Fremantle Arts Centre 15 May – 26 June 1994,* Fremantle Arts Centre, Fremantle, 1994, p. 4.
35   Geraldine Byrne, *Built on a Hilltop: A History of the Sisters of the Good Shepherd in Western Australia 1902-2002,* Sisters of the Good Shepherd, Leederville.
36   'THE HOME OF THE GOOD SHEPHERD: A NOBLE INSTITUTION. THE OPENING CEREMONY', *The West Australian,* Monday 3 October 1904, p. 5.
37   Ibid.
38   'POLICE COURTS', *The West Australian,* 4 July 1902, p. 3.
39   Alana Piper, '"A growing vice": the *Truth* about Brisbane girls and drunkenness in the early twentieth century', *Journal of Australian Studies,* 34 (2010): 486.
40   Shani D'Cruze and Louisa A. Jackson, 'Introduction: "Vice" and "Virtue"?' in Shani D'Cruze and Louisa A. Jackson (eds) *Women, Crime and Justice in England Since 1660,* Palgrave Macmillan, Hampshire, 2009, p. 3.
41   Description of Mary Collins in *The West Australian,* Tuesday 2 September 1919, p. 6.
42   The Perth and Fremantle underclass are defined within general concepts of the underclass. See: John Welshman, *Underclass,* Hambledon

Continuum, London, 2006, pp. xii-xv.

43 See chapter one for discussions of the underclass and dangerous classes and references to the following works: Lydia Morris, *The Dangerous Classes: the underclass and social citizenship*, Routledge, London and New York, 1994; Rita Farrell, 'Dangerous Women: constructions of female criminality in Western Australia 1915-1945', Murdoch University, PhD Thesis, 1997.

44 Graeme Davison, David Dunstan and Chris McConville (eds) *The Outcasts of Melbourne: Essays in Social History*, Allen & Unwin, Sydney, 1985, p. 23.

45 'POLICE COURTS', *The West Australian*, Thursday 16 October 1902, p. 2.

46 'PERTH POLICE COURT', *The West Australian*, Wednesday 25 September 1925, p. 5.

47 Mary S. Hartman, *Victorian Murderesses: A True History of Thirteen Respectable French and English Women Accused of Unspeakable Crimes*, Robson Books, London, 1985, p. 2.

48 Vicinus, 'Introduction: The Perfect Victorian Lady', p. x, xiii.

49 Matthews, *Good & Mad Women*, p. 88.

50 Marilyn Lake, *Getting Equal: The history of Australian feminism*, Allen & Unwin, St Leonard's, 1999, p. 53.

51 Lake, *Getting Equal*, p. 53.

52 Martin Crotty, *Making the Australian Male: middle-class masculinity 1870-1920*, Melbourne University Press, Carlton, 2001.

53 Angela Woollacott, 'Gender and Sexuality' in Deryck M. Schreuder and Stuart Ward, *Australia's Empire*, Oxford University Press, Oxford, 2008, (2009 edition), pp. 324-325.

54 Quoted in Patricia Grimshaw, 'Gendered Settlements' in Patricia Grimshaw, Marilyn Lake, Ann McGrath and Marian Quartly, *Creating a Nation 1788-1990*, McPhee Gribble, Ringwood, 1994, p. 178.

55 Jill Julius Matthews, 'Dancing modernity' in Barbara Caine and Rosemary Pringle (eds) *Transitions: New Australian Feminisms*, Allen & Unwin, St Leonards, 1995, pp. 74- 87.

56 Lake, *Getting Equal*, p. 93.

57 Ibid, pp. 93-94.

58 Melissa Bellanta, *Larrikins A History*, University of Queensland Press, St. Lucia, 2012, chapter 2; Melissa Bellanta, 'The larrikin girl', *Journal of Australian Studies*, 34:4 (2010): 499-512.

59 Bellanta, *Larrikins*, p. 47.

60 Rae Frances, *Selling Sex: A Hidden History of Prostitution*, UNSW Press, Sydney, 2007, p. 29.

61 Frances, *Selling Sex*, pp. 244-247.

62 Bill Marks, *The Fall of the Dice*, Fremantle Arts Centre Press, Fremantle, pp. 8-10.

63 Matthews, *Good & Mad Women*, p. 88.

64 D'Cruze and Jackson, 'Introduction: "Vice" and "Virtue"?', p. 1.

65 Judith A. Allen, *Sex & Secrets: Crimes involving Australian Women since 1880*, Oxford University Press, Oxford and New York, 1990, p. 11.

66 Janet K. Swim and Lauri L. Hyers, 'Sexism' in Todd D. Nelson (ed) *Handbook of Prejudice, Stereotyping and Discrimination*, Psychology Press,

New York, 2009, p. 407.

67 'A Police Court Identity' in *The West Australian,* Wednesday 17 March 1920, p. 8.
68 Yvonne Jewkes, *Crime and Media,* Sage Publications, London, 2004, p. 3.
69 Jewkes, *Crime and Media,* p. 200.
70 Davidson, 'Prostitution in Perth and Fremantle and on the Eastern Goldfields', p. 51.

Chapter 1

71 From an article on crime and vice on the streets of Perth around Melbourne Road (later renamed Milligan Street). See: *The Sunday Times,* Sunday 22 September 1912, p. 6.
72 'HIGH LIFE IN KING STREET: A PESTILENT SPOT', *The West Australian,* Wednesday 4 July 1900, p. 2.
73 Western Australia Police Department, *Report of Const. Robert Love. Reg. No.63. Relative to three houses in King St East Side near Hay Street,* SROWA, Perth, Consignment No. 430, Item no. 1900/1744.
74 *Truth,* Saturday 25 July 1903, p. 2.
75 R. T. Appleyard, 'Foundation and Early Settlement' in Jenny Gregory and Jan Gothard (eds) *Historical Encyclopedia of Western Australia,* University of Western Australia Press, Crawley, 2009, p. 383.
76 Simon J. Nevill, *Perth and Fremantle: Past and Present,* Simon Nevill Publications, Fremantle, 2007, p. 15.
77 *The Perth Gazette,* Saturday 24 April 1847.
78 Quoted in Ron Davidson, *Fremantle Impressions,* Fremantle Arts Centre Press, Fremantle, 2008, p. 18.
79 Quoted in Gwen Chessel, *Alexander Collie: Colonial Surgeon, Naturalist & Explorer,* UWA Publishing, Crawley, 2008, p. 118.
80 Chessel, *Alexander Collie,* p. 188.
81 Davidson, *Fremantle Impressions,* p. 95.
82 Ibid, p. 60
83 Ibid, pp. 61, 64
84 Ibid, p. 64
85 Ibid, p. 63
86 Ibid, pp. 166-168
87 Ibid, pp. 233-234, 246.
88 Ibid, p. 224.
89 *Statistical Register of Western Australia,* Part 1 – Population and Vital Statistics, Population, Government Printer, Perth, p. 3.
90 *The Western Mail,* Thursday 22 November 1928, p. 55;
91 *Pocket Year Book of Western Australia, 1923,* Government Printer, Perth, 1923, pp. 15-16.
92 Ibid, pp. 16, 20, 21.
93 Ibid, pp. 16, 20, 21.
94 Similar to urban patterns set out in: Michael Pacione, *Urban Geography: a global perspective,* Routledge, London, 2005, pp. 142-143.

95   C. T. Stannage, *The People of Perth: A Social History of Western Australia's Capital City*, Carroll's for Perth City Council, Perth, 1979, p. 243.

96   Stannage, *The People of Perth*, pp. 288, 293.

97   Davidson, *Fremantle Impressions*, p. 16

98   Charles Wittenoom's sketch of Fremantle around 1838 in Davidson, *Fremantle Impressions*, p. 14.

99   Reece, 'Fremantle', pp. 387-388.

100   Davidson, *Fremantle Impressions*, p. 122.

101   Patricia M. Brown, *The Merchant Princes of Fremantle: The rise and decline of a colonial elite 1870-1900*, University of Western Australia Press, Nedlands, 1996.

102   Davidson, *Fremantle Impressions*, p. 78.

103   Ibid, p. 30; Reece, 'Fremantle', p. 388.

104   Ibid.

105   Reece, 'Fremantle', p. 388.

106   Ibid.

107   Geoffrey Bolton, *Land of Vision and Mirage: Western Australia since 1826*, University of Western Australia Press, Crawley, 2008, p. 53.

108   Pacione, *Urban Geography: a global perspective*, p. 167.

109   Stannage, *The People of Perth*, p. 243.

110   *The West Australian*, Friday 15 December 1899, p. 6.

111   Stannage, *The People of Perth*, p. 241

112   *The West Australian*, Saturday 20 November 1937, p. 22.

113   Stannage, *The People of Perth*, p. 246.

114   *Truth*, Saturday 27 February 1904, p. 2.

115   *The West Australian*, Friday 14 November 1919, p. 6.

116   *The West Australian*, Saturday 18 September 1935, p. 20.

117   *The West Australian*, Wednesday 17 June 1936, p. 16.

118   *The Sunday Times*, Sunday 5 December 1920, p. 5.

119   *The Sunday Times*, Sunday 3 October 1920, p. 1.

120   Ibid.

121   Ibid.

122   *Sunday Times*, Sunday 8 July 1928, p. 9.

123   Ibid.

124   *The Sunday Times*, Sunday 1 February 1903, p. 13.

125   Penelope Hetherington, *Paupers, Poor Relief and Poor Houses in Western Australia 1829-1910*, UWA Publishing, Crawley, 2009.

126   *The West Australian*, 22 June 1927.

127   Davidson, *Fremantle Impressions*, p. 234.

128   Ibid, p. 233.

129   *The West Australian*, Friday 14 November 1919, p. 6.

130   Welshman, *Underclass*, pp. xii-xiii

131   Ibid, p. xvii

132   Ibid, p. xv

133   Robert MacDonald, 'Dangerous Youth and the dangerous class' in MacDonald (Ed), *Youth, the 'Underclass' and Social Exclusion*, Routledge, London, p. 4. Also quoted in: Robert MacDonald, '"Essentially Barbarians"? Researching the "Youth Underclass" in Pamela Davies, Peter

Francis and Victor Jupp (Ed), *Doing Criminological research*, Sage, London and Singapore, 2011, p. 181.

134 Welshman, *Underclass*, p. xiv

135 Emsley, *Crime and Society in Twentieth-Century England*, Pearson Longman, London, 2011, p. 55.

136 Eric H. Monkkonen, *The Dangerous Class: Crime and Poverty in Columbus, Ohio, 1860-1885*, Harvard University Press, Cambridge, 1975, pp. 151-152

137 Morris, *The Dangerous Classes*.

138 Ibid.

139 *The West Australian*, Tuesday 20 April 1880, p. 2.

140 Welshman, *Underclass*, pp. xxviii, 1

141 *Western Australian Parliamentary Debates*, 8th Parliament, 1st Session, 1911, pp. 283, 286.

142 *The West Australian*, Friday 19 July 1912, p. 6

143 *The West Australian*, Friday 14 November 1919, p. 6.

144 *The West Australian*, Wednesday 10 September 1913, p. 5

145 Monkkonen, *The Dangerous Class*, p. 150.

146 Ibid, p. 151

147 Ibid, p. 152

148 *The West Australian*, Wednesday 26 March 1930, p. 7.

149 Welshman, *Underclass*, pp. xvii-xviii

150 Roger Hopkins Burke, 'Policing Bad Behaviour – Interrogating the Dilemmas' in Judith Rowbotham and Kim Stevenson (eds) *Behaving Badly: Social Panic and Moral Outrage, Victorian and Modern Parallels*, Ashgate, Hampshire, 2003, p. 70

151 *Truth*, Sunday 16 December 1928, p. 13.

152 William Julius Wilson writing on the underclass in 1985, quoted in Welshman, *Underclass*, p. xiii

153 *Truth*, Saturday 15 August 1903, p. 2.

154 *The West Australian*, Monday 9 September 1929, p. 6.

155 *The West Australian*, Saturday 3 June 1911, p. 9.

156 *Truth*, Saturday 15 August 1903, p. 4.

157 *The West Australian*, Tuesday 28 March 1916, p. 6; *The West Australian*, Wednesday 12 April 1916, p. 8.

158 *The West Australian*, Saturday 8 June 1907, p. 2.

159 Ibid.

160 *The Sunday Times*, Sunday 21 July 1912, p. 11.

161 Ibid.

162 *The Sunday Times*, Sunday 5 December 1920, p. 5.

163 Magistrate quoted in *The West Australian*, Wednesday 26 July 1933, p. 16.

164 *The West Australian*, Monday 18 October 1937, p. 11.

165 Stannage, *The People of Perth*, p. 291.

166 One example: *The West Australian*, Tuesday 21 December 1897, p. 3.

167 *The West Australian*, Wednesday 22 May 1935, p. 17.

168 *The Sunday Times*, Sunday 22 September 1912, p. 6.

169 Ibid.

170 *The West Australian*, Monday 3 January 1938, p. 3.

171 *The West Australian*, Saturday 18 November 1905, p. 8.

172   *The West Australian,* Monday 27 November 1905, p. 4.
173   *Truth,* Saturday 7 May 1904, p. 3.
174   *The West Australian,* Tuesday 24 April 1917, p. 5.
175   *The West Australian,* Thursday 29 march 1900, p. 2.
176   'Lawlessness in the Streets', *The West Australian,* Tuesday 31 August 1909, p. 2.
177   Ibid.
178   *Truth,* Saturday 29 August 1903, p. 2.
179   *The West Australian,* Friday 2 July 1926, p. 8.
180   'A Fremantle Robbery', *The West Australian,* Thursday 1 January 1903, p. 4.
181   *The West Australian,* Friday 4 April, p. 10.
182   Ibid.
183   Ibid.
184   *The West Australian,* Tuesday 12 May 1903, p. 7.
185   Davidson, *Fremantle Impressions,* p. 228
186   Ibid, p. 240
187   *Truth,* Sunday 16 December 1928, p. 13.
188   Pacione, *Urban Geography: a global perspective,* pp. 62-62; Stannage, pp. 152, 291.
189   Department of Indigenous Affairs, *Noongar Prohibited Map 1927-1954,* State Records Office. Online: South West Aboriginal Land and Sea Council, Kaartdijin Noongar: Sharing Noongar Culture, *Contact History: Impacts of the law from the Aboriginal Protection Act 1905 onwards,* http://www. noongarculture.org.au/media/6233/prohibitedmap%20final%20new.pdf, accessed 15 February 2011.
190   *The West Australian,* Monday 29 July 1918, p. 6.
191   Gaol Department Western Australia, 'F317 – Morris, Lilly', Series 678, Con 4186/1.
192   *The West Australian,* Wednesday 13 May 1903, p. 4.
193   *Truth,* Saturday 7 May 1904, p. 193.
194   Ibid.
195   *Statistical Register of Western Australia,* Part 1 – Population and Vital Statistics, Population, Government Printer, Perth, p. 3.
196   Stannage, *The People of Perth,* p. 139.
197   Ian vanden Driesen, 'Population' in Gothard and Gregory, *Historical Encyclopedia of Western Australia,* p.713.
198   *Pocket Year Book of Western Australia, 1939,* Government Printer, Perth, 1939, p. 24.
199   Analysis of warrant notices in the *Western Australian Police Gazette,* various volumes, 1900-1939, State Library of Western Australia, Perth.
200   Farrell, 'Dangerous Women', p. 118.
201   Analysis of apprehensions and discharge details in the *Western Australian Police Gazette,* various volumes, 1900-1939; Gaol Department Western Australia, *'Register of Local Prisoners (Male),* SROWA, Perth, Series 672, Consignment 4173/1-15.
202   Comparison of discharge details in the *Western Australian Police Gazette,* various volumes, 1900-1939 with crime reports in *The West Australian, Truth and The Sunday Times,* 1900-1939.

203 Gaol Department Western Australia, *Register of Local Prisoners (Female)*, Series 678, Con 4186/1-2.

204 Farrell, 'Dangerous Women', p. 392.

205 *The West Australian*, 7 December 1935; *The West Australian*, 5 November 1937.

206 Farrell, 'Dangerous Women', p. 370: *Statistical Register of Western Australia, Part VIII– Law, Crime, etc*, Government Printer, Perth, volumes 1900-1940.

207 Julia Ball, David Kelsall and John Pidgeon, *Statewide Survey of Hotels, 1829-1939: Southern Region Western Australia, volume 1*, National Trust Australia (WA), November 1997, p. 18.

208 Ball, Kelsall and Pidgeon, *Statewide Survey of Hotels, 1829-1939*, p. 18.

209 *The West Australian*, Thursday 12 February 1903, p. 2.

210 *The West Australian*, Friday 3 February 1939, p. 16.

211 *The West Australian*, Wednesday 28 February 1900, p. 7.

212 *The West Australian*, Monday 22 October 1913, p. 8.

213 *The West Australian*, Friday 22 January 1915, p. 4.

214 *The West Australian*, Friday 14 February 1913, p. 8.

215 *The West Australian*, Thursday 14 March 1918, p. 6.

216 Farrell, 'Dangerous Women', p. 368.

217 *Truth*, Saturday 25 July 1903, p. 2.

218 Ibid.

219 Rae Frances, *Selling Sex: A Hidden History of Prostitution*, UNSW Press, Sydney, 2007, p. 205.

220 Elaine McKewon, 'The historical geography of prostitution in Perth, Western Australia', *Australian Geographer*, vol. 34 (3), pp. 300-302.

221 Frances, *Selling Sex*, p. 208.

222 McKewon, 'The historical geography of prostitution', p. 299.

223 Davidson, 'Prostitution in Perth and Fremantle and on the Eastern Goldfields, 1895-September 1939', p. 95.

224 Frances, *Selling Sex*, p. 211.

225 *The West Australian*, Thursday 20 November 1902, p. 5.

226 *The Sunday Times*, Sunday 8 February 1903, p. 1.

227 *The West Australian*, Tuesday 5 August 1919, p. 6.

228 *The West Australian*, Monday 9 February 1925, p. 9.

229 *The West Australian*, Monday 25 August 1902, p. 5.

230 Lynette McLaughlin, personal communication with author, 5 January 2012. Lynette is Mary Ann Sweetman's great-granddaughter.

231 *The West Australian*, Thursday 13 February 1930, p. 7.

232 Marks, *The Fall of the Dice*, p. 8.

233 *West Australian*, Saturday 3 January 1903.

234 *The West Australian*, Friday 13 June 1902, p. 7.

235 *The West Australian*, Wednesday 16 January 1918, p. 6.

236 *The West Australian*, Wednesday 8 January 1930, p. 7.

Chapter 2

237 Police description of Esther Warden used as title to report of court appearance: *The Daily News*, Tuesday 20 January 1914, p. 3.

238 *The Daily News*, Tuesday 20 January 1914, p. 3; Gaol Department Western Australia, 'F209 Warden, Esther Muriel', Series 678, Con 4186/1.

239 Rules for Female Prisoners, Fremantle Prison in Fremantle Arts Centre, *Absence of Evidence*, p. 3.

240 *The Sunday Times*, Sunday 9 January 1915, p. 7.

241 Government of Western Australia, *Registry of Births, Deaths & Marriages*, Birth Certificate for Warden, Stillborn Male, Registration Number 1737; 'PRISONERS DISCHARGED' in *Police Gazette Western Australia For The Year 1911*, Government Printer, Perth, 5 April 1911.

242 Gaol Department Western Australia, 'F209 Warden, Esther Muriel', Series 678, Con 4186/1.

243 *The West Australian*, Thursday 4 April 1918, p. 6.

244 Rica Erickson, *Dictionary of Western Australians 1829-1914*, volume 4, part 2, L-Z, University of Western Australia Press, Nedlands, 1985, p. 1745.

245 *Statistical Register of Western Australia for the year 1916*, 'Part 1, Population and Vital Statistics', p. 3.

246 Frances, *Selling Sex*, p. 129.

247 Ibid, p. 144.

248 *The West Australian*, Wednesday 5 December 1900, p. 5.

249 Government of Western Australia, *Registry of Births, Deaths & Marriages*, Birth Certificate for Warden, Stillborn Male, Registration Number 1737.

250 Gaol Department Western Australia, '6127 – O'Sullivan, Plunkett', *Register of Local Prisoners (Male)– Fremantle Prison*, Series 672, 4173/7.

251 *The West Australian*, Wednesday 20 February 1901, p. 12.

252 'F206 – Claffey, Eva', *Register of Local Prisoners (Female)– Fremantle Prison*, Series 678, Con 4186/1.

253 *The West Australian*, Friday 12 April 1901, p. 3.

254 *Truth*, Saturday 23 January 1904, p. 3; *Truth*, 13 February 1904, p. 2.

255 *The West Australian*, Wednesday 2 July 1902, p. 5.

256 *Truth*, Saturday 23 January 1904, p. 3; *Truth*, 13 February 1904, p. 2.

257 *The West Australian*, Thursday 12 February 1903, p. 2.

258 *The West Australian*, Wednesday 15 April 1903, p. 3.

259 *The West Australian*, Thursday 30 July 1903, p. 7.

260 *The Daily News*, Wednesday 29 July 1903, p. 1.

261 *The West Australian*, Monday 13 June 1904, p. 3.

262 Gaol Department Western Australia, '6127 – O'Sullivan, Plunkett', Series 672, Con 4173/7.

263 Ibid.

264 *The West Australian*, Friday 6 April 1906, p. 3.

265 *The West Australian*, Tuesday 23 February 1909, p. 7.

266 Gaol Department Western Australia, 'F209 Warden, Esther Muriel', Series 678, Con 4186/1.

267 *The West Australian*, Thursday 17 June 1909, p. 6.

268 *The West Australian*, Thursday 9 June 1910, p. 2.

269 Editorial, *The Western Australian Times*, Tuesday 28 March 1876, p. 2

270 *The Perth Gazette*, Saturday 24 April 1847, p. 3.

271 Ibid.

272 Ross Fitzgerald and Trevor L. Jordan, *Under the Influence: A history of*

alcohol in Australia, ABC Books, Sydney, 2009, p. 89.

273   Joseph Christensen, 'Drinking' in Gothard and Gregory, *Historical Encyclopedia of Western Australian History*, p. 287.

274   Mariana Valverde, *Diseases of the Will: Alcohol and the Dilemmas of Freedom*, Cambridge University Press, Cambridge, 1998, p. 39.

275   *The West Australian*, Thursday 7 May 1914, p. 6.

276   Ibid.

277   Farrell, 'Dangerous Women', p. 376.

278   Ibid.

279   Valverde, *Diseases of the Will*, p. 15.

280   *The West Australian*, Saturday 1 February 1930, p. 7.

281   *The Sunday Times*, Sunday 3 July 1927, p. 6.

282   G. F. Bodington, 'On The Control and Restraint of Habitual Drunkards', *The British Medical Journal*, 28 August 1875, pp. 255-256.

283   Valverde, *Diseases of the Will*, p. 48

284   Neil Davie, 'Born for Evil? Biological Theories of Crime in Perspective' in Shlomo Giova Shoham, Paul Knepper and Martin Kett, *International Handbook of Criminology*, CRC Press, London and New York, p. 38.

285   Davie, 'Born for Evil?', pp. 23-24

286   *The West Australian*, Friday 4 December 1903, pp. 5-6.

287   *The Sunday Times*, Sunday 12 February 1905, p. 9.

288   Police description of Esther Warden used as title to report of court appearance: *The Daily News*, Tuesday 20 January 1914, p. 3.

289   Quentin Beresford, 'Drinkers and the Anti-Drink Movement in Sydney', 1870-1930, PhD Thesis, Australian National University, Canberra, July 1984, pp. 1-2.

290   Fitzgerald and Jordan, *Under the Influence*, p. 156.

291   Annette Davis, 'Good Times for All? Popular Entertainment and Class Consciousness in Western Australian Society During the Interwar Years' in Jenny Gregory (ed) *Western Australia Between the Wars 1919-1939: Studies in Western Australian History*, (11) June 1990, p. 68.

292   Charlie Fox, '"Bookies, Punters and Parasites: Off-Course Betting, Conflict and Consensus in Western Australia Between the Wars"', *Western Australia Between the Wars 1919-1939: Studies in Western Australian History*, no. 11 (June 1990): p. 62.

293   Stuart Macintyre, *The Succeeding Age 1901-1942: The Oxford History of Australia*, Oxford University Press, Melbourne, 1993, p. 110.

294   *The West Australian*, Tuesday 8 November 1910, p. 2.

295   Ibid.

296   Ibid.

297   Dianne Davidson, 'Woman's Christian Temperance Union' in Gothard and Gregory, *Historical Encyclopedia of Western Australian History*, pp. 935-936.

298   Joyce R. Henderson, *The Strength of the White Ribbon: a year-by-year record of the centennial history of the Woman's Christian Temperance Union of Western Australia (Inc.): ten decades of service for "God, home and humanity" 1892-1992*, The Union, West Perth, c.1992, p. 60.

299   Fitzgerald and Jordan, *Under the Influence*, pp. 145-150.

300 Ibid, pp. 151-153.
301 Henderson, *The Strength of the White Ribbon*, p. 18.
302 Ibid, p. 21.
303 Ibid, p. 13.
304 Ibid, p. 59.
305 Ibid, p. 46.
306 Government Statistician's Office, *Statistical Register of Western Australia*, Perth, 1903-1920.
307 Fitzgerald and Jordan, *Under the Influence*, pp. 173-174.
308 Ibid, p.33.
309 Ibid, p. 36.
310 Ibid, pp. 37-39.
311 Ibid, p. 200.
312 Ibid, p. 170.
313 Public drunkenness was eventually decriminalised in Western Australia in 1989.
314 Farrell, 'Dangerous Women', p. 354.
315 Ibid, p. 368.
316 Satyanshu K. Mukherjee, *Crime Trends in Twentieth Century Australia*, Allen & Unwin, Sydney, 1981, pp. 82-83.
317 Mukherjee, *Crime Trends in Twentieth Century Australia*, p. 83.
318 Ibid.
319 Ibid, p. 80.
320 Ibid, p. 83.
321 Farrell, 'Dangerous Women', p. 114.
322 Ibid.
323 Ibid, p. 363.
324 *The West Australian*, Sunday 21 March 1908, p. 6.
325 Gaol Department Western Australia, 6127 – O'Sullivan, Plunkett', Series 672, Con 4173/7.
326 *The West Australian*, Sunday 21 March 1908, p. 6.
327 *The Daily News*, Wednesday 29 September 1909, p. 6.
328 *The Daily News*, Monday 26 September 1910, p. 5.
329 *The Daily News*, Friday 21 June 1912, p. 3.
330 *The Daily News*, Monday 5 February 1912, p. 2.
331 *The Daily News*, Tuesday 17 October 1911, p. 1.
332 Ibid.
333 *The Daily News*, 31 October 1907, p. 7.
334 *The Daily News*, Monday 26 September 1910, p. 5.
335 R. Reece and R. Pascoe, *A Place of Consequence: A Pictorial History of Fremantle*, Fremantle Arts Centre Press, Fremantle, 1983, p. 50.
336 Ibid, p. 57.
337 Ibid, pp. 71-73.
338 Ibid, p. 79.
339 Ibid, p. 75; Davidson, *Fremantle Impressions*, p. 126.
340 Reece and Pascoe, *A Place of Consequence*, p. 53.
341 *The Sunday Times*, Sunday 27 July 1913, p. 15.
342 *The Daily News*, Monday 27 September 1909, p. 5.

343   Keith Amos, *The Fenians in Australia*, UNSW Press, Kensington, 1988, pp. 86-87, 147-173.

344   Ibid, pp. 227-257.

345   *The West Australian*, Friday 22 January 1915, p. 4.

346   Gaol Department Western Australia, 'F209 Warden, Esther Muriel', Series 678, Con 4186/1.

347   *The West Australian*, Thursday 4 April 1918, p. 6.

348   *The Daily News*, Tuesday 17 October 1911, p. 1.

349   *The Daily News*, Friday 21 June 1912, p. 3.

350   *The West Australian*, Thursday 4 April 1918, p. 6.

351   Bolton, *Land of Vision and Mirage*, p. 103; Suzanne Welborn, 'First World War' in Gothard and Gregory, *Historical Encyclopedia of Western Australia*, p. 370.

352   *The West Australian*, Saturday 4 December 1918, p. 8.

353   *The West Australian*, Monday 8 January 1917, p. 8.

354   *The West Australian*, Monday 1 October 1917, p. 3.

355   *The West Australian*, Saturday 4 December 1918, p. 8.

356   Gaol Department Western Australia, 'F209 Warden, Esther Muriel', Series 678, Con 4186/1.

357   *Hull Advertiser*, 26 August 1836. Quoted in Emsley, *Crime and Society in England 1750-1900*, p. 99.

358   *The West Australian*, Saturday 13 May 1922, p. 10.

359   Emsley, *Crime and Society in England 1750-1900*, p. 99.

360   *The Daily News*, Tuesday 20 August 1918, p. 6.

361   *The West Australian*, Tuesday 23 November 1926, p. 6.

362   *Truth*, Saturday 5 March 1904, p. 2.

363   Ibid.

364   Robert Bell, 'The Subculture Concept: A Genealogy' in Shoham, Knepper and Kett, *International Handbook of Criminology*, pp. 153, 165.

365   Robert K. Merton's work in the late 1930s quoted in Bell, 'The Subculture Concept: A Genealogy', p. 167.

366   Bell, 'The Subculture Concept: A Genealogy', p. 167.

367   Beresford, 'Drinkers and the Anti-Drink Movement in Sydney', p. 19.

368   Davison, Dunstan and McConville, *The Outcasts of Melbourne*; Julie Kimber, ''A nuisance to the community': policing the vagrant woman', *Journal of Australian Studies*, 34:3 (2010): 275-293.

369   *The Sunday Times*, 12 February 1905, p. 9.

370   Quoted in Farrell, 'Dangerous Women', p. 368.

371   Fitzgerald and Jordan, *Under the Influence*, p. 99.

372   Farrell, 'Dangerous Women', p. 376.

373   Ibid, p. 368.

374   Peter Kelly, Jenny Advocat, Lyn Harrison and Christopher Hickey, *Smashed! The Many Meanings of Intoxication and Drunkenness*, Monash University Publishing, Clayton, 2011, p. 11.

375   *Truth*, Saturday 5 March 1904, p. 2.

376   *The Sunday Times*, Sunday 9 January 1915, p. 7.

377   *Western Australian Police Gazette*, 5 April 1911, p. 103

Chapter 3

378   *The West Australian*, Monday 26 March 1917, p. 5.

379   *The West Australian*, Tuesday 27 March 1917, p. 7.

380   Ibid.

381   'PERTH POLICE COURT', *West Australian*, Tuesday 27 March 1917, p. 7.

382   Gaol Department Western Australia, 'F322 Sweetman, Mary Ann', Series 678, Con 4186/1.

383   'AS OUR OWN SEE US', *The West Australian*, Monday 27 March 1916, p. 3.

384   Ibid.

385   Ibid.

386   'THE SINFUL CITY OF PERTH', *The West Australian*, Wednesday 6 December 1922, p. 10.

387   *The West Australian*, Wednesday 12 January 1927, p. 10.

388   'DRUNKENNESS IN THE CITY', *The West Australian*, Thursday 12 January 1933, p. 5

389   Government Statistician's Office, *Statistical Register of Western Australia*, 1903-1939.

390   Kelly, Advocat, Harrison and Hickey, *Smashed! The Many Meanings of Intoxication and Drunkenness*, p. xvi.

391   For a similar study of this see: Kimber, ''A nuisance to the community', 281.

392   Rica Erickson (ed), *Bicentennial Dictionary of Western Australians, pre-1829-1888, volume IV, R-Z*, University of Western Australia Press, Nedlands, 1988, p. 2995.

393   Erickson, *Bicentennial Dictionary of Western Australians, pre-1829-1888, volume IV, R-Z*, p. 2995.

394   Ibid; Emma Mould is featured on the Welcome Walls at the Maritime Museum in Victoria Quay, Fremantle.

395   Erickson, *Bicentennial Dictionary of Western Australians, pre-1829-1888, volume IV, R-Z*, p. 2995.

396   Ibid.

397   *The West Australian*, Wednesday 15 January 1902, p. 3.

398   *The West Australian*, Wednesday 5 February 1902, p. 11.

399   *The West Australian*, Wednesday 17 February 1904, p. 3.

400   *The West Australian*, Wednesday 7 September 1904, p. 9.

401   Lynette McLaughlin, personal communication with author, 5 January 2012.

402   *The West Australian*, Thursday 5 January 1905, p. 3.

403   Ibid.

404   Ibid.

405   Gaol Department Western Australia, 'F322 Sweetman, Mary Ann', *Register of Local Prisoners (Female)*, Series 678, Con 4186/1.

406   Lynette McLaughlin, personal communication with author, 5 January 2012.

407   'WOMEN IN PRISON: Conditions at Fremantle Gaol Described', *The West Australian*, Tuesday 27 April 1937, p. 6.

408   *The Daily News*, Friday 12 November 1912, p. 8.

409   *The Daily News,* Wednesday 20 March 1907, p. 11.

410   *The Daily News,* Monday 28 July 1913, p. 4.

411   *The Daily News,* Saturday 20 November 1909, p. 8.

412   Fitzgerald and Jordan, *Under the Influence,* p. 190.

413   Quoted in Emsley, *Crime and Society in England, 1750-1900,* pp. 92-93.

414   Gregory Durstan, *Victims and Viragos: Metropolitan Women, Crime and the Eighteenth-Century Justice System,* Arima Publishing, Suffolk, 2007.

415   Kelly, Advocat, Harrison and Hickey, *Smashed!,* p. 7.

416   *The West Australian,* Friday 15 January 1915, p. 9.

417   Ibid.

418   'THE DRUNKARD AS CRIMINAL' in *West Australian,* Monday 18 January 1915, p. 6.

419   Kelly, Advocat, Harrison and Hickey, *Smashed!,* p. 7.

420   Quoted in Farrell, 'Dangerous Women', p. 354.

421   'THE DRUNKARD AS CRIMINAL' in *West Australian,* Monday 18 January 1915, p. 6.

422   Ibid.

423   Valverde, *Diseases of the Will,* pp. 51-52.

424   *The West Australian,* Wednesday 7 February 1917, p. 8.

425   Valverde, *Diseases of the Will,* pp. 54, 59.

426   Ibid, p. 57.

427   Stannage, *The People of Perth,* pp. 88-89.

428   Ibid.

429   Ibid, p. 89.

430   *The West Australian,* Tuesday 8 January 1884, p. 3.

431   Norman Megahey, 'Convict labour' in Gregory and Gothard, *Historical Encyclopedia of Western Australia,* pp. 236-237.

432   Stannage, *The People of Perth,* p. 89.

433   *The West Australian,* Tuesday 8 January 1884, p. 3.

434   Stannage, *The People of Perth,* p. 89.

435   Details of Mary Ann's family life and the murder to follow in this section are taken from reports of the murder and trial. See: *The West Australian,* Saturday 20 October 1883, p. 3; *The West Australian,* Tuesday 8 January 1884, p. 3; *The West Australian,* Thursday 10 January 1884, p. 3; *The West Australian,* Tuesday 22 January 1884, p. 3.

436   *The West Australian,* Thursday 24 January 1884, p. 3.

437   Mary Ann Sweetman's court evidence reported in *The West Australian,* Saturday 7 December 1918, p. 8.

438   *Western Australian Police Gazette,* 5 April 1911, p. 103

439   *The West Australian,* Monday 1 December 1913, p. 6.

440   Ibid.

441   *The Daily News,* Monday 28 August 1911, p. 3.

442   *The Daily News,* Tuesday 12 September 1911, p. 3.

443   Gaol Department Western Australia, 'F565 Mattson, Sarah Jane', Series 678, Con 4186/2; Registry of Births, Deaths and Marriages, Sarah Jane Mattson - Death Certificate WA, 2474/1951.

444   Registry of Births, Deaths and Marriages, Sarah Jane Mattson - Death Certificate WA, 2474/1951.

445 Frances Finnegan, *Poverty and prostitution: A Study of Victorian prostitutes in York*, Cambridge, Cambridge University Press, 1979, p. 24.

446 Ibid, p. 23.

447 Ibid, p. 24.

448 Ibid.

449 Gaol Department Western Australia, 'F565 Mattson, Sarah Jane', Series 678, Con 4186/2.

450 William Power Register Report, unpublished family history, courtesy of Diane Anderson, 2011.

451 *The Western Mail*, Thursday 22 November 1928, p. 55; Stannage, *The People of Perth*, p. 193.

452 William Power Register Report, unpublished family history, courtesy of Diane Anderson, 2011.

453 Stannage, *The People of Perth*, pp. 240-241.

454 Ibid, p. 273.

455 Unnamed Mattson Triplet, Death Certificate WA, 2642/1904; Unnamed Mattson Triplet, Birth Certificate WA, 6183/1904; Unnamed Mattson Triplet, Death Certificate WA, 2640/1904.

456 Frederick G. Mattson, Birth Certificate WA, 57/1906; William Frederick, Birth Certificate WA, 56/1906.

457 William Power Register Report, unpublished family history, courtesy of Diane Anderson, 2011.

458 Birth Certificate WA, 23/1913; Birth Certificate WA, 24/1913.

459 *The West Australian*, Wednesday 21 May 1913, p. 1.

460 *The West Australian*, Wednesday 21 May 1913, p. 1.

461 Susannah Thompson, 'Infant mortality' in Gregory and Gothard, *Historical Encyclopedia of Western Australia*, p. 478.

462 Thompson, 'Infant mortality', p. 478.

463 *The West Australian*, Thursday 12 June 1902, p. 2.

464 *The West Australian*, Thursday 5 February 1914, p. 8.

465 *The West Australian*, Tuesday 9 February 1915, p. 5.

466 *The West Australian*, Saturday 1 May 1915, p. 10.

467 *The West Australian*, Saturday 18 September 1915, p. 10.

468 Gaol Department Western Australia, 'F565 Mattson, Sarah Jane', Series 678, Con 4186/2; William Power Register Report, unpublished family history, courtesy of Diane Anderson, 2011.

469 *The West Australian*, Wednesday 10 May 1916, p. 1.

470 *The Police Gazette*, 5 July 1916, p. 183.

471 *The West Australian*, Monday 4 December 1916, p. 4.

472 Ernest Carl Mattson, Death Certificate WA, 96/1918

473 *The West Australian*, Monday 20 January 1919, p .8.

474 *The Daily Mail*, Saturday 18 January 1919, p. 10.

475 *Hull Advertiser*, 26 August 1836. Quoted in Emsley, *Crime and Society in England 1750-1900*, p. 99.

476 *The West Australian*, Monday 4 December 1922, p. 10.

477 *The West Australia*, Monday 21 May 1923, p. 8.

478 *The Daily Mail*, Thursday 20 December 1923, p. 6.

479 *The West Australian*, Friday 1 August 1924, p. 13.

480   *The West Australian,* Tuesday 10 February 1925, p. 8.
481   *The West Australian,* Monday 14 December 1925, p. 11.
482   *The West Australian,* Friday 4 January 1929, p. 17.
483   *The West Australian,* Tuesday 10 February 1931, p. 9.
484   *The West Australian,* 6 October 1943, p. 2; *The West Australian,* 9 October 1943, p. 4.
485   William Power Register Report, unpublished family history, courtesy of Diane Anderson, 2011.
486   Fitzgerald and Jordan, *Under the Influence,* p. 214.
487   Ibid, p. 284.
488   Marilyn Lake, 'The Politics of Respectability: Identifying the Masculinist Context', *Historical Studies,* vol. 22, no 86 (1986): 116-131; Judith Allen, '"Mundane Men": Historians, Masculinity and Masculinism', *Historical Studies,* vol. 22, no 89 (1987): 617-628.
489   Kelly, Advocat, Harrison and Hickey, *Smashed!,* pp. xvi, 131.
490   Ibid, p. 131.
491   Chris McConville, 'Rough Women, Respectable Men and Social Reform: A Response to Lake's "Masculinism"', Historical Studies, vol. 22, no 88 (1987): 432-440.
492   Clare Wright, *Beyond the Ladies Lounge: Australia's Female Publicans,* Melbourne University Press, Melbourne, 2003.
493   *The West Australian,* Tuesday 18 October 1927, p. 12.
494   Kelly, Advocat, Harrison and Hickey, *Smashed!,* p. 9.
495   Ibid, p. 184.
496   Ibid, p. 127.
497   Ibid, p. 134.
498   Ibid, p. 129.
499   *The Sunday Times,* Sunday 9 October 1910, p. 5.
500   *Truth,* Sunday 30 December 1928, p. 7.
501   'Dangerous student drinking targeted in hard-hitting campaign', *Perthnow,* 26 September 2009, http://www.perthnow.com.au/news/western-australia/dangerous-student-drinking-targeted-in-hard-hitting-campaign/story-e6frg153-1225779965829, viewed 23 February 2011; 'WA young in binge drinking crisis', *Perthnow,* 22 June 2007, http://www.perthnow.com.au/news/western-australia/wa-young-in-binge-drinking-crisis/story-e6frg13u-1111113810177, viewed 23 February 2011.
502   Glenn Cordingley, 'Bank worker Eva Scolaro, 24, jailed for glassing, disfiguring young woman', *Perthnow,* 14 April 2010, retrieved from http://www.perthnow.com.au/news/bank-worker-eva-scolaro-24-jailed-for-glassing-another-woman/story-e6frg12c-1225853627296.
503   Cynthia A. Robbins and Steven S. Martin, 'Gender, Styles of Deviance and Drinking Problems', *Journal of Health and Social Behaviour,* vol. 34 (December 1993): 304.
504   Ibid, p. 305.
505   Ibid, p. 317.

Chapter 4

506　*The West Australian*, Wednesday 25 September 1918, p. 5.

507　*The West Australian*, Friday 13 December 1918, p. 8.

508　*The West Australian*, Saturday 15 November 1919, p. 12.

509　*The West Australian*, Wednesday 25 September 1918, p. 5.

510　Helen J. Self, *Prostitution, Women and the Misuse of the Law: The Fallen Daughters of Eve*, Frank Cass Publishers, London, 2003, pp. 24-25

511　Nina Auerbach, 'The Rise of the Fallen Woman', *Nineteenth-Century Fiction*, Vol. 35, No. 1 (June, 1980): 34.

512　Frances, *Selling Sex*, p. 162.

513　Emsley, *Crime and Society in England, 1750-1900*, p. 97.

514　Lucy Bland, 'Purifying' the public world: feminist vigilantes in late Victorian England', *Women's History Review*, 1:3(1992): 399.

515　Emsley, *Crime and Society in England, 1750-1900*, p. 79.

516　Matthews, *Good & Mad Women*, p. 125.

517　Vicinus, 'Introduction', p. xiv.

518　Matthews, *Good & Mad Women*, p. 127.

519　Bland, '"Purifying" the public world', p. 407.

520　*The Sunday Times*, Sunday 12 January 1908, p. 6.

521　*The West Australian*, Tuesday 23 December 1902, p. 7.

522　Paula Bartley, *Prostitution: Prevention and Reform in England, 1860-1914*, Routledge, London, 2000, pp. 1-2.

523　Ibid, p. 2.

524　G. O. Ferguson, letter to *The West Australian*, Saturday 16 February 1918, p. 8.

525　*The West Australian*, Monday 4 September 1899, p. 6.

526　Durstan, *Victims and Viragos*, pp. 198-199.

527　Bartley, *Prostitution: Prevention and Reform in England, 1860-1914*, p. 4.

528　Edward J. Bristow, *Vice and vigilance: purity movements in Britain since 1700*, Gill and Macmillan, Dublin, 1977, p. 189.

529　Kathleen Barry, *Female Sexual Slavery*, Prentice Hall, New Jersey, 1979, p. 283.

530　Roger Matthews, *Prostitution, Politics & Policy*, p. 39.

531　Ibid, p. 491.

532　Rae Frances, '"White Slaves" and White Australia: Prostitution and Australian Society', *Australian Feminist Studies*, Vol. 19, No. 44 (July 2004): 189-190.

533　Frances Ibid.

534　Frances, *Selling Sex*, p. 140.

535　Piper, '"A growing vice": the *Truth* about Brisbane girls and drunkenness in the early twentieth century', p. 490.

536　Jan Ryan, 'She lives with a chinaman': Orient-ing 'white' women in the courts of law', *Journal of Australian Studies*, 23:60 (1990): p. 151.

537　Ibid, p.151.

538　*Truth*, 3 January 1920.

539　*The Sunday Times*, Sunday 20 March 1910, p. 3.

540　Ryan, 'She lives with a chinaman': Orient-ing 'white' women in the courts of law', p. 159.

541 *Truth*, Saturday 23 January 1904, p. 3; *Truth*, 13 February 1904, p. 2.
542 *The West Australian*, Wednesday 2 July 1902, p. 5.
543 Frances, *Selling Sex*, p. 190.
544 Davidson, 'Prostitution in Perth and Fremantle and on the Eastern Goldfields, 1895-September 1939', p. 8.
545 *The West Australian*, Wednesday 14 June 1905, p. 2.
546 *The West Australian*, Friday 27 January 1905, p. 6.
547 Melissa Hope Ditmore, *Prostitution and Sex Work*, Greenwood, Oxford, 2011, p. 43.
548 Frances, *Selling Sex*, p. 129.
549 *Statistical Register of Western Australia for the year 1916*, 'Part 1, Population and Vital Statistics', p. 3.
550 Frances, *Selling Sex*, p. 129.
551 Ibid, p. 144.
552 Davidson, 'Dealing with the "Social Evil": Prostitution and the police in Perth and on the Eastern goldfields, 1895-1924', pp. 163-164.
553 *The West Australian*, Friday 29 May 1925, p. 8.
554 Henderson, *The Strength of the White Ribbon*, p. 131.
555 Frances, *Selling Sex*, p. 162.
556 Bartley, *Prostitution: Prevention and Reform in England, 1860-1914*, p. 2.
557 *The West Australian*, Friday 2 March 1900, p. 2.
558 Ibid.
559 *The Sunday Times*, Sunday 12 January 1908, p. 6.
560 Matthews, *Good & Mad Women*, p. 127.
561 Davidson, 'Dealing with the "Social Evil"', p. 165.
562 Ibid.
563 Davidson, 'Prostitution in Perth and Fremantle and on the Eastern Goldfields, 1895-September 1939', p. 8.
564 *The Sunday Times*, Sunday 12 January 1908, p. 6.
565 Davidson, 'Prostitution in Perth and Fremantle and on the Eastern Goldfields, 1895-September 1939', p. 47.
566 Ibid, p. 42.
567 Davidson, 'Dealing with the "Social Evil"', p. 173.
568 Farrell, 'Dangerous Women', p. 387.
569 Davidson, 'Prostitution in Perth and Fremantle and on the Eastern Goldfields, 1895-September 1939', p. 114.
570 *The West Australian*, Saturday 29 September 1900, p. 2.
571 Ibid.
572 Ibid.
573 Chris McConville, 'The location of Melbourne's prostitutes', *Historical Studies*, vol. 19, no. 74 (1980), p. 90.
574 Davidson, 'Dealing with the "Social Evil"', p. 118.
575 Davidson, 'Prostitution in Perth and Fremantle and on the Eastern Goldfields, 1895-September 1939', pp. 58-59.
576 Frances, *Selling Sex*, p. 211.
577 Ibid.
578 Davidson, 'Prostitution in Perth and Fremantle and on the Eastern Goldfields, 1895-September 1939', p. 95.

579　Frances, *Selling Sex*, p. 211.
580　*The West Australian,* Wednesday 3 September 1919, p. 8; *The West Australian,* Friday 12 September 1919, p. 8.
581　Judith Walkowitz, *Prostitution and Victorian Society: Women, class and the state,* Cambridge University Press, Cambridge, 1980 (2001 edition), p. 3.
582　Frances, *Selling Sex*, p. 131.
583　*The West Australian,* Tuesday 5 August 1919, p. 6.
584　Sharyn L. Anleu, *Deviance, Conformity & Control,* Pearson, Frenchs Forest, 2006, p. 198.
585　Ibid.
586　Frances, *Selling Sex*, p. 154.
587　Davidson, 'Dealing with the "Social Evil", p. 90.
588　Ibid, pp. 8, 90.
589　Police vs Winter, Perth Police Court Minutes, Acc. 1386/41, 10 July 1919.
590　*The West Australian,* Saturday 19 October 1901, p. 11.
591　Matthews, *Good & Mad Women*, p. 142.
592　*The Sunday Times,* Sunday 9 October 1910, p. 5.
593　Frances, *Selling Sex*, p. 155.
594　Davidson, 'Prostitution in Perth and Fremantle and on the Eastern Goldfields, 1895-September 1939', p. 98.
595　Davidson, 'Dealing with the "Social Evil", pp. 120, 110-111.
596　Ibid, p. 116.
597　Ibid.
598　*The Sunday Times,* Sunday 3 October 1909, p. 4.
599　SROWA, 'F209 – Warden, Esther Muriel', *Register of Local Prisoners (Female)*– Gaol Department Western Australia, Perth, Series 678, Con 4186/1.
600　*The West Australian,* Wednesday 5 December 1900, pp. 4-5.
601　Walkowitz, *Prostitution and Victorian Society*, p. 4.
602　*The Sunday Times,* Sunday 12 January 1908, p 6.
603　Davidson, 'Dealing with the "Social Evil", p. 174.
604　*The Sunday Times,* Sunday 12 January 1908, p. 6.
605　Ibid.
606　Frances, *Selling Sex*, p. 158.
607　*The Sunday Times,* Sunday 12 January 1908, p. 6.
608　Ibid.
609　Paul McHugh, *Prostitution and Victorian Social Reform,* Croom Helm, London, 1980, p. 17.
610　E. M. Sigsworth and T. J. Wyke, 'A Study of Victorian Prostitution and Venereal Disease' in Vicinus, *Suffer and Be Still,* p. 77.
611　Bland, '"Purifying" the public world', p. 400.
612　D'Cruze and Jackson, *Women, Crime and Justice in England since 1660,* p. 72.
613　Davidson, 'Dealing with the "Social Evil", p. 175.
614　Frances, *Selling Sex*, p. 209.
615　Davidson, 'Dealing with the "Social Evil", p. 179.
616　*Health Act 1911, Amendment Act 1915,* Part XI – Venereal diseases and disorders affecting the generative organs, http://www.austlii.edu.au/au/legis/wa/consol_act/ha191169/, accessed 31 October 2011.

617 Davidson, 'Prostitution in Perth and Fremantle and on the Eastern Goldfields, 1895-September 1939', p. 74.

618 Davidson, 'Dealing with the "Social Evil", pp. 176-177.

619 *The West Australian,* Friday 28 January 1916, p. 5.

620 Frances, *Selling Sex,* pp. 162, 197.

621 *The Sunday Times,* Sunday 21 July 1918, p. 5.

622 Ibid.

623 Ibid.

624 Ibid.

625 Anleu, *Deviance, Conformity & Control,* p. 197.

626 Select Committee findings in *The West Australian,* Friday 1 March 1918, p. 7.

627 Frances, *Selling Sex,* p. 160.

628 *The West Australian,* Saturday 16 February 1918, p. 8.

629 Ibid.

630 *The West Australian,* Saturday 9 July 1938, p. 22.

631 Legislative Council of Western Australia, *REPORT OF THE ROYAL COMMISSION APPOINTED TO INQUIRE INTO The Administration of the Municipal Council of the City of Perth,* Government Printer, Perth, 1938, p. 16.

Chapter 5

632 *Truth,* 3 January 1920.

633 Ibid.

634 Ibid.

635 Ibid.

636 Ibid.

637 Ibid.

638 Gaol Department Western Australia, 'F459 – Ahern, May', Series 678, Con 4186/1.

639 Matthews, *Good & Mad Women,* p. 125.

640 Roger Matthews, *Prostitution, Politics & Policy,* Routledge-Cavendish, Hoboken, 2008, p. 22.

641 For a similar study see: Finnegan, *Poverty and prostitution: A study of Victorian prostitutes in York.*

642 Bartley, *Prostitution: Prevention and Reform in England, 1860-1914,* p. 3.

643 Walkowitz, *Prostitution and Victorian Society,* p. 8.

644 Anleu, *Deviance, Conformity & Control,* pp. 197-198.

645 Detectives Office, *Return of brothels and prostitutes in the city, November 14, 1898,* SROWA, Perth, Consignment No. 430, Item no. 1898/4389.

646 Walkowitz, *Prostitution and Victorian Society,* p. 15.

647 Detectives Office, *Return of brothels and prostitutes in the city, November 14, 1898,* Item no. 1898/4389.

648 *The West Australian,* Saturday 19 October 1901, p. 11.

649 Gaol Department Western Australia, *Register of Local Prisoners (Female0,* Series 678, Con 4186/1-2; Davidson, 'Prostitution in Perth and Fremantle

and on the Eastern Goldfields, 1895-September 1939', chapter 5; various newspaper crime reports from *The West Australian, The Sunday Times* and *Truth,* 1900-1939.

650   Cresswell was born in Sydney. See: Gaol Department Western Australia, 'F173 Cresswell, Emily', Series 678, Con 4186/1; *The West Australian,* Monday 16 May 1904, p. 2.

651   Davidson, 'Prostitution in Perth and Fremantle and on the Eastern Goldfields, 1895-September 1939', chapter 5.

652   Ibid, p. 139.

653   Gaol Department Western Australia, *Register of Local Prisoners (Female)– Gaols Department, Western Australia,* SROWA, Series 672, Con 4186/1-2.

654   Davidson, 'Prostitution in Perth and Fremantle and on the Eastern Goldfields, 1895-September 1939', p. 142.

655   *The West Australian,* Monday 1 October 1917, p. 3.

656   Davidson, 'Prostitution in Perth and Fremantle and on the Eastern Goldfields, 1895-September 1939', p.167.

657   *Kalgoorlie Western Argus,* Tuesday 28 June 1904, p. 26.

658   Ibid.

659   *The West Australian,* Monday 27 March 1905, p. 2.

660   *Police Gazette,* 1 September 1909, p. 227; *Police Gazette,* 8 December 1909, p. 320.

661   *Kalgoorlie Western Argus,* Tuesday 6 October 1908, pp. 16-17; *The West Australian,* 14 April 1915, p. 9.

662   Gaol Department Western Australia, *Register of Local Prisoners (Female),* Series 672, Con 4186/1-2; Davidson, 'Prostitution in Perth and Fremantle and on the Eastern Goldfields, 1895-September 1939', pp. 150-151.

663   Ibid.

664   Ibid, p. 145.

665   Frances, *Selling Sex,* p. 131.

666   Gaol Department Western Australia, 'F186 – Dreardon, Kate', Series 678, Con 4186/1.

667   Quoted in Davidson, 'Prostitution in Perth and Fremantle and on the Eastern Goldfields, 1895-September 1939', p. 168.

668   Ibid, p. 169.

669   Ibid, p. 52.

670   Ibid.

671   Gaol Department Western Australia, *Register of Local Prisoners (Female),* Series 678, Con 4186/1-2; Analysis of apprehensions and discharge details in the *Western Australian Police Gazette,* annual volumes 1900-1939; Crime reports in *The West Australian, Truth* and *The Sunday Times,* 1900-1939;

672   Walkowitz, *Prostitution and Victorian Society,* p. 15.

673   Gaol Department Western Australia, *Register of Local Prisoners (Female),* Series 678, Con 4186/1-2.

674   Walkowitz, *Prostitution and Victorian Society,* p. 16.

675   *Truth,* 12 September 1903, p. 2.

676   Michael Ryan, *Prostitution in London, with a comparative view of that of Paris and New York,* H. Baillière, London, 1839, p. 170.

677   Walkowitz, *Prostitution and Victorian Society,* p. 13.

678 Ibid.
679 Bartley, *Prostitution: Prevention and Reform in England, 1860-1914*, p. 10.
680 Davidson, 'Prostitution in Perth and Fremantle and on the Eastern Goldfields, 1895-September 1939', p. 166.
681 Havelock Ellis, *The Criminal*, Walter Scott, London, 1890, p. 218.
682 *Truth*, Saturday 23 January 1904, p. 3; *Truth*, 13 February 1904, p. 2.
683 Gaol Department Western Australia, 'F206 Claffey, Eva', Series 678, Con 4186/1.
684 Bartley, *Prostitution: Prevention and Reform in England, 1860-1914*, p. 6.
685 Ibid.
686 Anleu, *Deviance, Conformity and Control*, p. 199.
687 Davidson, 'Prostitution in Perth and Fremantle and on the Eastern Goldfields, 1895-September 1939', pp. 160-161.
688 Ibid, p. 162.
689 Ibid, p. 160.
690 *Truth*, 23 July 1904, p. 2.
691 Ibid.
692 *The West Australian*, Tuesday 8 September 1914, p. 9.
693 Gaol Department Western Australia, *Register of Local Prisoners (Female)*, Series 678, Con 4186/1-2
694 Bartley, *Prostitution: Prevention and Reform in England, 1860-1914*, p. 9.
695 *The West Australian*, 12 April 1923, p. 9.
696 Gaol Department Western Australia, 'F865 - Bonner, Sadie', Series 678, Con 4186/2.
697 Kay Daniels, 'Introduction' in Daniels, *So Much Hard Work*, p. 2.
698 Gaol Department Western Australia, 'F136 Jones, Rose', Series 678, Con 4186/1.
699 Gaol Department Western Australia, 'F173 Cresswell, Emily', Series 678, Con 4186/1.
700 Gaol Department Western Australia, 'F459 Ahern, May', Series 678, Con 4186/2.
701 Analysis of warrants, apprehensions and discharge details in the *Western Australian Police Gazette*, annual volumes 1900-1939.
702 Gaol Department Western Australia, *Register of Local Prisoners (Female)*, Series 678, Con 4186/1-2.
703 *The West Australian*, Thursday 19 June 1902, p. 7.
704 *The West Australian*, Tuesday 14 January 1913, p. 8.
705 Gaol Department Western Australia, 'F249 'Warnock, Mary Louisa', Series 678, Con 4186/1.
706 *The West Australian*, Wednesday 15 July 1903, p. 3.
707 *The West Australian*, Monday 16 January 1911, p. 3; *The West Australian*, Monday 18 September 1911, p. 5.
708 *The West Australian*, Friday 18 June 1909, p. 5; *The West Australian*, 4 September 1909, p. 9.
709 *The Sunday Times*, Sunday 26 January 1913, p. 11.
710 Gaol Department Western Australia, 'F249 'Warnock, Mary Louisa', Series 678, Con 4186/1.
711 SROWA, *Register of Local Prisoners (Female)*– Gaol Department Western

Australia, Perth, Series 678, Con 4186/1-2.

712   Davidson, 'Prostitution in Perth and Fremantle and on the Eastern Goldfields, 1895-September 1939', p. 168.

713   Gaol Department Western Australia, 'F322 Sweetman, Mary Ann', Series 678, Con 4186/1.

714   Gaol Department Western Australia, 'F44 – Lawson, Alice', Series 678, Con 4186/1.

715   Ibid.

716   *The West Australian*, Friday 23 January 1903, p. 7.

717   *The Inquirer and Commercial News*, Friday 19 May 1899, p. 13.

718   *The Inquirer and Commercial News*, Friday 5 April 1901, p. 15.

719   *The Inquirer and Commercial News*, Friday 3 May 1901, p. 15.

720   *The West Australian*, Friday 23 January 1903, p. 7.

721   *Kalgoorlie Western Argus*, Tuesday 26 July 1904, p. 15.

722   *The West Australian*, Monday 2 June 1902, p. 7.

723   *The West Australian*, Monday 1 January 1900, p. 4.

724   Geoffrey Pearson, *Hooligan: A History of Respectable Fears*, Palgrave Macmillan, Hampshire, 1983.

725   Bellanta, 'The larrikin girl', p. 499.

726   Larry Writer, *Razor: Tilly Devine, Kate Leigh and the razor gangs*, Pan Macmillan, Sydney, 2001, p. 8.

727   *The West Australian*, Monday 18 May 1925, p. 7.

728   *Truth*, Saturday 7 May 1904, p. 3.

729   Ibid.

730   Ibid.

731   *Truth*, Saturday 23 January 1904, p. 3.

732   Ibid.

733   Bellanta, 'The larrikin girl', p. 500.

734   Andrew Davies, '"THESE VIRAGOES ARE NOT LESS CRUEL THAN THE LADS": Young women, Gangs and Violence in Late Victorian Manchester and Salford', *British Journal of Criminology*, vol. 39, no. 1, (1999): 74; Bellanta, 'The larrikin girl', pp. 499-512.

735   Emsley, *Crime and Society in England, 1750-1900*, p. 96.

736   Ibid, p. 80.

737   Gaol Department Western Australia, 'F284 Forrester, Minnie', Series 678, Con 4186/1.

738   *The West Australian*, Thursday 2 April 1903, p. 7.

739   Ibid.

740   *The West Australian*, Friday 6 December 1901, p 3.

741   *The West Australian*, Wednesday 29 July 1908, p. 3.

742   Ibid.

743   *The West Australian*, Wednesday 22 April 1914, p. 11.

744   Bellanta, 'The larrikin girl', p. 504.

745   Ibid.

746   A Reverend of the Home of the Good Shepherd in Leederville referred to inmates there as 'wretched and sinful' in the eyes of the world but remained the children of Jesus. See: *The West Australian*, Monday 3 October 1904, p. 5.

747 Steve Garton, The rise of the therapeutic state: Psychiatry and the system of criminal jurisdiction in New South Wales, 1890–1940', *Australian Journal of Politics and History*, vol. 32, no. 3 (1986): 378–388.

748 Wimshurst, 'Punishment, Welfare and Gender Ordering in Queensland, 1920-1940', 312.

749 Eamonn Carrabine, Pam Cox, Maggy Lee, Ken Plummer and Nigel South, *Criminology: A sociological introduction,* Routledge, London and New York, 2009 (second edition), pp. 293-294.

750 Ibid, pp. 359-362.

751 Ibid, p. 309.

752 Ibid, p. 309.

753 Ibid, pp. 309-310.

754 Ibid, p. 310.

755 Kerry Wimshurst, 'Punishment, Welfare and Gender Ordering in Queensland, 1920-1940', *The Australian and New Zealand Journal of Criminology*, vol. 34, no. 3 (2002): 310.

756 D'Cruze and Jackson, *Women, Crime and Justice in England Since 1660*, p. 137.

757 Carrabine *et al., Criminology,* p. 313.

758 Ibid, p. 363-364.

759 *The West Australian,* Wednesday 24 July 1912, p. 4.

760 Wimshurst, 'Punishment, Welfare and Gender Ordering in Queensland, 1920-1940', 323.

761 *The Sunday Times,* Sunday 31 July 1904, p. 10.

762 Sherrill Cohen, *The Evolution of Women's Asylums since 1500: From Refuges for Ex-Prostitutes to Shelters for Battered Women,* Oxford University Press, New York and Oxford, 1992, pp. 3, 8, 166.

763 Ibid, p. 6.

764 Ibid, p. 165.

765 Kellie Louise Toole, 'Innocence and Penitence Hand Clasped in Hand: Australian Catholic Refuges for Penitent Women, 1848-1914', Master of Arts Thesis, University of Adelaide, 2010, p. 2.

766 Ibid, p. 16.

767 Ibid, p. 3.

768 Ibid, p. 27.

769 Ibid, p. 63.

770 Ibid, p. 67.

771 Ibid, pp. 64-65.

772 Ibid, p. 79.

773 *The Daily News,* Thursday 4 April 1912, p. 6.

774 John O'Brien, 'The Founding and Early Years of the Convent of the Good Shepherd, Leederville' in John Tonkin (ed) *Religion and Society in Western Australia: Studies in Western Australian History,* vol. 9 (1987): 46.

775 Toole, 'Innocence and Penitence Hand Clasped in Hand: Australian Catholic Refuges for Penitent Women, 1848-1914', p. 9.

776 *The West Australian,* Monday 3 October 1904, p. 5.

777 Ibid.

778 O'Brien, 'The Founding and Early Years of the Convent of the Good

Shepherd, Leederville', p. 47.

779   Ibid.

780   Ibid.

781   Toole, 'Innocence and Penitence Hand Clasped in Hand: Australian Catholic Refuges for Penitent Women, 1848-1914', p. 22.

782   *The Daily News*, Monday 4 March 1912, p. 5.

783   Toole, 'Innocence and Penitence Hand Clasped in Hand: Australian Catholic Refuges for Penitent Women, 1848-1914', p. 22.

784   Cohen, *The Evolution of Women's Asylums since 1500*, p. 169.

785   *The West Australian*, Saturday 23 March 1907, p. 4.

786   Ibid.

787   *The West Australian*, Thursday 4 April 1907, p. 3.

788   O'Brien, 'The Founding and Early Years of the Convent of the Good Shepherd, Leederville', p. 49.

789   Toole, 'Innocence and Penitence Hand Clasped in Hand: Australian Catholic Refuges for Penitent Women, 1848-1914', p. 56.

790   'POLICE COURTS', *The West Australian*, 4 July 1902, p. 3.

791   Frances, *Selling Sex*, p. 162.

792   *The West Australian*, Wednesday 20 July 1904, p. 3.

793   Gaol Department Western Australia, 'F173 – Cresswell, Emily', Series 678, Con 4186/1.

794   *The West Australian*, Wednesday 20 July 1904, p. 3.

795   Ibid.

796   Cohen, *The Evolution of Women's Asylums since 1500*, p. 169.

797   *The West Australian*, Thursday 1 June 1922, p. 8.

798   Frances, *Selling Sex*, pp. 166-167.

799   Wimshurst, 'Punishment, Welfare and Gender Ordering in Queensland, 1920-1940', 325.

800   Ibid, 322.

801   *The West Australian*, Monday 15 January 1923, p. 7.

802   *Kalgoorlie Western Argus*, Tuesday 21 January 1908, p. 35.

803   Gaol Department Western Australia, 'F459 Ahern, May', Series 678, Con 4186/1.

804   Daniels, 'Introduction' in Daniels, *So Much Hard Work*, p. 4.

805   *The West Australian*, Wednesday 15 January 1908, p. 5.

806   *The Sunday Times*, 20 March 1910, p. 3.

807   *The West Australian*, Wednesday 13 October 1900, p. 3.

Chapter 6

808   Description of Rose Skivington, *The West Australian*, Saturday 20 June 1903, p. 11.

809   Ibid.

810   Mary Anne Poutanen, 'The Homeless, the Whore, the Drunkard and the Disorderly: Contours of Female Vagrancy in the Montreal Courts, 1810-1842' in Kathryn McPherson, Cecilia Morgan and Nancy M. Forrestell (eds) *Gendered Pasts: Historical Essays Femininity and Masculinity in Canada*,

University of Toronto Press, Toronto, 2003, pp. 29-30.

811 Anne O'Brien, *Poverty's Prison: The Poor in New South Wales, 1880-1918*, Melbourne University Press, Melbourne, 1988; Christina Twomey, *Deserted and Destitute: Motherhood, Wife Desertion and Colonial Welfare*, Australian Scholarly Publishing, Melbourne, 2002.

812 Poutanen, 'The Homeless, the Whore, the Drunkard and the Disorderly: Contours of Female Vagrancy in the Montreal Courts, 1810-1842', p. 30.

813 Pacione, *Urban Geography: a global perspective*, p. 167.

814 Stannage, *The People of Perth*, p. 269.

815 Ibid.

816 *The West Australian*, Tuesday 5 January 1904, p. 4.

817 Heather Shore, *Artful Dodgers: Youth and Crime in early nineteenth-century London*, Boydell Press, London, 1998, p. 35.

818 Statistics compiled from annual registers covering the years 1900-1939. See: Government Statistician's Office, *Statistical Register of Western Australia*, Perth, 1903-1939.

819 *The West Australian*, Tuesday 18 October 1927, p. 12.

820 *The West Australian*, Wednesday 12 July 1905, p. 8.

821 *The West Australian*, Saturday 4 December 1915, p. 8.

822 *The West Australian*, Saturday 19 December 1989, p. 6.

823 *The West Australian*, Friday 12 November 1920, p. 8.

824 *The West Australian*, Thursday 16 October 1902, p. 2.

825 Gaol Department Western Australia, 'F21- Pirie, Ellen', Series 678, Con 4186/2.

826 Ibid.

827 Ibid.

828 Ibid.

829 Ibid.

830 *The West Australian*, Tuesday 3 August 1915, p. 4.

831 *The West Australian*, Friday 14 March 1919, p. 6.

832 *The West Australian*, 9 September 1921, p. 8.

833 It seems the couple had a daughter. Davey, under name Caroline Hewitt, was mentioned in an assault case as mother to Elizabeth C. Hart. Annie Owens was charged in 1917 with assaulting Caroline and Elizabeth at their residence in Royal Street, East Perth. Davey's entry in the Fremantle Prison Register lists Caroline Hewitt as an alias. See: *The West Australian*, Tuesday 19 March 1918, p. 4; *The West Australian*, Wednesday 7 February 1917, p. 8; Gaol Department Western Australia, 'F614 – Davey, Elizabeth', Series 678, Con 4186/2.

834 *The West Australian*, Monday 30 May 1938, p. 11.

835 Susanne Davies, '"Ragged, Dirty...Infamous and Obscene" The Vagrant in Late-Nineteenth-Century Melbourne' in David Phillips and Susanne Davies (eds) *A Nation of Rogues: Crime, Law and Punishment in Colonial Australia*, Melbourne University Press, Carlton, 1994, p. 145.

836 Western Australian Parliament, *Western Australian Police Act (1892)*, sections 65, 66 and 67.

837 Gaol Department Western Australia, 'F173 – Cresswell, Emily', Series 678,

Con 4186/2.

838 Stannage, *The People of Perth*, p. 268.

839 Statistics compiled from annual registers covering the years 1900-1939. See: Government Statistician's Office, *Statistical Register of Western Australia*, Perth, 1903-1939.

840 Anleu, *Deviance, Conformity and Control*, p. 403

841 Kellie Abbott and Celia Chesney, '"I AM A POOR WOMAN": Gender, Poor Relief and the Poorhouse in Late Nineteenth and Early Twentieth-Century Western Australia' in Charlie Fox (ed) *Studies in Western Australian History: Social Policy in Western Australia*, no, 25 (2007): 27.

842 Davies, '"Ragged, Dirty...Infamous and Obscene" The Vagrant in Late-Nineteenth-Century Melbourne', p. 147.

843 Abbott and Chesney, '"I AM A POOR WOMAN": Gender, Poor Relief and the Poorhouse in Late Nineteenth and Early Twentieth-Century Western Australia', pp. 29-30.

844 Welshman, *Underclass*, p. 2.

845 Ibid, p. 3.

846 Ibid, p. 21.

847 Ibid, p. 22.

848 Beier, '"Takin' It to the Streets": Henry Mayhew and the Language of the Underclass in Mid-Nineteenth-Century London', pp. 93-94.

849 *The West Australian*, Saturday 19 January 1929, p. 4.

850 Welshman, *Underclass*, p. 32.

851 Ibid, p. 43.

852 Anleu, *Deviance, Conformity and Control*, p. 402.

853 Paul Ocobock, 'Introduction: Vagrancy and Homelessness in a Global and Historical Perspective' in A. L. Beier and Paul Ocobock (eds), *Cast Out: Vagrancy and Homelessness in Global and Historical Perspective*, Ohio University Press, Ohio, 2008, p. 2.

854 Kimber, '"A nuisance to the community': policing the vagrant woman', p. 278.

855 Anleu, *Deviance, Conformity and Control*, p. 403.

856 Davies, '"Ragged, Dirty...Infamous and Obscene" The Vagrant in Late-Nineteenth-Century Melbourne', p. 143.

857 Ocobock, 'Introduction: Vagrancy and Homelessness in a Global and Historical Perspective', p. 9.

858 Ibid, p. 26.

859 Davies, '"Ragged, Dirty...Infamous and Obscene" The Vagrant in Late-Nineteenth-Century Melbourne', p. 145.1

860 *The West Australian*, Tuesday 2 September 1919, p. 6.

861 *The West Australian*, Friday 10 August 1900, p. 6.

862 *The West Australian*, Tuesday 4 July 1899, p. 3.

863 Wimshurst, 'Punishment, Welfare and Gender Ordering in Queensland, 1920-1940', 310.

864 Ibid, 311.

865 Gaol Department Western Australia, 'F15 – Curedale, Marion', Series 678, Con 4186/1.

866 Mary Ann Hardman and George Curedale Marriage Record, *Births, Deaths and Marriages Western Australia,* http://www.bdm.dotag.wa.gov.au/_apps/pioneersindex/default.aspx, accessed 28 February 2012.

867 Ward Curedale, *Vikings, Normans and Lancashire Lords,* Ward Curedale, Applecross, 2008, p. 363.

868 Ibid, p. 364.

869 Ibid.

870 Ibid, pp. 373-374.

871 Ibid, p. 368.

872 Ibid, p. 401.

873 Ibid, p. 405.

874 Ibid, p. 409.

875 George Curedale Death Certificate, *Births, Deaths and Marriages Western Australia,* http://www.bdm.dotag.wa.gov.au/_apps/pioneersindex/default.aspx, accessed 28 February 2012.

876 Curedale, *Vikings, Normans and Lancashire Lords,* p. 405.

877 Colonial Secretary's Office, *The Widow Curedale's application for support: copy of correspondence from Colonial Secretary's Office, 1887/88 / compiled with notes by J.R. Cook,* SROWA, PR11645.

878 Curedale, *Vikings, Normans and Lancashire Lords,* pp. 407-408.

879 *The Daily News,* Monday 20 July 1903, p. 3.

880 Curedale, *Vikings, Normans and Lancashire Lords,* p. 451.

881 *The West Australian,* Friday 14 December 1900, p. 6.

882 Gaol Department Western Australia, 'F15 – Curedale, Marion', Series 678, Con 4186/1.

883 Allen, *Sex & Secrets,* p. 155.

884 Leonie Stella, 'Policing Women: Women's Police in Western Australia 1917-1943', Honours thesis, Murdoch University, 1990, p. 7.

885 Ibid, p. 22.

886 Ibid, p. 24.

887 Ibid, p. 30.

888 Ibid, pp. 40-42.

889 Ibid, p. 50.

890 Ibid, p. 58.

891 Ibid, p. 68.

892 Ibid, p. 69.

893 Ibid, pp. 244-246.

894 Ibid, pp. 120-122.

895 Ibid, pp. 251-252.

896 *The Daily News,* Tuesday 17 February 1931, p. 2.

897 *The West Australian,* Tuesday 9 August 1927, p. 12.

898 *The West Australian,* Saturday 12 September 1936, p. 13.

899 Gaol Department Western Australia, 'F99 – Doyle, Lilly', Series 678, Con 4186/1.

900 *The West Australian,* Tuesday 9 July 1912, p. 6.

901 Gaol Department Western Australia, 'F99 – Doyle, Lilly', Series 678, Con 4186/1.

902   Ibid.
903   *The West Australian*, Wednesday 3 April 1895, p .2.
904   Gaol Department Western Australia, 'F99 – Doyle, Lilly', Series 678, Con 4186/1.
905   *The West Australian*, Monday 9 December 1895, p. 3.
906   *The West Australian*, Monday 18 April 1900, p. 4.
907   http://www.bdm.dotag.wa.gov.au/_apps/pioneersindex/default.aspx
908   Metropolitan Cemeteries Board, 'Research and Genealogy', Summary of Record Information, http://www2.mcb.wa.gov.au/NameSearch/details. php?id=FB00013774, retrieved 3 February 2012.
909   *The West Australian*, Thursday 27 February 1902, p .6.
910   *The West Australian*, Thursday 8 November 1923, p. 7.
911   *The West Australian*, Thursday 24 February 1910, p. 5.
912   Ibid.
913   Bill Marks, *Fall of the Dice*, Fremantle Arts Centre Press, Fremantle, 1991, pp. 8-9.
914   Kimber, ''A nuisance to the community': policing the vagrant woman', pp. 286-287.
915   *The West Australian*, Tuesday 14 December 1915, p. 9.
916   *The West Australian*, Tuesday 30 April 1901, p. 7.
917   *The West Australian*, Tuesday 22 September 1908, p. 2.
918   Chris Chamberlain and David Mackenzie, 'Australian Census Analytical Program: Counting the Homeless Australia, 2006', Australian Bureau of Statistics, ACT, accessed 6 October 2012, < http://www.ausstats.abs.gov. au/Ausstats/subscriber.nsf/0/57393A13387C425DCA2574B900162DF0/$Fi le/20500-2008Reissue.pdf.> pp. 34-37.
919   Chamberlain and Mackenzie, 'Australian Census Analytical Program: Counting the Homeless Australia, 2006', p. 51.

Chapter 7

920   *The West Australian*, 17 March 17, p. 8.
921   Farrell, 'Dangerous Women', p. 120.
922   Ibid, pp. 435-436.
923   Walkowitz, *Prostitution and Victorian Society: Women, class and the state*, p. 8.
924   Yvonne Jewkes, *Crime and Media*, SAGE, Los Angeles and London, 2011, p. 37.
925   Ibid, p. 3.
926   David Whiteford, 'Newspapers, colonial' in Gregory and Gothard, *Historical Encyclopedia of Western Australia*, p. 632.
927   Ibid, p. 632.
928   Michael Sturma, *Vice in a vicious society: crime and convicts in mid-nineteenth century New South Wales*, University of Queensland Press, St Lucia, c.1983, p. 4.
929   Ulrike Tabbert, 'Crime through a Corpus: The Linguistic Construction of Offenders in the British Press' in Christiana Gregoriou (ed) *Constructing Crime: Discourse and Cultural Representations of Crime and Deviance*, Palgrave Macmillan, Basingstoke, 2012, p. 130.
930   Jock Young quoted in Chris Greer (ed) *Crime and Media: A Reader*,

Routledge, New York, 2010, p. 208.

931 Kimber, '"A nuisance to the community": policing the vagrant woman', p. 281.

932 Jewkes, *Crime and Media*, p. 109.

933 Tabbert, 'Crime through a Corpus: The Linguistic Construction of Offenders in the British Press', p. 131.

934 Ibid.

935 Pamela Davies, Peter Francis and Victor Jupp (Ed), *Doing Criminological research*, Sage, London and Singapore, 2011; Ian Marsh and Gaynor Melville, *Crime, Justice and the Media*, Routledge, New York, 2009.

936 *The West Australian*, 2 June 1902, p. 7.

937 *The West Australian*, 3 August 1917, p. 6.

938 *The West Australian*, 9 February 1925, p. 9.

939 *The West Australian*, 1 August 1900, p. 3.

940 *The West Australian*, Thursday 1 September 1898, p. 3.

941 *The West Australian*, 1 October 1917, p. 3.

942 *Truth*, 3 January 1920.

943 *The Sunday Times*, 9 October 1910, p. 5.

944 *The Sunday Times*, 27 July 1913, p. 15.

945 *The West Australian*, 16 October 1902, p. 2.

946 Jewkes, *Crime and Media*, p. 200.

947 Ibid, p. 109.

948 *The West Australian*, Tuesday 9 July 1912, p. 6.

949 *The West Australian*, Friday 9 September 1921, p. 8.

950 *The West Australian*, Tuesday 22 November 1910, p. 4.

951 Davidson, 'Dealing with the "Social Evil", p. 90.

952 Ibid, pp. 8, 90.

953 Police vs. Winter, Perth Police Court Minutes, Acc. 1386/41, 10 July 1919.

954 *The West Australian*, 19 October 1901, p. 11.

955 *The West Australian*, 31 December 1914, p. 4.

956 *The West Australian*, 25 September 1918, p. 5.

957 Tabbert, 'Crime through a Corpus: The Linguistic Construction of Offenders in the British Press', p. 141.

958 *The West Australian*, Monday 8 January 1917, p. 8.

959 *The Daily News*, Tuesday 7 April 1903, p. 1.

960 *The West Australian*, Tuesday 17 January 1899, p. 4.

961 Ibid.

962 *The West Australian*, Friday 16 June 1899, p. 2.

963 *The West Australian*, Tuesday 24 March 1908, p. 7.

964 Ruth Penfold-Mounce, *Celebrity, Culture and Crime: The Joy of Transgression*, Palgrave Macmillan, Basingstoke, 2009, p. 74.

965 Ibid, pp. 73-74.

966 Ibid, pp. 63, 68, 69.

967 Ibid, pp. 63-64.

968 *The Sunday Times*, Sunday 9 January 1915, p. 7.

969 *The West Australian*, 18 August 1908, p. 6.

970 *The West Australian*, 28 May 1909, p. 3.

971 *The Daily News*, Monday 4 April 1910, p. 4.

972   *The Daily News*, Friday 3 March 1911, p. 3.
973   Davidson, 'Prostitution in Perth and Fremantle and on the Eastern Goldfields, 1895-September 1939', p. 176.
974   *The West Australian*, 6 August 1907, p. 7.
975   *The Daily News*, Wednesday 31 August 1910, p. 6.
976   *The Daily News*, Saturday 10 January 1914, p. 16.
977   Ibid.
978   *Kalgoorlie Western Argus*, Tuesday 25 December 1906, p. 12.
979   Ibid.
980   *The West Australian*, Thursday 1 September 1898, p. 3.
981   *The Sunday Times*, Wednesday 21 October 1903, p. 2.
982   *The West Australian*, Thursday 13 January 1910, p. 4.
983   *The West Australian*, Tuesday 22 November 1910, p. 4.
984   *The West Australian*, Thursday 22 October 1903, p. 6.
985   *The West Australian*, Friday 28 June 1907, p. 4.
986   *The Daily News*, Monday 1 August 1910, p. 6.
987   *The Daily News*, Friday 23 September 1910, p. 2.
988   Kelly, Advocat, Harrison and Hickey, *Smashed! The Many Meanings of Intoxication and Drunkenness*, p. xvi.
989   Christensen, 'Drinking' in Gregory and Gothard, *Historical Encyclopedia of Western Australian History*, p. 287; Dianne Davidson, 'Woman's Christian Temperance Union' in Gothard and Gregory, *Historical Encyclopedia of Western Australian History*, pp. 935-936.
990   Tabbert, 'Crime through a Corpus: The Linguistic Construction of Offenders in the British Press', p. 142.
991   Simon Adams, *The Unforgiving Rope: Murder and Hanging on Australia's Western Frontier*, UWA Publishing, Crawley, 2009, p. 217.
992   *The Daily News*, Tuesday 7 April 1903, p. 1.
993   Bellanta, 'The larrikin girl', p. 509.

Chapter 8

994   *The West Australian*, Tuesday 18 October 1949, p. 10.
995   *The West Australian*, Friday 9 September 1921, p. 8.
996   *The West Australian*, Thursday 27 April 1933, p. 10.
997   *The West Australian*, Tuesday 9 May 1933, p. 10.
998   *The West Australian*, Wednesday 30 June 1937, p. 8.
999   *The West Australian*, Saturday 31 December 1938, p, 7.
1000 Gaol Department Western Australia, 'F565 Mattson, Sarah Jane', Series 678, Con 4186/2.
1001 Sarah Jane Mattson, Death Certificate WA, 2474/1951; *The West Australian*, Friday 16 November 1951, p. 23.
1002 *The West Australian*, Thursday 5 January 1939, p. 9.
1003 *The West Australian*, Tuesday 15 August 1939, p. 1.
1004 Gaol Department Western Australia, 'F333 'Roots, Patricia', Series 678, Con 4186/1.
1005 *The West Australian*, Friday 9 September 1921, p. 8.

1006 Ibid.

1007 *The West Australian,* Monday 30 May 1938, p. 11.

1008 *The West Australian,* Wednesday 18 September 1946, p. 12.

1009 *The West Australian,* Friday 8 September 1950, p. 4.

1010 *The West Australian,* Tuesday 31 October 1950, p. 7.

1011 *The Daily News,* Saturday 22 September 1906, p. 8.

1012 *The West Australian,* Tuesday 22 November 1910, p. 4.

1013 *The West Australian,* Thursday 27 March 1913, p. 6.

1014 Gaol Department Western Australia, 'F92 – Reilly Cecilia', Series 678, Con 4186/1.

1015 *The West Australian,* Thursday 31 December 1914, p 4.

1016 *The West Australian,* Wednesday 15 April, p. 8.

1017 *The West Australian,* Wednesday 5 May, p. 5.

1018 *The West Australian,* Thursday 31 December, p. 4.

1019 *The West Australian,* Monday 15 November, p. 3.

1020 *The Sunday Times,* Sunday 19 December 1920, 14.

1021 *The West Australian,* Thursday 5 January 1905, p. 3.

1022 *The West Australian,* Wednesday 1 March 1922, p. 1.

1023 Lynette McLaughlin, personal communication with author, 5 January 2012.

1024 Ibid.

1025 'A Drink Victim', *West Australian,* Saturday 6 January 1906, p. 13.

1026 R. E. N. Twopenny, *Town Life in Australia,* Sydney University Press, Sydney, 1973 edition, p. 169.

1027 *The West Australian,* Saturday 8 July 1933, p. 16.

1028 *Western Argus,* Tuesday 31 July 1934, p. 15.

1029 *The West Australian,* Monday 30 September 1935, p. 19.

1030 Gaol Department Western Australia, 'F209 – Warden, Esther', Series 678, Con 4186/1.

1031 *The West Australian,* Tuesday 29 January 1935, p. 12.

1032 Gaol Department Western Australia, 'F209 Warden, Esther Muriel', Series 678, Con 4186/1.

1033 Gaol Department Western Australia, 'F42 – Lawson, Alice', Series 678, Con 4186/1.

1034 *The West Australian,* Friday 29 November 1918, p. 8.

1035 *The West Australian,* Friday 29 November 1918, p. 8.

1036 Gaol Department Western Australia, 'F42 – Lawson, Alice', Series 678, Con 4186/1.

1037 Gaol Department Western Australia, 'F99 – Doyle, Lilly', Series 678, Con 4186/1.

1038 Metropolitan Cemeteries Board, 'Summary of Record Information, Elizabeth Doyle', Research and Genealogy online, application number FB00013774, accessed 1 September 2012, http://www2.mcb.wa.gov.au/NameSearch/details.php?id=FB00013774>

1039 *The Daily News,* Monday 4 April 1910, p. 4.

1040 *The Daily News,* Saturday 30 October 1920, p. 4.

1041 *The West Australian,* Friday 17 October 1924, p. 12.

1042 *The West Australian,* Tuesday 14 March 1933, p. 15.

1043 *The West Australian,* Tuesday 20 March 1888, p. 3.

1044 *The West Australian,* Tuesday 16 February 1897, p. 2
1045 *The West Australian,* Friday 14 December 1900, p. 6.
1046 *The West Australian,* Tuesday 24 June 1902, p. 7.
1047 *The West Australian,* Tuesday 10 February 1903, p. 7.
1048 *The West Australian,* Saturday 25 December 1909, p. 7.
1049 Ibid.
1050 Ibid.
1051 Ibid.
1052 Ibid.
1053 Ibid.
1054 Ibid.

Epilogue

1055 *The Daily News,* Wednesday 5 October 1910, p. 4.
1056 *The Daily News,* Monday 20 January 1902, p. 2.
1057 Kimber, ''A nuisance to the community': policing the vagrant woman', p. 288.
1058 *The West Australian,* Thursday 4 April 1907, p. 3.
1059 Description of Esther Warden in *The West Australian,* April 4, 1918, 6.
1060 Evidence Policewoman Dugdale, 'Select Committee into Health Act Amendment Act', *Votes and Proceedings,* 1917-18, vol. II, p. 835. Quoted in Davidson, 'Prostitution in Perth and Fremantle and on the Eastern Goldfields, 1895-September 1939', p. 174.
1061 *The Sunday Times,* Sunday 26 January 1913, p. 11.
1062 Emma Ogilvie and Mark Lynch, 'Gender, Race, Class, and Crime in Australia' in Graycar and Grabosky *The Cambridge Handbook of Australian Criminology,* p. 197.
1063 I agree with recent research into women and crime in England. See: D'Cruze and Jackson, *Women, crime and justice in England since 1660,* p. 163.
1064 Hutter and Williams quoted in Frances Heidensohn, *Women & Crime,* Macmillan, Hampshire and London, 1996 (second edition), p. 194.
1065 *The Daily News,* Tuesday 17 October 1911, p. 1.
1066 *The Daily News,* Thursday 4 April 1918, p. 17.

Bibliography

NEWSPAPERS

Albany Advertiser
Argus (Melbourne)
Bunbury Herald
Daily News
Inquirer
Kalgoorlie Western Argus
Mirror
Perth Gazette
Sunday Times
Sydney Morning Herald
Truth
West Australian
Western Mail

ARCHIVE COLLECTIONS

State Records Office of Western Australia

Detectives Office, *Return of brothels and prostitutes in the city, November 14, 1898,* Perth, Consignment No. 430, Item no. 1898/4389.

Fremantle Court of Petty Sessions, *Evidence Books, 1911-1923,* Acc 2952, AN 17.

Government of Western Australia, Department of the Attorney General, *Registry of Births, Deaths and Marriages,* Perth, Western Australia.

Magistrates' Evidence Books – Local Court, 1 April 1897-20 August 1920, Consignment No. 786, Items 17-18.

Perth Police Court Minutes, Acc. 1386.

Records of Conviction, 1866-1909, Series 272, Consignment 3663-3664.

Gaol Department Western Australia, *Register of Local Prisoners (Female),* Series 678, Consignment 4186/1-2.

Gaol Department Western Australia, *Register of Local Prisoners (Male)– Fremantle Prison –* Gaol Department Western Australia, Perth, Series 672, Consignment 4173/1-9.

Perth Police Court, *Charge Books, 1853-1917*, Consignment 1386, 1052 and 3146, AN 17.

Western Australia Police Department, *Report of Const. Robert Love. Reg. No.63. Relative to three houses in King St East Side near Hay Street*, SROWA, Perth, Consignment No. 430, Item no. 1900/1744.

Western Australian Police Department, *General Files, 1876-1971*, Series 76, Consignment 430.

State Library of Western Australia

Government Statistician's Office, *Statistical Register of Western Australia*, Perth, 1903-1939.

Legislative Council of Western Australia, *REPORT OF THE ROYAL COMMISSION APPOINTED TO INQUIRE INTO The Administration of the Municipal Council of the City of Perth*, Government Printer, Perth, 1938.

Pocket Year Book of Western Australia, Government Printer, Perth.

Western Australian Police Gazette, various volumes, 1900-1939, Government Printer, Perth.

Western Australian Parliament, *Western Australian Police Act (1892)*, sections 65, 66 and 67.

Western Australian Parliamentary Debates, 8th Parliament, 1st Session, 1911

PERSONAL COMMUNICATION

Lynette McLaughlin, personal communication with author, 5 January 2012.

THESES

Beresford, Quentin, 'Drinkers and the Anti-Drink Movement in Sydney', 1870-1930, PhD Thesis, Australian National University, Canberra, July 1984.

Davidson, Raelene. 'Prostitution in Perth and Fremantle and on the Eastern Goldfields, 1895-September 1939', MA thesis, University of Western Australia, 1980.

Farrell, Rita, 'Dangerous Women: constructions of female criminality in Western Australia 1915-1945', Murdoch University, PhD Thesis, 1997.

Toole, Kellie Louise, 'Innocence and Penitence Hand Clasped in Hand: Australian Catholic Refuges for Penitent Women, 1848-1914', Master of Arts Thesis, University of Adelaide, 2010.

BOOKS

Adler, Freda and Rita James Simon, *The Criminology of Deviant Women*, Houghton Mifflin Company, Boston, 1979.

Adams, Simon, *The Unforgiving Rope: Murder and Hanging on Australia's Western Frontier*, UWA Publishing, Crawley, 2009.

Allen, Judith A, *Sex & Secrets: Crimes involving Australian Women since 1880*, Oxford University Press, Oxford and New York, 1990.

Amos, Keith, *The Fenians in Australia*, UNSW Press, Kensington, 1988

Anleu, Sharyn L, *Deviance, Conformity & Control*, Pearson, Frenchs Forest, 2006.

Arnold, Catharine, *Underworld London: Crime and Punishment in the Capital City*, Simon & Schuster, London, 2012.

Baldwin, John, A. E. Bottoms in collaboration with Monica A. Walker, *The Urban Criminal: A study in Sheffield*, Tavistock Publications, London, 1976.

Ball, Julia, David Kelsall and John Pidgeon, *Statewide Survey of Hotels, 1829-1939: Southern Region Western Australia, volume 1*, National Trust Australia (WA), November 1997.

Barrie, David G, *Police in the Age of Improvement: Police Development and the Civic Tradition in Scotland, 1775-1865*, Willan Publishing, Cullompton, 2008.

Barry, Kathleen, *Female Sexual Slavery*, Prentice Hall, New Jersey, 1979.

Bartley, Paula, *Prostitution: Prevention and Reform in England, 1860-1914*, Routledge, London, 2000.

Bellanta, Melissa, *Larrkins: A History*, University of Queensland Press, St. Lucia, 2012.

Beier, A. L and Paul Ocobock (eds) *Cast Out: Vagrancy and Homelessness in Global and Historical Perspective*, Ohio University Press, Ohio, 2008.

Bolton, Geoffrey, *Land of Vision and Mirage: Western Australia since 1826*, University of Western Australia Press, Crawley, 2008.

Bristow, Edward J, *Vice and vigilance: purity movements in Britain since 1700*, Gill and Macmillan, Dublin, 1977.

Brown, Patricia M, *The Merchant Princes of Fremantle: The rise and decline of a colonial elite 1870-1900*, University of Western Australia Press, Nedlands, 1996.

Byrne, Geraldine, *Built on a Hilltop: A History of the Sisters of the Good Shepherd in Western Australia 1902-2002*, Sisters of the Good Shepherd, Leederville.

Caine, Barbara and Rosemary Pringle (eds) *Transitions: New Australian Feminisms*, Allen & Unwin, St Leonards, 1995.

Carrabine, Eamonn, Cox, Pam, Lee, Maggy, Plummer, Ken and Nigel South, *Criminology: A sociological introduction*, Routledge, London and New York, 2009 (second edition).

Chesney, Kellow, *The Victorian Underworld*, Penguin, London, 1970.

Chessel, Gwen, *Alexander Collie: Colonial Surgeon, Naturalist & Explorer*, UWA Publishing, Crawley, 2008.

Cohen, Sherrill, *The Evolution of Women's Asylums since 1500: From Refuges for Ex-Prostitutes to Shelters for Battered Women*, Oxford University Press, New York and Oxford, 1992.

Coleborne, Catharine and Dolly MacKinnon (eds), *'Madness' in Australia: histories, heritage and the asylum*, University of Queensland Press, St. Lucia, 2003.

Crotty, Martin, *Making the Australian Male: middle-class masculinity 1870-1920*, Melbourne University Press, Carlton, 2001.

Curedale, Ward, *Vikings, Normans and Lancashire Lords*, Ward Curedale, Applecross, 2008.

D'Cruze, Shani and Louisa A. Jackson (eds) *Women, Crime and Justice in England Since 1660*, Palgrave Macmillan, Hampshire, 2009.

Daniels, Kay (ed) *So Much Hard Work: Women and Prostitution in Australian History*, Fontana Books, Sydney, 1984.

Davidson, Ron, *Fremantle Impressions*, Fremantle Arts Centre Press, Fremantle, 2008.

Davies, Pamela, Peter Francis and Victor Jupp (Ed), *Doing Criminological research*, Sage, London and Singapore, 2011.

Davison, Graeme, David Dunstan and Chris McConville (eds) *The Outcasts of Melbourne: Essays in Social History*, Allen & Unwin, Sydney, 1985.

Ditmore, Melissa Hope *Prostitution and Sex Work*, Greenwood, Oxford, 2011.

Durstan, Gregory, *Victims and Viragos: Metropolitan Women, Crime and the Eighteenth-Century Justice System*, Arima Publishing, Suffolk, 2007.

Ellis, Havelock, *The Criminal*, Walter Scott, London, 1890.

Emsley, Clive, *Crime and Society in England, 1750-1900*, Pearson Longman, Harlow, 2005 (third edition).

Emsley, Clive, *Crime and Society in Twentieth-Century England*, Pearson Longman, London, 2011.

Erickson, Rica (ed), *Bicentennial Dictionary of Western Australians, pre-1829-1888, volume IV, R-Z*, University of Western Australia Press, Nedlands, 1988.

Erickson, Rica, *Dictionary of Western Australians 1829-1914*, volume 4, part 2, L-Z, University of Western Australia Press, Nedlands, 1985.

Finnegan, Frances, *Poverty and prostitution: A Study of Victorian prostitutes in York*, Cambridge, Cambridge University Press, 1979.

Fitzgerald, Ross and Trevor L. Jordan, *Under the Influence: A history of alcohol in Australia*, ABC Books, Sydney, 2009.

Frances, Rae, *Selling Sex: A Hidden History of Prostitution*, UNSW Press, Sydney, 2007.

Fremantle Arts Centre, *Absence of Evidence: Fremantle Arts Centre 15 May – 26 June 1994*, Fremantle Arts Centre, Fremantle, 1994.

Godfrey, Barry, Paul Lawrence and Chris A. Williams, *History & Crime*, Sage Publication, London, 2008.

Graycar, Adam and Peter Grabosky (ed) *The Cambridge Handbook of Australian Criminology*, Cambridge University Press, Cambridge, 2009 digitally printed version.

Greer, Chris (ed) *Crime and Media: A Reader*, Routledge, New York, 2010.

Gregoriou, Christiana (ed) *Constructing Crime: Discourse and Cultural Representations of Crime and Deviance*, Palgrave Macmillan, Basingstoke, 2012.

Gregory, Jenny and Jan Gothard (eds) *Historical Encyclopedia of Western Australia*, University of Western Australia Press, Crawley, 2009.

Grimshaw, Patricia, Marilyn Lake, Ann McGrath and Marian Quartly, *Creating a Nation 1788-1990*, McPhee Gribble, Ringwood, 1994.

Hartman, Mary S, *Victorian Murderesses: A True History of Thirteen Respectable French and English Women Accused of Unspeakable Crimes*, Robson Books, London, 1985.

Heidensohn, Frances, *Women & Crime*, Macmillan, Hampshire and London, 1996 (second edition).

Henderson, Joyce R, *The Strength of the White Ribbon: a year-by-year record of the centennial history of the Woman's Christian Temperance Union of Western Australia (Inc.): ten decades of service for "God, home and humanity" 1892-1992*, The Union, West Perth, c.1992.

Hetherington, Penelope, *Paupers, Poor Relief and Poor Houses in Western Australia 1829-1910*, UWA Publishing, Crawley, 2009.

Jewkes, Yvonne, *Crime and Media,* Sage Publications, London, 2004.

Kelly, Peter, Jenny Advocat, Lyn Harrison and Christopher Hickey, *Smashed! The Many Meanings of Intoxication and Drunkenness,* Monash University Publishing, Clayton, 2011.

Lake, Marilyn, *Getting Equal: The history of Australian feminism,* Allen & Unwin, St Leonard's, 1999.

MacDonald, Robert (Ed), *Youth, the 'Underclass' and Social Exclusion,* Routledge, London.

Macintyre, Stuart, *The Succeeding Age 1901-1942: The Oxford History of Australia,* Oxford University Press, Melbourne, 1993.

Marks, Bill *Fall of the Dice,* Fremantle Arts Centre Press, Fremantle, 1991.

Marsh, Ian and Gaynor Melville, *Crime, Justice and the Media,* Routledge, New York, 2009.

Matthews, Jill Julius, *Good & Mad Women: The Historical Construction of Femininity in Twentieth-Century Australia,* Allen & Unwin, North Sydney, 1984, (1992 edition).

Matthews, Roger, *Prostitution, Politics & Policy,* Routledge-Cavendish, Hoboken, 2008.

McHugh, Paul, *Prostitution and Victorian Social Reform,* Croom Helm, London, 1980.

McPherson, Kathryn, Cecilia Morgan and Nancy M. Forrestell (eds) *Gendered Pasts: Historical Essays Femininity and Masculinity in Canada,* University of Toronto Press, Toronto, 2003.

Monkkonen, Eric H, *The Dangerous Class: Crime and Poverty in Columbus, Ohio, 1860-1885,* Harvard University Press, Cambridge, 1975.

Morris, Lydia, *The Dangerous Classes: the underclass and social citizenship,* Routledge, London and New York, 1994.

Mukherjee, Satyanshu K, *Crime Trends in Twentieth Century Australia,* Allen & Unwin, Sydney, 1981

Nelson, Todd D, (ed) *Handbook of Prejudice, Stereotyping and Discrimination,* Psychology Press, New York, 2009.

Nevill, Simon J, *Perth and Fremantle: Past and Present,* Simon Nevill Publications, Fremantle, 2007.

O'Brien, Anne, *Poverty's Prison: The Poor in New South Wales, 1880-1918,* Melbourne University Press, Melbourne, 1988.

Pacione, Michael, *Urban Geography: a global perspective,* Routledge, London, 2005.

Pearson, Geoffrey, *Hooligan: A History of Respectable Fears,* Palgrave Macmillan, Hampshire, 1983.

Penfold-Mounce, Ruth, *Celebrity, Culture and Crime: The Joy of Transgression,* Palgrave Macmillan, Basingstoke, 2009.

Phillips, David and Susanne Davies (eds) *A Nation of Rogues: Crime, Law and Punishment in Colonial Australia,* Melbourne University Press, Carlton, 1994.

Power Family Archives, unpublished family history, courtesy of Diane Anderson, 2011.

Reece, R and R. Pascoe, *A Place of Consequence: A Pictorial History of Fremantle,* Fremantle Arts Centre Press, Fremantle, 1983.

Rowbotham, Judith and Kim Stevenson (eds) *Behaving Badly: Social Panic and Moral Outrage, Victorian and Modern Parallels,* Ashgate, Hampshire, 2003.

Ryan, Michael, *Prostitution in London, with a comparative view of that of Paris and New York*, H. Baillière, London, 1839.

Sangster, Joan, *Through Feminist Eyes: Essays on Canadian Women's History*, Edmonton, AB, Athabasca University Press, 2011.

Schreuder, Deryck M and Stuart Ward, *Australia's Empire*, Oxford University Press, Oxford, 2008, (2009 edition).

Self, Helen J, *Prostitution, Women and the Misuse of the Law: The Fallen Daughters of Eve*, Frank Cass Publishers, London, 2003.

Shoham, Shlomo Giovam Paul Knepper and Martin Kett, *International Handbook of Criminology*, CRC Press, London and New York.

Shore, Heather, *Artful Dodgers: Youth and Crime in early nineteenth-century London*, Boydell Press, London, 1998.

Stannage, C. T, *The People of Perth: A Social History of Western Australia's Capital City*, Carroll's for Perth City Council, Perth, 1979.

Sturma, Michael, *Vice in a vicious society: crime and convicts in mid-nineteenth century New South Wales*, University of Queensland Press, St Lucia, c.1983.

Taylor, David, *Crime, Policing and Punishment in England, 1750-1914*, Palgrave Macmillan, Hampshire, 1998.

Thomas, Donald, *The Victorian Underworld*, John Murray, London, 1998.

Twomey, Christina, *Deserted and Destitute: Motherhood, Wife Desertion and Colonial Welfare*, Australian Scholarly Publishing, Melbourne, 2002.

Twopenny, R. E. N. *Town Life in Australia*, Sydney University Press, Sydney, 1973 edition.

Valverde, Mariana, *Diseases of the Will: Alcohol and the Dilemmas of Freedom*, Cambridge University Press, Cambridge, 1998.

Vicinus, Martha (ed), *Suffer And Be Still: Women in the Victorian Age*, Indiana University Press, Bloomington and Indianapolis, 1973 edition.

Walkowitz, Judith, *Prostitution and Victorian Society: Women, class and the state*, Cambridge University Press, Cambridge, 1980 (2001 edition).

Welshman, John, *Underclass*, Hambledon Continuum, London, 2006.

Wright, Clare, *Beyond the Ladies Lounge: Australia's Female Publicans*, Melbourne University Press, Melbourne, 2003.

Writer, Larry, *Razor: Tilly Devine, Kate Leigh and the razor gangs*, Pan Macmillan, Sydney, 2001.

JOURNAL ARTICLES

Abbott, Kellie and Celia Chesney, '"I AM A POOR WOMAN": Gender, Poor Relief and the Poorhouse in Late Nineteenth and Early Twentieth-Century Western Australia' in Charlie Fox (ed) *Studies in Western Australian History: Social Policy in Western Australia*, no, 25 (2007): 24-39.

Allen, Judith, '"Mundane Men": Historians, Masculinity and Masculinism', *Historical Studies*, vol. 22, no 89, (1987): 617-628.

Auerbach, Nina, 'The Rise of the Fallen Woman', *Nineteenth-Century Fiction*, Vol. 35, No. 1 (June 1980): 29-52.

Bashford, Alison, 'At the border: contagion, immigration, nation', *Australian Historical Studies*, vol. 33, no. 120 (2002): 344-358.

Bellanta, Melissa, 'The larrikin girl', *Journal of Australian Studies*, vol. 34, no. 4 (2010): 499-512.

Bland, Lucy, 'Purifying' the public world: feminist vigilantes in late Victorian England', *Women's History Review*, 1:3(1992): 397-412.

Bodington, G. F, 'On The Control and Restraint of Habitual Drunkards', *The British Medical Journal*, 28 August 1875, pp. 255-256.

Boritch, Helen and John Hagan, Crime and the Changing Forms of Class Control: Policing Public Order in "Toronto the Good,"1859-1955', *Social Forces*, vol. 66, no. 2 (December 1987): 307-335.

Chesney-Lind, Meda, '"Women and Crime": The Female Offender, *Signs*, vol. 12, no. 1, (Autumn 1986): 78-96.

Davies, Andrew, '"THESE VIRAGOES ARE NOT LESS CRUEL THAN THE LADS": Young women, Gangs and Violence in Late Victorian Manchester and Salford', *British Journal of Criminology*, vol. 39, no. 1 (1999): 72-89.

Davis, Annette, 'Good Times for All? Popular Entertainment and Class Consciousness in Western Australian Society During the Interwar Years' in Jenny Gregory (ed) *Western Australia Between the Wars 1919-1939: Studies in Western Australian History*, no. 11 (June 1990): 68-82.

Feeley, Malcolm M and Deborah L. Little, 'The Vanishing Female: The Decline of Women in the Criminal Process, 1687-1912', *Law & Society Review*, vol. 25, no. 4 (1991): 719-758.

Fox, Charlie, '"Bookies, Punters and Parasites: Off-Course Betting, Conflict and Consensus in Western Australia Between the Wars"', in Gregory, *Western Australia Between the Wars 1919-1939: Studies in Western Australian History*, no. 11 (June 1990): 57-67.

Frances, Rae, '"White Slaves" and White Australia: Prostitution and Australian Society', *Australian Feminist Studies*, Vol. 19, No. 44 (July 2004): 189-190.

Hay, Douglas, 'Crime and Justice in Eighteenth- and Nineteenth-Century England', *Crime and Justice*, vol. 2 (1980): 45-84.

Kaladelfos, Amanda, 'Murder in Gun Alley: girls, grime and gumshoe history', *Journal of Australian Studies*, vol. 34, no. 4 (2010): 471-484.

Kimber, Julie, '"A nuisance to the community': policing the vagrant woman', *Journal of Australian Studies*, 34:3 (2010): 275-293.

Lake, Marilyn, 'The Politics of Respectability: Identifying the Masculinist Context', *Historical Studies*, vol. 22, no 86 (1986): 116-131.

McConville, Chris, 'The location of Melbourne's prostitutes', *Historical Studies*, vol. 19, no. 74 (1980): 86-97.

McKewon, Elaine, 'The historical geography of prostitution in Perth, Western Australia', *Australian Geographer*, vol. 34 (3): 297-310.

O'Brien, Anne, 'Pauperism Revisited', *Australian Historical Studies*, vol. 42, no. 2 (2011): 212-229.

O'Brien, John, 'The Founding and Early Years of the Convent of the Good Shepherd, Leederville' in John Tonkin (ed) *Religion and Society in Western Australia: Studies in Western Australian History*, vol. 9 (1987): 45-53.

Piper, Alana, '"A growing vice": the *Truth* about Brisbane girls and drunkenness in the early twentieth century', *Journal of Australian Studies*, 34 (2010): 485-497.

Piper, Alana, '"I Go Out Worse Every Time: Connections and Corruption in a Female Prison', *History Australia*, vol. 9, no. 3 (2012): 132-153.

Robbins, Cynthia A. and Steven S. Martin, 'Gender, Styles of Deviance and Drinking Problems', *Journal of Health and Social Behaviour*, vol. 34 (December 1993): 302-321.

Ryan, Jan, 'She lives with a chinaman': Orient-ing 'white' women in the courts of law', *Journal of Australian Studies*, 23:60 (1999): 149-159.

Tennent, Margaret, '"Magdalens and moral imbeciles": Women's homes in nineteenth-century New Zealand', *Women's Studies International Forum*, Vol. 9, Issues 5-6 (1986): 491-502.

Wimshurst, Kerry, 'Punishment, Welfare and Gender Ordering in Queensland, 1920-1940', *The Australian and New Zealand Journal of Criminology*, vol. 34, no. 3 (2002): 308-329.

'Women in Policing Exhibit', *Journal for Women and Policing*, no. 11 (2002): 43.

ONLINE RESOURCES

Chamberlain, Chris and David Mackenzie, 'Australian Census Analytical Program: Counting the Homeless Australia, 2006', Australian Bureau of Statistics, ACT, accessed 6 October 2012, <http://www.ausstats.abs.gov.au/Ausstats/subscriber.nsf/0/57393A13387C425DCA2574B900162DF0/$File/20500-2008Reissue.pdf.> pp. 34-37.

Cordingley, Glenn, 'Bank worker Eva Scolaro, 24, jailed for glassing, disfiguring young woman', *Perthnow*, 14 April 2010, retrieved from http://www.perthnow.com.au/news/bank-worker-eva-scolaro-24-jailed-for-glassing-another-woman/story-e6frg12c-1225853627296.

Curedale, George Death Certificate, *Births, Deaths and Marriages Western Australia*, http://www.bdm.dotag.wa.gov.au/_apps/pioneersindex/default.aspx, accessed 28 February 2012.

'Dangerous student drinking targeted in hard-hitting campaign', *Perthnow*, 26 September 2009, http://www.perthnow.com.au/news/western-australia/dangerous-student-drinking-targeted-in-hard-hitting-campaign/story-e6frg153-1225779965829, viewed 23 February 2011

Department of Indigenous Affairs, *Noongar Prohibited Map 1927-1954*, SROWA. South West Aboriginal Land and Sea Council, Kaartdijin Noongar: Sharing Noongar Culture, *Contact History: Impacts of the law from the Aboriginal Protection Act 1905 onwards*, http://www.noongarculture.org.au/media/6233/prohibitedmap%20final%20new.pdf, accessed 15 February 2011.

Hardman, Mary Ann and George Curedale Marriage Record, *Births, Deaths and Marriages Western Australia*, http://www.bdm.dotag.wa.gov.au/_apps/pioneersindex/default.aspx, accessed 28 February 2012.

Health Act 1911, Amendment Act 1915, Part XI – Venereal diseases and disorders affecting the generative organs, http://www.austlii.edu.au/au/legis/wa/consol_act/ha191169/, accessed 31 October 2011.

Metropolitan Cemeteries Board, 'Summary of Record Information', Karrakatta Cemetery, Research and Genealogy online <http://www2.mcb.wa.gov.au/NameSearch>

'WA young in binge drinking crisis', *Perthnow*, 22 June 2007, http://www.perthnow.com.au/news/western-australia/wa-young-in-binge-drinking-crisis/story-e6frg13u-1111113810177, viewed 23 February 2011.

Index